T0070603

ENEMIES *of* PROMISE

Other Books by Cyril Connolly

The Rock Pool
The Unquiet Grave
The Selected Essays of Cyril Connolly

ENEMIES *of* PROMISE

CYRIL CONNOLLY

"Quando sovviemmi di cotanta speme"

REVISED EDITION

With a New Foreword by Alex Woloch

The University of Chicago Press

To Logan Pearsall Smith

Alex Woloch is associate professor of English at Stanford University.

The University of Chicago Press, Chicago 60637
© 1983 by Deidre Levi
New Foreword © 2008 by Alex Woloch
All rights reserved

Revised edition first published in 1948
University of Chicago Press edition 2008
Printed in the United States of America

17 16 15   3 4 5

ISBN-13: 978-0-226-11504-7
ISBN-10: 0-226-11504-6

Library of Congress Cataloging-in-Publication Data

Connolly, Cyril, 1903–74.
  Enemies of promise / Cyril Connolly ; with a new foreword by Alex Woloch.
— Rev. ed.
      p. cm.
  Originally published: New York : Macmillan, 1948.
  Includes index.
  ISBN-13: 978-0-226-11504-7 (pbk. : alk. paper)
  ISBN-10: 0-226-11504-6 (pbk. : alk. paper)   1. English literature—20th
century—History and criticism.   I. Title.
  PR471.C65 2008
  820'.9'00912 22

                                              2008005378

♾ The paper used in this publication meets the minimum requirements of the
American National Standard for Information Sciences—Permanence of Paper for
Printed Library Materials, ANSI Z39.48-1992.

CONTENTS

v

PART THREE
A GEORGIAN BOYHOOD

FOREWORD

"[T]he best work explodes with a delayed impact."

Cyril Connolly, *Enemies of Promise*

I.

WHY READ CYRIL CONNOLLY'S *Enemies of Promise* IN 2008, A LIFETIME after it first appeared? Books fall out of print all the time; far fewer are reissued. But the 1938 *Enemies of Promise* actually concerns the way that books fall out of print: how they last, fade, became dated, or die. What kind of writing, Connolly begins by asking, can survive ten years—particularly in the face of looming global war? "Contemporary books do not keep. The quality in them which makes for their success is the first to go; they turn over night" (4). With this quirky comparison of a short-lived book to spoiled food, Connolly embarks on his own most ambitious piece of writing: a perverse study of how books fail to endure, how talent or "promise" can be extinguished, and how writing is torn between its allegiance to the present and a more impalpable futurity.

A second run of *Enemies of Promise* appeared, appropriately, in 1948, and Connolly begins that edition by putting his own work forward as writing that has lasted for the elusive ten years. In fact, within these same ten years Connolly had moved to the center of literary culture in England: as a critic, essayist, reviewer, and, most importantly, editor of the journal *Horizon*. But, as though following the script laid out in *Enemies of Promise*, Connolly was always tormented by the directions his talent took him in, constantly worrying whether all his dispersed creative work would end up as mere "journalism," forgotten once a little time had passed, or survive as "literature," enduring beyond the historical framework that generated it.

Connolly's intermediate state between these two kinds of writing continues to characterize his work and its legacy. Today *Enemies of Promise* is, at best, half-remembered: a book that many people might admire but few people still seem to read, perhaps invoked in discussions of other, more critically fashionable 1930s texts (if only for its endless supply of striking aphorisms) but almost never made the center of attention itself. Yet Connolly's book, always tottering near the obscurity that it examines, is also resiliently contemporary: it has things to say both as, and about, literary criticism that are more current than ever.

Connolly explores his central question—how to write a book that will last ten years—in two initial ways. In Part One, "Predicament," he considers the essential stylistic tendencies of literature in the 1920s and 30s, organizing his analysis around two newly coined categories: the Vernacular (pared-down or documentary writing that directly engages the contemporary world) and the Mandarin (stylized writing that is committed above all to its own formal or verbal elegance). In Part Two, the virtuoso discussion that gives the book its title and central focus, Connolly shifts his attention from the substance of writing to the creative act itself. "The Charlock's Shade" catalogues the various interests, distractions, experiences, and dilemmas that endanger the aspiring writer's promise: politics, "day-dreams, conversation, drink and other narcotics," "the clarion call of journalism," worldly success, escapism, "sex with its obsessions," and "the ties of duty and domesticity" (85–86).

As even this preliminary list suggests, Connolly blends together numerous and, crucially, various kinds of obstacles that face writing. This variety is a key to the book, as Connolly teases out a kaleidoscopic range of ways in which the world can disrupt, and become fatally intertwined with, the act of writing. If failure endangers the writer, so can too much success. Having no one to speak to might distort the writer's creative process, but so can an overly solicitous audience—or even simply a facility at talking (106–7). By the end of Part Two, Connolly has transformed writing from a simple or stable action into something more akin to an acrobatic feat—a tightrope walk that needs to avoid any number of potential slips. Similarly, a continual range of dangers looms over the written word itself in Part One. For Connolly, both the Mandarin and the Vernacular styles have any number of potential shortcomings. Addison's elegant eighteenth-century essays are as treacherously contingent, in their own way, as Hemingway's pared-down modernist prose. And, again, Connolly wants to show how any style of writing can fail in varied ways: as it drifts off-course, betrays itself, dilutes itself, or, conversely, becomes too accomplished (and, potentially, in this accomplishment, too rigid, mechanical, or complacent).

The enemies that Connolly conjures up proliferate. What is the best time of day to write? he asks on the opening page of his book, immediately signaling the idiosyncratic kind of question that *Enemies of Promise* seeks to make room for within literary criticism. Like most of the questions that Connolly poses, this one receives no purely satisfying answer: writing in the mornings, the afternoons, or at night each offers a specific set of quandaries and possibilities. *Enemies of Promise* prompts the reader to move from this kind of playful and delimited question about writing to more urgent and essential ones. How should writers support themselves or earn money—again, only imperfect choices. Relying on an inheritance, commercial sales, or different possible "second" careers—teaching, publishing, advertising, journalism, even the civil service—all come in for specific scrutiny. How much—or little—should a writer produce? How do a host of other activities and interests both intersect with and disrupt the process of writing? And for what kind of audience does the writer write: "himself, his friends, his teachers, his God, an educated upper-class, a wanting to be educated lower-class, a hostile jury" (10)?

This list, so typical of *Enemies of Promise,* does more than sketch different types of reader that any writer might choose. For Connolly, most interesting writing will reach out toward a range of contrasting readers, and the complicated, perhaps futile, effort to address all these intersecting audiences will work its way into the very texture of the writing. There is no neat division between the essential inside of writing—style, word-choices, the rhythms of form, the contours of imagination itself—and the outside of writing: in this case, the conflicting audiences that any work of writing tries to keep in view. For this reason, Connolly also offers a catalogue of the different (and all imperfect) stances that writing might take toward its audience: a writer can "flatter . . . scream . . . beg . . . lecture . . . or play confidence tricks" with his or her readers (5).

Every aspect of writing, for Connolly, involves its own hazards. Travel, journalism, political activism, religion, daydreaming, hobbies: each of these can spring out of but also bring an end to creative struggle. (Touching on "hobbies" Connolly offers another, embedded catalogue, from the writers who "collect first editions or old dust-wrappers" through the ones "who run chicken-farms" [109]). Cliques of writers can "ascend" the "moving staircase . . . in groups of four or five"(123), which poses a different set of dangers. Economic duress will almost always, of course, be devastating, but spending money also can be a "substitute for creation"(136). Connolly's beautiful description of good talkers, or writers who lose their creative potential through the very eloquence and power of their conversation, is one highlight in this gloomily exuberant recitation of the ways in which writing can fail (106–7).

2.

What drives Connolly's originality here? Why does he concentrate on showing all the ways in which writing might fall short (rather than how it can succeed) and the range of dead-ends into which the promising writer can wander (rather than the heights to which the writer could ascend)? At the center of this lighthearted and deftly pragmatic book is a deeply negative principle. The act of writing (in Part Two), like literary style itself (in Part One), unfolds in an extremely uncertain state, precarious and contingent. And criticism best grasps the elusive quality that makes a work literary not by directly adumbrating its characteristics or confidently theorizing its essence, but by paying rigorous and flexible attention to these "enemies" of promise, to the points where the literary stumbles or lapses. Any theory of writing that was more fixed or more positive would miss the essentially dynamic nature of the literary text. Instead, *Enemies of Promise* tackles its real subject—the nature of literariness—through a classic *via negativa*. Connolly takes on his intractable question not by cataloguing the transcendent or fixed qualities that define literature but by bringing out literary value in relief, against the various obstacles, pitfalls, and dangers that can send the writer, and writing itself, off a "promising" course.

This strategy connects Connolly's work to a rich tradition of aesthetic and formal criticism but also offers a crucial distinction. Like the best formalists and New Critics (many of whom are writing at this same period), Connolly emphasizes the specificity of literary language as it differentiates itself from all the given and ossified languages of the world (the discourses of advertising, propaganda, commerce, tradition, etc). But unlike critics who monumentalize the written work—elaborating a novel or a poem as a sealed-off and self-sufficient object—Connolly brings out the intrinsic *fragility* of the literary text and its necessary and complicated intertwining with the world. For this reason it is striking that Connolly titles Part One simply "Predicament": as though literature doesn't face one particular, delimited problem, or a set of contingent challenges, but rather finds itself in a persistently problematic state. Writing will never fully outstrip or elude its "predicament" (or vanquish all of its "enemies"): it doesn't succeed by transporting itself into a realm in which its dilemmas and difficulties have disappeared. Despite its professed "didactic" strain (vii), the hidden, aesthetic force of Connolly's book rests in its cumulative suggestion that the wrong turns and bitter traps that seem to endanger the literary are also—simultaneously—the very conditions through which art thrives. Safe writing, entirely "unendangered" by the enemies that Connolly enumerates, would be anodyne, self-satisfied, uninteresting. The "promise" of writing is only fulfilled, paradoxically, through its peril.

Just as Connolly shies away from constructing an exhaustive or simple definition of literary value, we shouldn't take the catalogue of "enemies" that he enumerates to be closed or complete. On the contrary, the book urges the reader to consider how the obstacles it describes might intersect with his or her own creative efforts, and to imagine any number of other ways in which writing becomes entangled with the world. What sort of enemies, to put this most obviously, would e-mail, the Internet, or text-messaging be to today's aspiring writer? Or, since Connolly has often been critiqued for saying that "there is no more somber enemy of good art than the pram in the hall" (116)—how, rather than jettisoning Connolly's model altogether, could we imagine the specific enemies of a female writer's promise (something untouched on in this book)? And how do the currents of United States culture—so often anti-intellectual and reactionary, but also potentially multiethnic and heterogeneous—create a different set of enemies, and even different kinds of promise, than the late 1930s British cultural landscape that Connolly is investigating? These questions open up this book's enduring relevance, not merely as they provide "updated" or relocated versions of Connolly's enemies, but also as they remind us of its subtle generosity toward the implied reader. This reader, in order even to follow or become absorbed into Connolly's argument, must also understand him- or herself to be a potentially creative agent. *Enemies of Promise* insists on being reimagined through the ambitions, desires, and potential promise of each individual who engages it. Thus unlike much of the New Criticism, which tends to emphasize the singularity of a privileged, and rare, literary object, Connolly's book distributes "promise" in a wide and democratic manner.

3.

Between the first and second editions of *Enemies of Promise* Connolly edits the influential literary monthly *Horizon,* which begins its run at the outbreak of World War II, at a moment when many journals from the 1930s—including T. S. Eliot's *Criterion*—are closing down. We might understand the very enterprise of *Horizon* as an odd sequel to Connolly's most famous work, in part because it provides a welcome and supportive site for so many gifted poets, novelists, and critics to exercise their "promise" during and immediately after the war. Connolly prefaces most monthly issues of *Horizon* with often

brilliant editorial "Comments," many of which share that same striking mixture of formal and sociological concerns as *Enemies of Promise*.
But, as I've suggested, Connolly's own ambivalence about his success
as a journalist and an editor in the 1940s also underscores his concern
with the stark difference between ephemeral and durable forms of
writing. Throughout his own career, Connolly stigmatizes his usually
fragmented and episodic work against the standard of an unfinished,
never-to-be-written masterpiece. *Enemies of Promise* starts with Connolly getting up too late in the morning (in order to write), and circles
back several times to his professed laziness and psychological restlessness. And in the autobiographical Part Three, "A Georgian Childhood," *Enemies of Promise* explicitly shifts to the grounds of the author's self: critically, but also nostalgically, examining how Connolly's
own psychological formation was shaped by the rarified educational
institutions through which he passed.

Connolly sums up this autobiographical section, which offers a detailed reconstruction of his experiences at preparatory school and
Eton College, quite bluntly: "I have always disliked myself at any
given moment; the total of such moments is my life" (143). But it
would be a mistake simply to take Connolly's often dismissive self-
presentation at face value, or to see the psychological dissociation that
Connolly here foregrounds (life as merely a series of disjointed "moments," each shaped by the author both considering and "disliking"
himself) as the key to his interest in how writing, too, can fall apart.
First, and most obviously, *Enemies of Promise*, for all its attention to
the author's failings (both moral and artistic), is at the same time an
extremely ambitious book. If the *longeurs* in Connolly's text suggest a
pose of ease and lassitude, they only serve to intensify the pounce
when his critical perception does inexorably strike. And in his discussion, too, Connolly insists several times that "industriousness" can
easily sap literary promise ("what ruins the writer is over-production"
[87]; "the health of a writer should not be too good. . . . Rude health,
as the name implies, is averse to culture" [135]) while what looks like
inaction often underlies an intensity that characterizes the very best
work: "like many lazy people, once I started working I could not stop;

perhaps that is why we avoid it" (232). Health is here an obstacle to writing, while "laziness" is a potentially valuable accomplice. It is very hard to distinguish enemy and friend in moments like this, a blurring of the lines that is crucial to the achievement of this book.

It would be folly to consider the conceptual significance of *Enemies of Promise*—its sustained efforts to understand the nature and fragility of literary writing—without calling attention to its own accomplished style. Connolly writes extremely well. His deft phrasing, rhetorical unpredictability, and agile, insistent humor underlie a prose-style that is at once strikingly epigrammatic and disarmingly familiar. The odd mixture of ease and pointedness creates an uncanny reading experience. Echoing the fundamental tension investigated in *Enemies of Promise,* Connolly's thoughts about literature seem both offhand and meant to be remembered. The work bristles with conceptual intelligence but never loses its studied veneer of effortlessness or sprezzatura. The combination can be quite seductive, as the reader engages ideas which, as they are articulated, work to both strike and relax our faculties of reflection. In this way, the fragility that concerns Connolly so much in this book is also woven into the unfolding of the text itself. Like "the best work," Connolly's phrases tend to "explode with a delayed impact" (6).

As one example of this relationship between style and criticism we might consider the interesting passage in which Connolly imagines having read "The Love Song of J. Alfred Prufrock" upon its initial publication:

> I have often wondered what it must have felt like to discover these opening lines of *Prufrock* in *Blast* or the *Catholic Anthology* in 1914–15 with the Rupert Brooke poems, Kitchener's Army and *Business as Usual* everywhere. Would we have recognised that new, sane, melancholy, light-hearted and fastidious voice? (40)

Connolly's unsated desire to have "recognised" or "discover[ed]" Eliot's poem in this way suggests that part of *Prufrock's* value would have been discernable only against, and thus in subtle relation to, the

surrounding, more transient material. Once again, Connolly offers us
a compelling interplay between endurance and fragility, or promise
and its enemies. After all, to encounter a literary text that is self-
evidently or unproblematically "beautiful" would leave no room for
the recognition or discovery that Connolly understandably high-
lights. At the same time, Connolly's own tricky description of Eliot's
voice—as "new, sane, melancholy, light-hearted and fastidious"—
poses a subtle challenge for the reader of *Enemies of Promise*. The
words unfold with sinuous ease, but it is difficult to synthesize this
complicated, shifting description into a fixed or stable sense of the
poem. Each of the five adjectives takes up the poem from a slightly
different position and the description hinges on a stark, but almost
unnoticeable, tension between "melancholy" and "light-hearted."
Through this instability, Connolly's description of the poem works to
reenergize his reader's own sense of "recognition" and "discovery."

   Enemies of Promise is full of prose that works in this way: simultaneously precise and open-ended. It's something we can see not just in
other versions of such five-fingered phrases ("the equipment of the
homosexual writer: combativeness, curiosity, egotism, intuition, and
adaptability, is greatly to be envied" [113]), but, more generally, in
Connolly's consistent reliance on and mastery of anaphora—prose
constructions built around modulated repetition. Connolly's writing
is saturated with quietly complex iterations, lists, and catalogues, at
once easy to understand but hard to simplify, with nuanced, subtly
shifting terms that work to provoke thought in the reader without de-
termining all the contours or limits of this thought. The overarching,
three-part structure of *Enemies of Promise* allows Connolly to enact a
still larger version of this thought-provoking simultaneity. How do
we fit these elegant parts together? This question operates like a bass-
line underneath the reading of the entire book. Even in the first section, while pursuing that distinction between Vernacular and Mandarin styles, Connolly's relaxed prose veers off into radically different
forms several times. He offers chronological lists (27–29, 62–63), a
chart that maps out the shared plot structure of seven different texts
(43), and one memorable "experiment" (70) that fuses together mate-

rial from three different books (*Goodbye to Berlin, To Have and Have Not*, and *The Road to Wigan Pier*). The odd compendium of catalogues, quotations, and tables—at once logical and devious, systematic and whimsical—has a striking effect, suggesting that literary criticism, properly pursued, is always threatening (or aspiring) to turn into a different mode of writing altogether. Such generic uncertainty is much more pronounced when we read *Enemies of Promise* in full, with its three parts cutting across established or entrenched genres. Each section is odd in its own way: for instance, it is unsettlingly ambiguous whether the autobiographical Part Three is meant as a sentimental memoir or a quasi-sociological critique of the institutions that Connolly passes through. But the combination of these three sections into one book is certainly odder and more unsettling still. The reader passes from Part to Part with a mixture of admiration and bafflement. These disruptive shifts signal both the author's own ambition to endure and his failure to cohere—and in this combination of reach and strain they once again locate the text itself within the predicaments it explores.

This kind of experimental structure connects Connolly's work to a constellation of writing from the late 1930s that was marked by a peculiar mixture of confidence and anxiety. The puzzling form of Connolly's book suggests a literary mind confident enough to dream of a book that would have a unique and original form but anxious enough to call into question the different modes that it deploys—and, in this way, to take no modality of writing, or cultural authority, for granted. Such a tension is central to the energies of the 1930s British cultural left, and the experimental form of Connolly's book resonates most clearly with other important texts of this tradition: Stephen Spender's *Forward From Liberalism* (1937), which, like *Enemies of Promise*, has three different sections that articulate shifts not just in topic but in genre and tone; W. H. Auden and Christopher Isherwood's *Journey to a War* (1940), which combines lyric poetry, photography, and documentary prose in a jagged, tentative book that is simultaneously a travelogue and a record of emerging global catastrophe; or George Orwell's *The Road to Wigan Pier* (1937), which is so controversially and memorably welded together across two different parts, the first documentary and factual, and the second autobiographical, essayistic, and speculative. (All of these authors—Spender, Auden, Isherwood, and, in particular, Orwell, who was Connolly's close childhood friend—also play important and interesting "roles" within *Enemies of Promise*.) In all of these centaur-like texts we can find that same combination of confidence and uncertainty; a commitment to form and a radicalized suggestion that it is largely through form and structure that imagination and expression must take place; a wary but still insistent personal idiosyncrasy; and, intertwined with all this, a sustained interest in social class and the social bases of writing itself. The shifts from section to section, in all of these books, mark the limits of the self in relation to class. As Connolly writes at the beginning of Part Three: "A critic is a product of his time who may affect impartiality but who while claiming authority over the reader projects his doubt and aspiration. . . . [N]ow is the moment to step down from the pulpit, to disrobe in the vestry. The autobiography which follows . . . is meant to be an analysis of the grounding in life and art which the critic received. . . . We grow up among theories and illusions common to our class, our race, our time. We absorb them unawares and their effect is incalculable" (141–42).

Part Three of *Enemies of Promise* gestures at a history that lies, in part, outside of any writer's critical grasp—a history of those institutions and social structures that, "absorb[ed] unawares," have preceded and shaped the writer's own faculties of perception and expression. For this reason, as Connolly points out in his 1948 preface, it is crucial that the autobiographical section comes only at the *end* of the book, even though the events it describes are chronologically first. Having considered all the ways in which writing is vulnerably intertwined with the outside world, Connolly shifts in Part Three toward the world of his own childhood and education. In other words, he tries to encompass the context that has shaped the writing of the earlier sections themselves. Even while revealing the most personal details of his earliest friendships and desires, Connolly demonstrates here a much larger point. If we look carefully enough, Connolly suggests, every act of writing expresses the social history that lies behind it and that is threaded into the writing's own form, assumptions, and point-of-view. By elongating his book in this way, Connolly makes the second half of *Enemies of Promise* at once uncompromisingly personal and strangely universal. Any book could, as Connolly's book does, "double" itself by unearthing the hidden story of its own composition. It's a beautiful if impossible idea, and the final way in which Connolly demonstrates the fragility that rests at the center of writing's promise.

ALEX WOLOCH
Stanford University, March 2008

INTRODUCTION

Enemies of Promise WAS FIRST PUBLISHED IN 1938 AS A DIDACTIC
enquiry into the problem of how to write a book which lasts ten
years. That limit is now reached and the book has survived; the
proof lying in the fact that it has been republished. The original
edition appeared in the week of the Munich crisis and, despite
some very favourable and some very offensive reviews, sold extremely badly. One provincial reviewer attacked me for daring
to eat peaches for lunch on the first page, though in the South of
France that summer they were cheaper than potatoes. Another
accused me of plagiarising Valéry who in an essay which I had not
read made use of the Mandarin image for some kinds of writing.
A more general criticism was that the autobiographical section of
Part III should precede the rest of the book or alternatively be
published separately, since it had nothing to do with it.

The objection to beginning with Part III, aside from the fact
that I wrote it in the position which it now occupies, is that a section dealing with life and living people would make the ensuing
literary criticisms seem dry and insipid. And in fact there is a
very intentional harmony, if not an obvious one, between the last
section and the others, to which it stands in the relationship of
illustrations to text. Thus several writers who appear as text-book
names in Part I occur as people in Part III. Literary theories mentioned in Part I are seen originating from existence itself in Part
III. Romanticism is measured against a romantic education—and the
autobiography is essentially an autobiography of ideas and one
which deliberately leaves out all those episodes in my life which

do not further the growth of those literary speculations on which the first part is based. Even the title "A Georgian Boyhood" and the chapter headings are meant to shed an ironical emphasis on the Pater-Ruskin-Mackenzie autobiographical pastiche that was the fashion of the day.

One more point: the enquiry into the nature of contemporary prose style and the recommendation towards a certain solution in Parts I and II is meant to be illustrated by the style which emerges in Part III. The autobiography is intended to be composed in a language which combines the rapidity of the colloquial with an elasticity permitting incursions into the Mandarin of prose poetry. It should be felt evolving as it goes along. Were the first and second halves of the book to be separated there would result a very indifferent and incomplete work of criticism and a very evasive and partial autobiography; the poisons in the laurel would be segregated from its delights. I hope that my readers of to-day will be more perceptive.

What is much more disturbing is that I should have found it necessary to make so few alterations. On every page I have retouched the writing itself (it was Edmund Wilson who remarked that it was not a very well-written book and put me on to this) and I have cut out one or two rather dull passages and restored in their place one or two from the original manuscript. But I have not altered or inserted a single opinion. I have retained all the engagingly simple left-wing militancy since it breathes the air of the period, but I have found it quite unnecessary to modify any of my literary judgments. In other words I am unwilling to recognise any revolution in the reputation of modern authors over the last ten years. Yeats, Joyce, Virginia Woolf, alas, are dead. The Sitwells have grown enormously in stature, Aldous Huxley has made a brilliant recovery, Auden and Orwell added new triumphs —but with these modifications the literary values remain unaltered. Unless it is I who have been stationary, time would seem to have stood still—or rather literary time—for the effect of wars and catastrophes is to slow up the movement (so much more profound) of the human spirit. I would have preferred to re-write the whole book in order to bring it into line with a revolution in taste rather than be compelled only to revarnish it and send it forth into a stagnant world and a moribund society. But there is one change. In the autobiography I wrote of the premature death of one of my schoolmates as a momentous and distressing event, but in a year or so after its appearance death was to take a heavy toll of my generation and now I find the later chapters inexpressibly sad for me through the deaths of Denis Dannreuther my kind and loyal mentor, the gentle Peter Loxley, and the one whose friendship was the mainstay of my existence during the seven years after leaving Eton, Robert Longden killed—the only casualty—by a bomb splinter in a raid on the great school of which he was headmaster. To these I would now like to dedicate the last portion. Several others mentioned in these papers were to follow and this presence of death now lends a remoteness to the chronicles of what I see to be a far more weird and privileged and threatened and vanishing society than I ever realised—a doomed seminary of humanism singled out for especial displays of carnage in the chaotic liquidation of the West.

* * *

Sometimes I meet people who think the autobiography is meant to be an attack on Eton and as I understand that it was thrown out, with bell, book and candle on its appearance there, I expect the author would meet with the same fate. Of course it is not meant to be anything of the kind, it is an effort to tell the truth. The truth, I should have thought, emerges fairly clearly. It is possible to have a very bad time indeed in one's first year or so in a large public school if one's companions are bullies and there are bloody-minded people at the top. This would be avoided at a secondary school or an advanced school like Dartington. On the other hand my last two years at Eton, as I have tried to convey, were among the most interesting and rewarding of my whole life and I do not believe they could have been so at any other public school or in any other house than College. My criticism is not of Eton but of a system which tends to keep boys at school too late. I believe they should go at the age of twelve and leave at seventeen and go down from the university a year earlier, and I think that preparatory schools should be mostly for day-boys. And masters should all come up regularly before a psychiatrist. But parents who can send their children to Eton should at all costs do so; it may be their one chance of survival, and if they don't survive, their one moment of happiness. For, ten years after the threats of dictators and rumours of wars which toll through the opening and closing paragraphs of *Enemies of Promise*, the knell is heard again and when this reprint appears my subject may seem as trivial and superficial as in that terrible Munich week. But we must go on doing what we like doing best as if it were the illusions of humanism which are real and the realities of nihilism that prove a nightmare. *"Il faut tenter de vivre"*—we must try to live and that for many of us means we must try to write, and very difficult it is, as I found out during that Mediterranean summer especially in those moments when one leaves off telling others how to:

> As Helluo, late dictator of the feast
> The nose of Haut-gout and the tip of taste
> Critiqu'd your wine, and analysed your meat,
> Yet on plain pudding deigned at home to eat.

[1948]

PART ONE

PREDICAMENT

In vain do individuals hope for immortality, or any patent from oblivion, in preservations below the Moon.

SIR THOMAS BROWNE.

CHAPTER I

THE NEXT TEN YEARS

⅗⅗

THIS IS THE TIME OF YEAR WHEN WARS BREAK OUT AND WHEN A broken glass betrays the woodland to the vindictive sun. Already the forest fires have accounted for a thousand hectares of the Var. We fight them by starting little manageable blazes which burn a strip to ashes before the main conflagration has had time to arrive. These flames in turn must be extinguished and isolated by setting fire to other and still more obedient strips till the last cinders expire in the garden where I am writing.

It is after lunch (omelette, vichy, peaches) on a sultry day. Here is the plane tree with the table underneath it; a gramophone is playing in the next room. I always try to write in the afternoon for I have just enough Irish blood to be afraid of the Irish temperament. The literary form it takes, known as the "Celtic twilight", consists of an addiction to melancholy and to an exaggerated use of words and such good Irish writers as there have been exorcise the demon by disciplining themselves to an alien and stricter culture. Yeats translated Greek, while Joyce, Synge and George Moore fled to Paris. For myself I find Augustan Latin and Augustan English the best correctives. But they do not at all times function well and when I write after dark the shades of evening scatter their purple through my prose. Then why not write in the morning? Unfortunately in my case there is never very much of the morning, and it is curious that although I do not despise people who go to bed earlier than I, almost everyone is impatient with me for not getting up. I may be

working in bed on a wet morning and they have nothing to do yet
they cannot conceal their feelings of superiority and ill will.

But between the dissipated bedridden morning and the dangerous night fall the cicada hours of afternoon so pregnant in their
tedium and these I now have free for the problem that is obsess-
ing me.

THE NEXT TEN YEARS.

(1) What will have happened to the world in ten years' time?
(2) To me? To my friends?
(3) To the books they write?

Above all to the books—for, to put it another way, I have one
ambition—to write a book that will hold good for ten years afterwards. And of how many is that true to-day? I make it ten years
because for ten years I have written about books, and because I can
say, and this is the gravest warning, that in a short time the writing of books, especially works of the imagination which last that
long, will be an extinct art. Contemporary books do not keep. The
quality in them which makes for their success is the first to go; they
turn over night. Therefore one must look for some quality which
improves with time. The short-lived success of a book may be the
fault of the reader for newspapers, libraries, book-societies, broadcasting and the cinema have vitiated the art of reading. But the
books of which I am thinking have all been read once, and have all
seemed good to discriminating readers. They go bad just the same.

Suppose we were describing English literature in 1928. We
would mention Lawrence, Huxley, Moore, Joyce, Yeats, Virginia
Woolf and Lytton Strachey. If clever we would add Eliot, Wyndham Lewis, Firbank, Norman Douglas and, if solid, Maugham,
Bennett, Shaw, Wells, Galsworthy, Kipling. Of these Strachey,
Galsworthy, Bennett, Lawrence, Moore, Firbank are dead and also
out of fashion. They are as if they had never been. Suppose new
manuscripts were discovered, a *Five Towns* by Bennett, a *Forsyte* by
Galsworthy, even another novel by Lawrence, it would be a nightmare. We can discount for this prejudice as a natural reaction from

the work of yesterday to that of to-day but much of it is unnatural because during their life-time these writers were unnaturally praised. Since their booms, the reputations of Shaw, Joyce, Firbank and Huxley and many others have declined; in fact, of the eminent writers of ten years ago, only the fame of Eliot, Yeats, Maugham and Forster has increased. And the young writers of ten years ago are also stringing out.

My own predicament is—how to live another ten years.

Living primarily means keeping alive. The predicament is economical. How to get enough to eat? I assume however that most people who read this will have made some kind of adjustment, in fact I am writing for my fellow bourgeois. A writer has no greater pleasure than to reach people; nobody dislikes isolation more than an artist, a difficult artist most of all—but he must reach them by fair means—if he flatters them, if he screams at them, begs from them, lectures them or plays confidence tricks on them, he will appeal only to the worthless elements, and it is they who will throw him over. Meanwhile the way I write and the things I like to write about make no appeal to the working class nor can I make any bridge to them till they are ready for it. So I greet you my educated fellow bourgeois, whose interests and whose doubts I share.

Another way to keep alive is not to get killed. That is a political question. The official policy by which we are not to get killed is by keeping out of war, but in order to keep out of war it is necessary to avoid the rôle of the good samaritan; we have to pass by on the other side.

To have to dispense with their ideals and thus support a cynical policy in which they do not believe is a humiliating position for idealists. They therefore cannot be said to remain spiritually alive and this necessity of choosing between the perils of war and physical extermination and the dangers of an ostrich peace and spiritual stagnation, between physical death and moral death, is another predicament.

Since at present our own expectation of life is so insecure, the one way to make certain of living another ten years is to do work which will survive so long. For the best work explodes with a delayed impact. There is E. M. Forster, who has only produced two books since the last war, yet he is alive because his other books which are from twenty to thirty years old, are gaining ground among intelligent readers. Their pollen fertilises a new generation. There are reasons for this. To begin with, the novels of Forster state the general conflict which is localised in the political conflict of to-day. His themes are the breaking down of barriers: between white and black, between class and class, between man and woman, between art and life. "Only connect . . ." the motto of *Howard's End,* might be the lesson of all his work. His heroes and heroines, with their self-discipline, their warm hearts, their horror of shams and false emotion, of intellectual exclusiveness on the moral plane and of property, money, authority, social and family ties on the material one, are the precursors of the left-wing young people of to-day; he can be used by them as a take-off in whatever direction they would develop. Thus the parable form of Forster's novels may survive the pamphlet form of Shaw's plays, despite their vigorous thinking, because Forster is an artist and Shaw is not. Much of his art consists in the plainness of his writing for he is certain of the truth of his convictions and the force of his emotions. It is the writer who is not so sure what to say or how he feels who is apt to overwrite either to conceal his ignorance or to come unexpectedly on an answer. Similarly it is the novelist who finds it hard to create character who indulges in fine writing. This unemphatic, even style of Forster's makes him easy to re-read, for it contains nothing of which one can get tired except sprightliness. But there is another reason why the work of Forster remains fresh. His style has not been imitated.

What kills a literary reputation is inflation. The advertising, publicity and enthusiasm which a book generates—in a word its success—imply a reaction against it. The element of inflation in a writer's success, the extent to which it has been forced, is something that has to be written off. One can fool the public about a book but the public will store up resentment in proportion to its folly. The public can be fooled deliberately by advertising and publicity or it can be fooled by accident, by the writer fooling himself. If we look at the boom pages of the Sunday papers we can see the fooling of the public going on, inflation at work. A word like genius is used so many times that eventually the sentence "Jenkins has genius. *Cauliflower Ear* is immense!" becomes true because he has as much genius and is as immense as are the other writers who have been praised there. It is the words that suffer for in the inflation they have lost their meaning. The public at first suffers too but in the end it ceases to care and so new words have to be dragged out of retirement and forced to suggest merit. Often the public is taken in by a book because, although bad, it is topical, its up-to-dateness passes as originality, its ideas seem important because they are "in the air". *The Bridge of San Luis Rey, Dusty Answer, Decline and Fall, Brave New World, The Postman Always Rings Twice, The Fountain, Good-bye, Mr. Chips* are examples of books which had a success quite out of proportion to their undoubted merit and which now reacts unfavourably on their authors, because the overexcitable public who read those books have been fooled. None of the authors expected their books to become best-sellers but, without knowing it, they had hit upon the contemporary chemical combination of illusion with disillusion which makes books sell.

But it is also possible to write a good book and for it to be imitated and for those imitations to have more success than the original so that when the vogue which they have created and surfeited is past, they drag the good book down with them. This is what has happened to Hemingway who made certain pointillist discoveries in style which have almost led to his undoing. So much depends on style, this factor of which we are growing more and more suspicious, that although the tendency of criticism is to explain a writer either in terms of his sexual experience or his economic background, I still believe his technique remains the soundest base for a diagnosis, that it should be possible to learn as much about an author's income and sex-life from one paragraph of his writing as from his cheque stubs and his love-letters and that one should also be able to learn how well he writes, and who are his influences. Critics who ignore style are liable to lump good and bad writers together in support of pre-conceived theories.

An expert should be able to tell a carpet by one skein of it; a vintage by rinsing a glassful round his mouth. Applied to prose there is one advantage attached to this method—a passage taken from its context is isolated from the rest of a book, and cannot depend on the goodwill which the author has cleverly established with his reader. This is important, for in all the books which become best-sellers and then flop, this salesmanship exists. The author has fooled the reader by winning him over at the beginning, and so establishing a favourable atmosphere for putting across his inferior article—for making him accept false sentiment, bad writing, or unreal situations. To write a best-seller is to set oneself a problem in seduction. A book of this kind is a confidence trick. The reader is given a cigar and a glass of brandy and asked to put his feet up and listen. The author then tells him the tale. The most favourable atmosphere is a stall at a theatre, and consequently of all things which enjoy contemporary success that which obtains it with least merit is the average play.

A great writer creates a world of his own and his readers are proud to live in it. A lesser writer may entice them in for a moment, but soon he will watch them filing out.

But darkness falls, frogs croak, the martins bank and whistle over the terrace and the slanting hours during which I can be entrusted with a pen grow threatening with night.

CHAPTER II

THE MANDARIN DIALECT

⋈

BEFORE CONTINUING WITH OUR DIAGNOSIS IT BECOMES NECES-
sary to have a definition of style. It is a word that is beginning to
sound horrible, a quality which no good writer should possess.
Stephen Spender can even brashly say of Henry James:

As always with great æstheticians there is a certain vulgarity in his
work, and this vulgarity found its expression in violence. It is vulgarity
of a kind that we never find in the work of coarser writers like Fielding,
Smollett and Lawrence, but which we always are conscious of in
writers like Flaubert, or Jane Austen, or Wilde.

The dictionary defines style as the "collective characteristics of
the writing or diction or artistic expression or way of presenting
things or decorative methods proper to a person or school or period
or subject, manner of exhibiting these characteristics." This suggests a confusion since the word means both the collective characteristics and the manner of exhibiting them, and perhaps this
confusion may account for the distaste in which the topic is held.
For a surprising number of people to-day would agree in principle
with Spender, or would argue that the best writers have no style.
Style to them seems something artificial, a kind of ranting or of
preening. "The best writing, like the best-dressed man", as Samuel
Butler said, is sober, subdued and inconspicuous.

In point of fact there is no such thing as writing without style.
Style is not a manner of writing, it is a relationship; the relation
in art between form and content. Every writer has a certain capac-

9

ity for thinking and feeling and this capacity is never quite the same as any other's. It is a capacity which can be appreciated and for its measurement there exist certain terms. We talk of a writer's integrity, of his parts or his powers, meaning the mental force at his disposal. But in drawing from these resources the writer is guided by another consideration; that of his subject. Milton's prose style, for example, is utterly unlike his verse. Not because one is prose and the other poetry; it reveals a quite different set of qualities. The Milton of *Paradise Lost* is an aloof and dignified pontiff who makes no attempt to enter into a relationship with the reader, whose language exhibits a classical lack of detail, whose blank verse is restrained, and whose sublime sentences, often ending in the middle of a line, suggest the voice of a man who talks to himself trailing off into silence. The Milton of the pamphlets is out to persuade the reader and confute his enemy, the style is forceful, repetitive and prolix; he bludgeons away at his opponent until he is quite certain that there is no life left in him, the magnificent language is remarkable for detailed exuberance and masculine vitality. The same distinction can be made between the prose and verse style of Marvell. The style of these writers varies with their subject and with the form chosen. One might say that the style of a writer is conditioned by his conception of the reader, and that it varies according to whether he is writing for himself, or for his friends, his teachers or his God, for an educated upper class, a wanting-to-be-educated lower class or a hostile jury. This trait is less noticeable in writers who live in a settled age as they soon establish a relationship with a reader whom they can depend on and he, usually a man of the same age, tastes, education and income, remains beside them all their life. Style then is the relation between what a writer wants to say; his subject—and himself—or the powers which he has: between the form of his subject and the content of his parts.

Style is manifest in language. The vocabulary of a writer is his currency but it is a paper currency and its value depends on the reserves of mind and heart which back it. The perfect use of language is that in which every word carries the meaning that it is intended to, no less and no more. In this verbal exchange Fleet Street is a kind of Bucket Shop which unloads words on the public for less than they are worth and in consequence the more honest literary bankers, who try to use their words to mean what they say, who are always "good for" the expressions they employ, find their currency constantly depreciating. There was a time when this was not so, a moment in the history of language when words expressed what they meant and when it was impossible to write badly. This time I think was at the end of the seventeenth and the beginning of the eighteenth century, when the metaphysical conceits of the one were going out and before the classical tyranny of the other was established. To write badly at that time would involve a perversion of language, to write naturally was a certain way of writing well. Dryden, Rochester, Congreve, Swift, Gay, Defoe, belong to this period and some of its freshness is still found in the *Lives of the Poets* and in the letters of Gray and Walpole. It is a period which is ended by the work of two great Alterers, Addison and Pope.

Addison was responsible for many of the evils from which English prose has since suffered. He made prose artful, and whimsical, he made it sonorous when sonority was not needed, affected when it did not require affectation; he enjoined the essay on us so that countless small boys are at this moment busy setting down their views on Travel, the Great Man, Courage, Gardening, Capital Punishment to wind up with a quotation from Bacon. For though essay-writing was an occasional activity of Bacon, Walton and Evelyn, Addison turned it into an industry. He was the first to write for the entertainment of the middle classes, the new great power in the reign of Anne. He wrote as a gentleman (Sir Roger is the perfect gentleman), he emphasised his gentle irony, his gentle melancholy, his gentle inanity. He was the apologist for the New Bourgeoisie who writes playfully and apologetically about nothing, casting a smoke screen over its activities to make it seem harmless, genial and sensitive in its non-acquisitive moments; he anticipated Lamb and Emerson, Stevenson, *Punch* and the professional humorists, the delicious middlers, the fourth leaders, the memoirs of cabinet ministers, the orations of business magnates, and of chiefs of police. He was the first Man of Letters. Addison had the misuse of an extensive vocabulary and so was able to invalidate a great number of words and expressions; the quality of his mind was inferior to the language which he used to express it.

I am one, you must know, who am looked upon as a Humanist in Gardening. I have several Acres about my House, which I call my Garden, and which a skilful Gardener would not know what to call. It is a Confusion of Kitchen and Parterre, Orchard and Flower Garden, which lie so mixt and interwoven with one another, that if a Foreigner who had seen nothing of our Country should be conveyed into my Garden at his first landing, he would look upon it as a natural Wilderness, and one of the uncultivated Parts of our Country. My flowers grow up in several Parts of the Garden in the Greatest Luxuriancy and Profusion. I am so far from being fond of any particular one, by reason of its Rarity, that if I meet with any one in a Field which please me, I give it a place in my Garden. . . . I have always thought a Kitchen-garden a more pleasant sight than the finest Orangerie, or artificial Green-house [etc.].

Notice the presentation of the author (whose mind is also a *jardin anglais*); he is eccentric, unpractical, untidy but glories in it and implies superiority over the foreigner, he prefers home-grown vegetables to exotic fruits and in short flatters the Little Man and also the city Soames Forsytes of his day. The court jester with his cap and bells is now succeeded by the upper middle-class with his "awkward-squad" incompetence, his armchair, carpet slippers, and gardening gloves.[1]

I shall christen this style the Mandarin, since it is beloved by

---

[1] "For these reasons there are not more useful Members in a Commonwealth than Merchants. They knit Mankind together in a mutual Intercourse of good Offices, distribute the gifts of Nature, find Work for the Poor, add Wealth to the Rich, and Magnificence to the great." Compare Addison's attitude to the Merchants with Congreve's, for whom a decade earlier they were comic cuckolds.

literary pundits, by those who would make the written word as unlike as possible to the spoken one. It is the style of all those writers whose tendency is to make their language convey more than they mean or more than they feel, it is the style of most artists and all humbugs and one which is always menaced by a puritan opposition. To know which faction we should belong to at a given moment is to know how to write with best effect and it is to assist those who are not committed by their temperament to one party alone, the grand or the bald, the decorative or the functional, the baroque or the stream-lined that the following chapters are written.

Here are two more examples by Lamb and Keats of its misuse.

(I) My attachments are all local, purely local. I have no passion (or have had none since I was in love, and then it was the spurious engendering of poetry and books) to groves and vallies. The rooms where I was born, the furniture which has followed me about (like a faithful dog, only exceeding him in knowledge) wherever I have moved—old chairs, old tables, streets, squares, where I have sunned myself, my old school—these are my mistresses.

(II) I had an idea that a man might pass a very pleasant life in this manner. Let him on a certain day read a certain page of full Poesy or distilled Prose, and let him wander with it, and muse upon it, and reflect from it, and bring home to it, and prophesy upon it, and dream upon it, until it becomes stale—but when will it do so? Never! When Man has arrived at a certain ripeness in intellect any one grand and spiritual passage serves him as a starting-post towards all the two and thirty Palaces. How happy is such a voyage of conception, what delicious diligent indolence! A doze upon a sofa does not hinder it, and a nap upon Clover engenders ethereal finger-pointing. The prattle of a child gives it wings . . . [etc., etc.].

Notice how untrue these sentiments are. Lamb's old school is not a mistress, nor is an old book-case. The book-case has to be packed up and put on a van when it moves; to compare it to a faithful dog is to suggest that Lamb is beloved even by his furniture. The delicious middlers probably believe it, for Essayists must be lovable, it is part of their rôle.

"Until it becomes stale—but when will it do so? Never!" Now,
Keats is lying. "I am often hard put to it not to think that never
fares a Man so far afield as when he is anchored to his own
Armchair!" One could turn this stuff out almost fast enough to
keep up with the anthologies. "The Man," "your Man," always
occurs in these essayists. (Addison: "There is nothing in the
World that pleases a Man in Love so much as your Nightingale.")

Here are two recent examples (also from the *Oxford Book of
English Prose*). The authors are Compton Mackenzie and Rupert
Brooke.

(I) Some four and twenty miles from Curtain Wells on the Great
West Road is a tangle of briers among whose blossoms an old damask
rose is sometimes visible. If the curious traveller should pause and
examine this fragrant wilderness, he will plainly perceive the remains
of an ancient garden, and if he be of an imaginative character of mind
will readily recall the legend of the Sleeping Beauty in her mouldering
palace; for some enchantment still enthralls the spot, so that he who
bravely dares the thorns is well rewarded with pensive dreams, and,
as he lingers a while gathering the flowers or watching their petals flut-
ter to the green shadows beneath, will haply see elusive Beauty hurry
past. *The Basket of Roses* was the fairest dearest inn down all that
billowy London Road . . .

Heigh ho! Georgian prose! Notice the words, especially the
adverbs which do not aid but weaken the description, serving only
to preserve the architecture of the sentence. They are Addison's
legacy. A catalogue of flowers follows. I will begin at flower
thirty-five.

There was Venus' Looking-glass and Flower of Bristol, and Apple
of Love and Blue Helmets and Herb Paris and Campion and Love in
a Mist and Ladies' Laces and Sweet Sultans or Turkey Cornflowers,
Gillyflower Carnations (Ruffling Rob of Westminster amongst them)
with Dittany and Sops in Wine and Floramer, Widow Wail and Berga-
mot, True Thyme and Gilded Thyme, Good Night at Noon and

Flower de Luce, Golden Mouse-Ear, Prince's Feathers, Pinks and deep red Damask Roses.

It was a very wonderful garden indeed.

(II) He was immensely surprised to perceive that the actual earth of England held for him a quality which he found in A—— and in a friend's honour, and scarcely anywhere else, a quality which, if he'd ever been sentimental enough to use the word, he'd have called "holiness". His astonishment grew as the full flood of "England" swept him on from thought to thought. He felt the triumphant helplessness of a lover. Grey, uneven, little fields, and small, ancient hedges rushed before him, wild flowers, elms, and beeches. Gentleness, sedate houses of red brick, proudly unassuming, a countryside of rambling hills and friendly copses. He seemed to be raised high, looking down on a landscape compounded of the western view from the Cotswolds, and the Weald, and the high land in Wilshire, and the Midlands seen from the hills above Princes Risborough. And all this to the accompaniment of tunes heard long ago, an intolerable number of them being hymns.

"England has declared war," he says to himself, "what had Rupert Brooke better feel about it?" His equipment is not equal to the strain and his language betrays the fact by what might be described as the "Worthington touch". "If he'd ever been sentimental he'd have called it 'holiness'," i.e. he calls it holiness. "Triumphant helplessness of a lover" has no meaning. It is a try-on. "Little, small, grey, uneven, ancient, sedate, red, rambling, friendly, unassuming"—true escapist Georgian adjectives. They might all be applied to the womb.

Pope as an Alterer is a very different case. He is one of the great poets of all time and the injury he did to English Verse consisted in setting it a standard to which it could not live up. He drove lyricism out except from isolated artists like Burns and Blake, and left his successors the task of continuing in a form which he had already perfected, and for which they had neither the invention nor the ear.

> 'A waving glow the blooming beds display
> Blushing in bright diversities of day'

After this plenty poetry had become by the time of the Romantics barren and pompous, once again the content of the poetical mind was unequal to the form. The first Romantics, Wordsworth, Southey and Coleridge, therefore, set themselves to write simply, to entice poetry away from the notion of the Grand Style and the Proper Subject; their language was monosyllabic, plebeian, their subjects personal or everyday. They wore their own hair.

CHAPTER III

THE CHALLENGE TO THE MANDARINS

❧❧

THE QUALITY OF MIND OF A WRITER MAY BE IMPROVED THE
more he feels or thinks or, without effort, the more he reads and
as he grows surer of this quality so is he the better able to make
experiments in technique or towards a simplification of it even to
its apparent abandonment and the expression of strong emotion
or deep thought in ordinary language. The great speeches in *Lear*
and *Samson Agonistes* do not seem revolutionary to us because we
do not recognize them as superb and daring manipulations of the
obvious. Any poet of talent could write: "The multitudinous seas
incarnadine" or "Bid Amaranthus all his beauty shed", but only a
master could get away with "I pray you undo this button", or
Lear's quintuple "Never".

Style is a relation between form and content. Where the content
is less than the form, where the author pretends to emotion which
he does not feel, the language will seem flamboyant. The more
ignorant a writer feels, the more artificial becomes his style. A
writer who thinks himself cleverer than his readers writes simply
(often too simply), while one who fears they may be cleverer than
he will make use of mystification: an author arrives at a good style
when his language performs what is required of it without shy-
ness.

The Mandarin style at its best yields the richest and most complex expression of the English language. It is the diction of Donne,
Browne, Addison, Johnson, Gibbon, de Quincey, Landor, Carlyle

and Ruskin as opposed to that of Bunyan, Dryden, Locke, Defoe, Cowper, Cobbett, Hazlitt, Southey and Newman. It is character-ised by long sentences with many dependent clauses, by the use of the subjunctive and conditional, by exclamations and interjec-tions, quotations, allusions, metaphors, long images, Latin ter-minology, subtlety and conceits. Its cardinal assumption is that neither the writer nor the reader is in a hurry, that both are in possession of a classical education and a private income. It is Ciceronian English.

The last great exponents of the Mandarin style were Walter Pater and Henry James, who, although they wrote sentences which were able to express the subtlest inflexions of sensibility and mean-ing, at the worst grew prisoners of their style, committed to a tyranny of euphonious nothings. Such writers, the devotees of the long sentence, end by having to force everything into its frame-work, because habit has made it impossible for them to express themselves in any other way. They are like those birds that weave intricate nests in which they are as content to hatch out a pebble as an egg. But the case of Henry James is sadder still, for his best writing, that found in his later books, charged with all the wisdom and feeling of his long life, went unappreciated. As he reminded Gosse, he remained "insurmountably unsaleable", and of his col-lected edition of 1908 he could say, like Ozymandias, "Look on my *works* ye mortals and despair".

The reason for this failure of James to reach an audience lay in the change that had come over the reading public, a change to which he could not adapt himself. The early books of James ap-peared as three-volume novels which sold at thirty-one and six-pence. They reached a small leisured collection of people for whom reading a book—usually aloud—was one of the few diver-sions of our northern winters. The longer a book could be made to last the better, and it was the duty of the author to spin it out. But books grew cheaper, and reading them ceased to be a luxury; the reading public multiplied and demanded less exacting enter-tainment; the struggle between literature and journalism began.

Literature is the art of writing something that will be read twice; journalism what will be grasped at once, and they require separate techniques. There can be no delayed impact in journalism, no subtlety, no embellishment, no assumption of a luxury reader and since the pace of journalism waxed faster than that of literature, literature found itself in a predicament. It could react against journalism and become an esoteric art depending on the sympathy of a few or learn from journalism and compete with it. Poetry, which could not learn from journalism, ran away and so we find from the nineties to the last war, desolate stretches with no poets able to make a living and few receiving any attention from the public. The stage is held by journalist-poets like Kipling and Masefield, while Hopkins, Yeats, Bridges, de la Mare, Munro and a few others blossom in neglect.

Prose, with the exception of Conrad who tried to pep up the grand style, began to imitate journalism and the result was the "modern movement"; a reformist but not a revolutionary attack on the Mandarin style which was to supply us with the idiom of our age. Shaw, Butler, and Wells attacked it from the journalistic side—George Moore, Gissing and Somerset Maugham, admirers of French realism, of the Goncourts, Zola, Maupassant, from the æsthetic.

Only Wilde belonged to the other camp, and the style he created was his own variation of the introspective essayist:

On that little hill by the city of Florence, where the lovers of Giorgione are lying, it is always the solstice of noon, of noon made so languorous by summer suns that hardly can the slim naked girl dip into the marble tank the round bubble of clear glass, and the long fingers of the lute-players rest idly upon the chords. It is twilight also for the dancing nymphs whom Corot set free among the silver poplars of France. In eternal twilight they move, those frail diaphanous figures, whose tremulous white feet seem not to touch the dew-drenched grass they tread on.

Notice the amount of "romantic" words, now well-known hacks, "solstice, languorous, eternal, frail, diaphanous, tremulous", which help to date the passage, while Shaw, who was the same age, was then writing:

This is the true joy in life, the being used for a purpose recognised by yourself as a mighty one; the being thoroughly worn out before you are thrown on the scrapheap; the being a force of Nature instead of a feverish selfish little clod of ailments and grievances complaining that the world will not devote itself to making you happy. And also the only real tragedy in life is the being used by personally minded men for purposes which you recognise to be base. All the rest is at worst mere misfortune or mortality; this alone is misery, slavery, hell on earth; and the revolt against it is the only force that offers a man's work to the poor artist, whom our personally minded rich people would so willingly employ as pander, buffoon, beauty monger, sentimentaliser, and the like.

This sentence with its boisterous sentiments and creaking gerunds might have been written to-day. It is not a question of subject. The beauty of the Giorgione picture is just as alive as a sense of social injustice. Giorgione is not Sir Alma Taddema. But while the first passage is dead, constructed out of false sentiment and faulty linguistic material, the second is in the idiom of our time. For the idiom of our time is journalistic and the secret of journalism is to write the way people talk. The best journalism is the conversation of a great talker. It need not consist of what people say but it should include nothing which cannot be said. The Shaw passage could be talked; the Wilde passage would hardly stand recitation.

Moore also was not to remain a realist for long—but Moore, after his *Esther Waters* period, carried on his warfare against the Mandarin style from another position. In his *Ave, Salve, Vale* books he describes the Irish rebellion against the official literary language.

Alas, the efforts of the uneducated to teach the educated would be made in vain; for the English language is perishing and it is natural that. it should perish with the race; race and grammatical sense go together. The English have striven and done a great deal in the world;

the English are a tired race and their weariness betrays itself in the language, and the most decadent of all are the educated classes.

He perceived, however, the increasing unreality of Anglo-Irish, of Yeats and Synge filling their notebooks with scraps of tinker's dialogue which could be used only in plays, and in plays only about tinkers, and instead he moulded for himself a simplified prose in which he could describe pictures, books, people, places, and complex sensations—yet always maintain an unassuming unsophisticated equality with the reader.

The artist should keep himself free from all creed, from all dogma, from all opinion. As he accepts the opinions of others he loses his talent, all his feelings and ideas must be his own.

. . . .

I never knew a writer yet who took the smallest pains with his style and was at the same time readable. Plato's having had seventy shies at one sentence is quite enough to explain to me why I dislike him.

Men like Newman and R. L. Stevenson seem to have taken pains to acquire what they called a style as a preliminary measure—as something that they had to form before their writings could be of any value. I should like to put it on record that I never took the smallest pains with my style, have never thought about it, and do not know or want to know whether it is a style at all, or whether it is not, as I believe and hope, just common, simple straightforwardness. I cannot conceive how any man can take thought for his style without loss to himself and his readers.

Here in the colloquial English of 1897 is Samuel Butler attacking the Mandarin style. The musing introspective attitude of Pater and of Wilde's essays, is replaced by one more social and argumentative.[1] This *arguing* style (as opposed to the soliloquy) is typical of the new relationship with the reader which is to sweep over the twentieth century and dominate journalism and adver-

[1] "Mr. Walter Pater's style is, to me, like the face of some old woman who has been to Madam Rachel and had herself enamelled. The bloom is nothing but powder and paint and the odour is cherry blossom. Mr. Matthew Arnold's odour is as the faint sickliness of hawthorn."—Butler.

tising. It may be described as *you*-writing from the fact that there
is a constant tendency to harangue the reader in the second person.
It is a buttonholing approach. The Addison manner on the other
hand, has degenerated into whimsical *we*-writing. "We have the
best goods. We like quality. We're funny that way", is one sort
of advertising. "You realise the inconveniences of inadequate
plumbing. Then why not of inadequate underclothing?" is the
other.

Meanwhile, Wells, also, was not inactive (though it was not
till 1915 that he attacked Henry James in *Boon,* a bogus autobiography). Henry James, in two magnificent letters (Vol. II, pp.
503-8, of his letters) answers Wells's criticism.

Wells wrote:

To you literature, like painting, is an end, to us literature, is a means,
it has a use. Your view was, I felt, altogether too prominent in the
world of criticism and I assailed it in lines of harsh antagonism. I
had rather be called a journalist than an artist, that is the essence of it,
and there was no antagonist possible than yourself.

James replied that his view can hardly be so prominent or it
would be reflected in the circulation of his books.

But I have no view of life and literature, I maintain, other than
that our form of the latter (the novel) in especial is admirable exactly
by its range and variety, its plasticity and liberality, its fairly living on
the sincere and shifting experience of the individual practitioner . . .
Of course for myself I live, live intensely and am fed by life, and my
value, whatever it be, is in my own kind of expression of that . . . .
Meanwhile I absolutely dissent from the claim that there are any dif-
ferences whatever in the amenability to art of forms of literature
æsthetically determined, and hold your distinction between a form that
is (like) painting and a form that is (like) architecture for wholly null
and void. There is no sense in which architecture is æsthetically "for
use" that doesn't leave any other art whatever exactly as much so; and
so far from that of literature being irrelevant to the literary report upon
life, and to its being made as interesting as possible, I regard it as
relevant in a degree that leaves everything else behind. It is art that

makes life, makes interest, makes importance, for our consideration
and application of these things, and I know of no substitute whatever
for the force and beauty of its process. If I were Boon I should say that
any pretence of such a substitute is helpless and hopeless humbug; but
I wouldn't be Boon for the world, and am only yours faithfully, Henry
James.

The justification for Wells's attack must lie in the defence it
provoked, for these two majestic letters from the dying giant form
a creed which he might not otherwise have left us. One is reminded of a small boy teasing an elephant which gets up with a
noble bewilderment, gives him one look, and shambles away.

We are not concerned here with the people who prefer to be
journalists rather than artists, but with those who have tried to
make journalism into an art, and already it is possible to define
the opponents of the Mandarin style, all those who tried to break
it up into something simpler and terser, destroying its ornamen-
tation, attacking its rhythms and giving us instead the idiom of
to-day. Thus Moore's new language is somewhat lyrical, for his
standards are æsthetic. Norman Douglas is intellectual, with a
strong imaginative side. Maugham is also imaginative, though
play-writing interferes with his literary development, but Butler,
Shaw, Wells, Bennett, write as plainly as they can. If Henry James
could have given up all hope of being read, had abandoned novels
and written but a few magnificent pages about ideas that stirred
him, he might have been happier and had greater influence. But
he was obsessed with the novel to the neglect even of his long
short stories; he still considered the novel the supreme art form,
as it had been for Turgenev, Balzac and Flaubert. So he continued
to write novels which came into competition with the journalistic
novels of Wells and Bennett or the speeded-up Jamesian of Conrad, rather than take refuge in the strongholds of the leisurely
style—memoirs, autobiography, books of criticism, or else venture
out into the experimental forms of the short story. The younger
writers whom he patronised—Rupert Brooke, Compton Mackenzie

and Hugh Walpole [1]—were more remarkable for talent, personal charm and conventionality than for the "beginning late and long choosing" of genius, the crabwise approach to perfection.

[1] It is interesting to speculate on the effect Henry James might have had on, say, E. M. Forster, Virginia Woolf and Lytton Strachey had he bestowed on them the loving criticism which he lavished on his more personable disciples.

CHAPTER IV

THE MODERN MOVEMENT

❧❦

MEANWHILE BUTLER'S DICTUM "A MAN'S STYLE IN ANY ART
should be like his dress—it should attract as little attention as
possible," reigned supreme, though only since Brummel had this
stranglehold of convention been applied to what we wear.

Here, on these remote uplands, I prefer to turn my back on the
green undulations of Massa and Sorrento, on Vesuvius and Naples,
Ischia and Phlegræan fields: all these regions are trite and familiar. I
prefer to gaze towards the mysterious south, the mountains of Basilicata,
and the fabled headland Licosa, where Leucosia, sister-siren of Parthen-
ope, lies buried. At this height the sea's horizon soars into the firma-
ment smooth as a sheet of sapphire, and the eye never wearies of
watching those pearly lines and spirals that crawl upon its surface, the
paths of silver-footed Thetis—a restful prospect, with dim suggestions
of love and affinity for this encircling element that reach back, for aught
we know, to primeval days of Ascidian-life. There is a note of impotence in the sea's wintry storms, for it can but rage against its prison
bars or drown a few sailormen, an ignoble business: true grandeur is
only in its luminous calm.

.   .   .   .

This is a good example of the reformed Mandarin. It is leisurely
but not too leisurely, the syntax is easy, the thought simple, the
vocabulary humdrum. The use of classical names takes for granted
a reader who will accept this coin. The intellectual attitude is evi-
dent in the author's genial patronage of Nature and his calm

analysis. It is readable, good-mannered and seems to-day a little flat, for the coins mean less to us and yet it is redeemed by the lovely image of the patterns on the sea from a height—if we know who Thetis is. It comes from Norman Douglas's *Siren Land* (1911).

The poor little wife coloured at this, and, drawing her handkerchief from her pocket, shed a few tears. No one noticed her. Evie was scowling like an angry boy. The two men were gradually assuming the manner of the committee room. They were both at their best when serving on committees. They did not make the mistake of handling human affairs in the bulk, but disposed of them item by item, sharply. Calligraphy was the item before them now, and on it they turned their well-trained brains. Charles, after a little demur, accepted the writing as genuine, and they passed on to the next point. It is the best, perhaps the only way, of dodging emotion. They were the average human article, and had they considered the note as a whole it would have driven them miserable, or mad. Considered item by item, the emotional content was minimised, and all went forward smoothly. The clock ticked, the coals blazed higher, and contended with the white radiance that poured in through the windows. Unnoticed, the sun occupied his sky, and the shadows of the tree stems, extraordinarily solid, fell like trenches of purple across the frosted lawn. It was a glorious winter morning. Evie's fox terrier, who had passed for white, was only a dirty grey dog now, so intense was the purity that surrounded him. He was discredited, but the blackbirds that he was chasing glowed with Arabian darkness, for all the conventional colouring of life had been altered. Inside, the clock struck ten with a rich and confident note. Other clocks confirmed it, and the discussion moved towards its close.

To follow it is unnecessary. It is rather a moment when the commentator should step forward. Ought the Wilcoxes to have offered their home to Margaret? I think not. The appeal was too flimsy.

This is a passage from E. M. Forster's *Howard's End* (1910) and shows a great departure from the writing of the nineteenth century. Extreme simplicity, the absence of relative and conjunctive clauses, an everyday choice of words (Arabian darkness is the one romanticism, for darkness in Arabia can be no different from anywhere else) constitute a more revolutionary break from the Mandarin style than any we have yet quoted. Twenty-two short sentences follow. How remote it is from James, Meredith, Conrad, Walter Pater whom one cannot imagine interpolating themselves into a novel to ask a question, and answer "I think not"! From a passage like this derives much of the diction, the handling of emotional situations and the attitude to the reader of such writers as Virginia Woolf, Katherine Mansfield, David Garnett, Elizabeth Bowen.

The hardest task in modern criticism is to find out who were the true innovators. Forster I think was one. Novels like *The Longest Journey* and *Howard's End* established a point of view, a technique, and an attitude to the reader that were to be followed for the next thirty years by the psychological novelists. Intellectual rebels against the grand style, such as Norman Douglas, still wrote for Oxford and Cambridge graduates, for educated men, were but reformists. Forster wrote for men and women, chiefly women, of a larger though still cultured public, and evolved a more radically simplified, disintegrated, and colloquial form of art.

Now we are coming on the tracks of the writers of 1927-8. They are going to be judged by the contents of their minds and the form of their books and by what they make of them. From their failures and their successes we shall endeavour to learn how in the future to avoid failure, and so create that great book which will last a round ten years. This list forms the next stage in their pursuit.

Some Books in the Modern Movement—1900–22

1900. Dreiser, *Sister Carrie*; *Oxford Book of English Verse*.
1901. Gissing, *By the Ionian Sea*.
1902. James, *The Wings of the Dove*; Yeats, *The Celtic Twilight*; Maugham, *Mrs. Craddock*; Belloc, *The Path to Rome*.
1903. Butler, *Way of all Flesh*; Gissing, *Private Papers of Henry Rycroft*; James, *The Ambassadors*.
1904. Baron Corvo, *Hadrian VII*.

1905. Wilde, *De Profundis*; Forster, *Where Angels Fear to Tread*; Firbank, *Odette D'Antrevernes*; James, *The Golden Bowl*; H. G. Wells, *Kipps*.

1906. Galsworthy, *The Man of Property*.

1907. Forster, *The Longest Journey*; Beardsley, *Venus and Tannhäuser*; Gosse, *Father and Son*; James, *The American Scene*; Joyce, *Chamber Music*.

1908. Conrad, *A Set of Six*; Forster, *A Room with a View*.

1909. Stein, *Three Lives*; Beerbohm, *And Even Now*.

1910. Forster, *Howard's End*; Bennett, *Old Wives' Tale*; Wedgwood, *Shadow of a Titan*; Saki's Stories; Wells, *Mr. Polly*; Shaw, *Plays Pleasant and Unpleasant*.

1911. Beerbohm, *Zuleika Dobson*; Douglas, *Siren Land*; Lawrence, *The White Peacock*; Moore, *Ave*; Lytton Strachey, *Landmarks in French Literature*; Lowes Dickinson, *A Modern Symposium*; Hugh Walpole, *Mr. Perrin and Mr. Traill*.

1912. Douglas, *Fountains in the Sand*; Samuel Butler, *Notebooks*; Beerbohm, *Christmas Garland*; Moore, *Salve*; Forster, *Celestial Omnibus*; Stephens, *Crock of Gold*; *Georgian Poetry (to 1918)*.

1913. Conrad, *Chance*; Lawrence, *Sons and Lovers*; Mansfield, *In a German Pension*.

1914. Wyndham Lewis, *Blast*; Moore, *Vale*; Imagists' *Anthology* (Aldington, H. D., Pound, etc.); Monro, *Children of Love*; James Joyce, *Dubliners*; Compton Mackenzie, *Sinister Street*.

1915. Douglas, *Old Calabria*; Firbank, *Vain Glory*; Somerset Maugham, *Of Human Bondage*; *Catholic Anthology* (includes Eliot's *Prufrock*); Virginia Woolf, *The Voyage Out*; Brooke, *1914*, etc.; D. H. Lawrence, *The Rainbow*.

1916. Moore, *The Brook Kerith*; Firbank, *Inclinations*; Joyce, *A Portrait of the Artist*; *Ulysses* starts in the *Little Review*.

1917. Douglas, *South Wind*; Eliot, *Prufrock*; *Wheels* (includes the Sitwells); Firbank, *Caprice*.

1918. Strachey, *Eminent Victorians*; Lewis, *Tarr*; Pearsall-Smith, *Trivia*; Bridges, *The Poems of Gerard Manley Hopkins* and *The Spirit of Man*; Waley, *170 Chinese Poems*.

1919. Cabell, *Jurgen*; Firbank, *Valmouth*; Maugham, *The Moon and*

Sixpence; Daisy Ashford, *The Young Visiters*; Barbellion, *Diary of a Disappointed Man*; [Anderson, *Winesburg-Ohio*]; Beerbohm, *Seven Men*.

1920. Huxley, *Limbo* and *Leda*; Eliot, *The Sacred Wood*; Wilfrid Owen, *Poems*; Henry James, *Letters*.

1921. Huxley, *Crome Yellow*; Strachey, *Queen Victoria*; Virginia Woolf, *Monday or Tuesday, Poems of To-day*.

1922. Housman, *Last Poems*; Mansfield, *The Garden Party*; Garnett, *Lady Into Fox*; Strachey, *Books and Characters*; Beerbohm, *Rossetti and His Circle*; Yeats, *Later Poems*; Gerhardi, *Futility*; Galsworthy, *Forsyte Saga*; James Joyce, *Ulysses*; Virginia Woolf, *Jacob's Room*.

Not all of these books are of equal significance but they reveal how long ago most of our well-known writers began, how they overlap, how thick the field was before the Armistice. There will be several new names to talk about on our way to 1928.

I shall not group writers under movements, for the reason that between the nineties and the present day they scarcely exist. I recognise a complicating trend or inflation in the nineties, a simplifying one or deflation (realism, Georgian poetry) that followed. Then a further complicating process (Bloomsbury) and a further deflation (Hemingway), and I find the simplest guide the words used by writers themselves and the purposes for which they are employed. One faith unites all the writers discussed (with the exception of Shaw and Wells); whether realists, intellectuals or imaginative writers, from Pater to Joyce they believed in the importance of their art, in the sanctity of the artist and in his sense of vocation. They were all inmates of the Ivory Tower.

An "ivory tower" is a vague image and those who adopt it may take advantage of the vagueness. The image was taken by Flaubert from Alfred de Vigny and all who accept it are to some extent his pupils; if they do not admire *Bouvard*, they admit *Bovary*; if they reject *Bovary* they will recognise the *Letters*, *Salammbô*, the *Tentation*, or the *Education Sentimentale*.

We write in the language of Dryden and Addison, of Milton and Shakespeare, but the intellectual world we inhabit is that of Flaubert and Baudelaire; it is to them, and not to their English contemporaries that we owe our conception of modern life. The artist who accepts the religion of the Ivory Tower, that is of an art whose reward is perfection and where perfection can be attained only by a separation of standards from those of the non-artist is led to adopt one of four rôles: the High Priest (Mallarmé, Joyce, Yeats), the Dandy (Firbank, Beerbohm, Moore), The Incorruptible Observer (Maugham, Maupassant) or the Detached Philosopher (Strachey, Anatole France). What he will not be is a Fighter or a Helper.

The tradition of dandyism is purer in France. Baudelaire was obsessed with "l'éternel superiorité, du Dandy" as were Nerval, Laforgue, D'Aurevilly. When the wit and lyricism are shallow the resulting dandyism will have a popular success—and we get Noel Coward and Paul Morand—when deep, we find the most delicate achievements of conscious art. Meanwhile there are one or two more contributions to the idiom of our time to be considered.

The period 1900–14 was that of the Dublin School—Yeats, Moore, Joyce, Synge and Stephens. The sentiment of these writers was anti-English; they found the Mandarin style the language of their oppressors for they were sufficiently interested in the National Movement to consider themselves oppressed. For them England was the Philistine and since they could not use Gaelic, their aim was to discover what blend of Anglo-Irish and French would give them an explosive that would knock the pundits of London off their padded chairs. All had lived in Paris, and all had absorbed French culture. Moore kept strictly to it, using his Irish background as an excuse for spiteful criticism and ponderous ancestor-worship, but always preferring simple and racy expressions and unforced sentences as the basis of his style. Yeats was engrossed in his mysticism and Gaelic legends; the French influence is more apparent in his verse-forms, and in his cryptic utterances, sanctioned by Mallarmé. Synge went on from Villon to pick up peasant talk on the Aran islands and twine it into plays.

It isn't that I haven't prayed for you, Bartley, to the Almighty God. It isn't that I haven't said prayers in the dark till you wouldn't know what I'd be saying, but it's a great rest I'll have now, and it's time surely. It's a great rest I'll have now, and great sleeping in the long nights after Samhain, if it's only a bit of wet flour we do have to eat, and maybe a fish that would be stinking.

There could be no clearer example than this of the extent of that insurrection against the prose of the capital which was the Celtic movement.

James Stephens's *The Crock of Gold* was an attempt to reconcile Classical mythology with Celtic. It proved that the Irish could beat the English at whimsy and produce a rival to the *Wind in the Willows* and *Peter Pan*.

Of much greater importance are *Dubliners* and *A Portrait of the Artist*. These books are written in a reformed Mandarin, influenced by French Realism. The style is not as unconventional as Yeats's or Synge's, or even as Moore's, and fits in more with the English of Maugham (*Of Human Bondage*) and of the Lawrence of *Sons and Lovers*. The favourite epithet of all these writers at that time was "grey".

(I) The park trees were heavy with rain and rain fell still and even in the lake, lying grey like a shield. A game of swans flew there and the water and the shore beneath were fouled with their green-white slime. They embraced softly impelled by the grey rainy light, the shield-like witnessing lake, the swans.—Joyce, *Portrait of the Artist*.

(II) The day broke grey and dull. The clouds hung heavily, and there was a rawness in the air that suggested snow. A woman servant came into the room in which a child was sleeping, and drew the curtains.—*Of Human Bondage*, opening paragraph.

(III) I stood watching the shadowy fish slide through the gloom of the mill-pond. They were grey, descendants of the silvery things that had darted away from the monks in the young days when the valley was lusty. The whole place was gathered in the musing of old age. The

thick-piled trees on the far shore were too dark and sober to dally with
the sun; the weeds stood crowded and motionless.—Lawrence, *The
White Peacock*.

Nineteen fourteen-fifteen were important years in the Modern
Movement. Besides *Dubliners*, Joyce's first prose book, we have
Of Human Bondage, the first poems of Eliot, Firbank's *Vainglory*,
Lawrence's *Rainbow*, Douglas's *Old Calabria* and Virginia Woolf's
Voyage Out. Wyndham Lewis edits *Blast*. The most serious artists
among them continued to produce throughout the war. Joyce wrote
A Portrait of the Artist and *Ulysses*. From his rooms in Oxford
Firbank let slip a novel a year. In 1918 Lytton Strachey, a con-
scientious objector, was able to launch *Eminent Victorians* on a
war-weary world. Moore produced *The Brook Kerith* and Douglas
South Wind, perhaps their two greatest books, Huxley appears in
two slim volumes of poetry, Eliot in *Prufrock* while the Sitwells
emerge in *Wheels;* Lewis writes *Tarr*, and Pearsall-Smith publishes
Trivia in unashamed Mandarinese. Nineteen-fourteen was also the
year of an important bad book, *Sinister Street*. It is a work of
inflation, important because it is the first of a long line of
bad books, the novels of adolescence, autobiographical, romantic,
which squandered the vocabulary of love and literary appreciation
and played into the hands of the Levellers and Literary Puritans.

Three years afterwards came *South Wind*, a book, which although one now recognises in it reiterations and longueurs, remains
a flower of the intellectual school, a book that was to reform for
a while Compton Mackenzie and which stated for the first time
the predicament (when anxious to be successful in love or at
making a living) of the Petrouchka of the Twenties, the Clever
Young Man. The plight of Dedalus in revolt against the Jesuits
is too particular; Michael Fane of *Sinister Street* is a born success;
it is Denis of *South Wind* pursuing the Italian chambermaid and
cut out by the rough young scientist who is the hero of *South
Wind* and the years that follow, the Oxford Boy, the miserable
young man on the flying trapeze.

CHAPTER V

ANATOMY OF DANDYISM

⊱⊰

DANDIES IN LITERATURE HAVE OFTEN BEGUN BY MAKING FUN
of the Mandarin style, for it is the enemy of their qualities of wit
and lyricism, though in the end they come round to it. Dandyism
is capitalist, for the Dandy surrounds himself with beautiful
things and decorative people and remains deaf to the call of social
justice. As a wit he makes fun of seriousness, as a lyricist he exists
to celebrate things as they are, not to change them. Moore's *Confessions of a Young Man* is a typical dandy book but one finds
much dandyism in Wilde and some in Saki who, however, adul-
terated his Wilde to suit the *Morning Post* and to procure the
immediate impact of journalism. In his work the reactionary implication of dandyism is very clear.

Of the young men of these years (1914–18) Firbank, Eliot and
Huxley, the three most prominent, were dandies. Firbank followed
Beardsley and Apollinaire, Eliot followed Laforgue, Huxley Eliot
and Firbank. They were intellectuals, but in his writing Firbank
took pains to conceal the fact and so can best be taken as an
example of the type. He harked back to the dandyism of the
seventeenth century; his play *The Princess Zoubaroff* is based on
Congreve and among his few allusions are one to the Memoirs of
Grammont and another to the acting of Betterton. He was an
impressionist; his sentences are hit or miss attempts to suggest a
type of character or conversation, or to paint a landscape in a few
brush strokes. When something bored him, he left it out (a device

33

which might have improved the quality of innumerable novelists).
Firbank is not epigrammatic, he is not easily quotable, his object
was to cast a sheen of wit over his writing. Like all dandies, like
Horace, Tibullus, Rochester, Congreve, Horace Walpole and the
youthful Beckford, like Watteau and Guardi, he was obsessed
with the beauty of the moment, and not the beauty only, but the
problem of recording that beauty, for with one false touch the
description becomes ponderous and overloaded and takes on that
unreal but sickly quality often found in modern paganism. Firbank, like Degas, was aware of this and, like Degas, he used
pastel.

What is his contribution to modern literature? To what extent
can we profit from him if we wish to write well ourselves?

One thing which we recognise not to have kept in him is an
element of sexuality. Firbank was homosexual, which is not a
factor of importance in the assessment of a writer's style but he
was of the breed with a permanent giggle and the result is a
naughtiness in his books, a sniggering about priests and choir-
boys, nuns and flagellation, highbrows and ostlers which shocks
us because it does not come off. It is meant to be a joke but it
actually betrays the author, his inhibitions and his longings and
it is his capacity for not betraying himself that is the secret of his
art. It is this element which looks back to the nineties, to Beardsley and Corvo, when so much more looks forward. For the
"queen" or homosexual capon being usually a parasite on society,
a person with an inherited income and no occupation, can criticise
that society only in jest. When goaded by wars and slumps it will
become unfriendly and any criticism, however frivolous, will seem
impertinent. Firbank, like most dandies, disliked the bourgeoisie,
idealised the aristocracy and treated the lower classes as his brothel.

It is customary to assume that Firbank was frivolous because
frivolity was his only medium of self-expression. In fact he was
no less serious than Congreve or Horace Walpole but he recognised frivolity as the most insolent refinement of satire. The things
Firbank hated were the moral vices of the bourgeoisie, stupidity,

hypocrisy, pretentiousness, greed and the eye on the main chance. What distinguishes the characters he writes about is their unworld-liness and he believed that the most unworldly people are those who are born with everything. It was a complete vagueness about money, a warm erratic unjudging heart, a muddled goodness, an instinctive elegant disorder that he loved. The quality common to his characters is their impulsiveness; their virtue lies in their un-awareness of evil. Where they are ambitious, their ambitions are preposterous. To be perpetuated by a stained-glass window, to shine in the highest circles of Cuna-Cuna, to go to Athens, to be a great tragic actress and yet to remain unconscious of the difficulty of attaining these ends, was what appealed to him. Whom he disliked were the schemers, the Becky Sharps, the Babbitts. Here is Mrs. Sixsmith, thinking of her dead friend, Sally.

Those fine palatial houses, she reflected, must be full of wealth . . . old Caroline plate and gorgeous green Limoges: Sally indeed had proved it! The day she had opened her heart in the Café Royal she had spoken of a massive tureen *too heavy even to hold*.
Mrs. Sixsmith's eyes grew big.

Or:

And now a brief lull, as a brake containing various delegates and "representatives of English Culture" rolled by at a stately trot—Lady Alexander, E. V. Lucas, Robert Hichens, Clutton Brock, etc.—the en-semble, the very apotheosis of the worn-out *cliché*.

For what he hated was vulgarity and vulgarity of writing as much as vulgarity of the heart. Indeed, the writers with the most exquisite choice of words, those who take pains to avoid the outworn and the obvious to achieve distinction of phrasing, are equally susceptible to the fine points of the human heart. The world to Congreve is a sink out of which a few young people manage to drag themselves, to Horace Walpole an arena which friendship alone makes tolerable. They are strongly conscious of good and evil. "To write simply", explains Maugham, "is as difficult as to be good." Perhaps one requires the other. For

Dandies are perfectionists and Perfectionism involves disappointment and from the disappointments is built up the idea of an
elect, of a few human beings gifted with distinction of mind and
heart heaving themselves up from the general mud-bath. Some are
kept up for a few years by their beauty, breeding or charm, but
all those without moral qualities and a courageous intelligence are
bound to flop back.

"Now that the ache of life with its fevers, passions, doubts, its
routine, vulgarity and boredom was over, his serene unclouded
face was a marvelment to behold. Very great distinction and sweetness was visible there together with much nobility and love, all
magnified and commingled," writes Firbank of the death-mask
of Cardinal Pirelli and it was the last sentence but two he ever
wrote; his most serious, though not his most successful, for he is
nervous of his own seriousness and suddenly produces a word,
"marvelment" out of his old 1890 past to reassure him. But it is
the sentence of an ascetic, as must be all those who are dandies
in the fullest sense.

The lesson one can learn from Firbank is that of inconsequence.
There is the vein which he tapped and which has not yet been
fully exploited.

His method was to write in dialogue, and to omit what would
not fit in. Narrative prose as opposed to dialogue is used only for
vignettes of places or descriptions of characters when they first
appear. It is the most brisk and readable form of writing, making
demands on the reader's intelligence but none on his eye or ear:
and it is to Firbank that we owe the conception of dialogue—not
as a set-piece in the texture of the novel, as are the conversations
of Wilde and Meredith—but as the fabric itself. A book by Firbank is in the nature of a play where passages of descriptive prose
correspond to stage directions.

As a prose writer Firbank did not have a large or an interesting
vocabulary and his work is full of spelling mistakes, but he wrote
with a horror of the cliché and with a regard for the words he
used, achieving the freshness he needed by grammatical inversion,

and by experiments in order. He also applied impressionism with startling results.

The mists had fallen from the hills, revealing old woods wrapped in the blue doom of Summer.

Boats with crimson spouts, to wit, steamers, dotted the skyline far away, and barques with sails like the wings of butterflies, borne by an idle breeze, were winging more than one ineligible young mariner back to the prose of the shore.

It was the Feast night. In the grey spleen of evening through the dusty lanes towards Mediavilla, country-society flocked.

Do they come off? On the whole yes, much better than his over-loaded passages in *Cardinal Pirelli* and *Santal*, for it is one of the weaknesses of the dandy's position that the seriousness on which it is based must at all costs be concealed. The preoccupation of the dandy is with the moment.

Every moment some form grows perfect in hand or face; some tone on the hills or the sea is choicer than the rest; some mood or passion or insight or intellectual excitement is irresistibly real and attractive for us—for that moment only. Not the fruit of experience, but experience itself, is the end. A counted number of pulses only is given to us of a variegated dramatic life. How may we see in them all that is to be seen in them by the finest senses? How shall we pass most swiftly from point to point, and be present always at the focus where the greatest number of vital forces unite in their purest energy? To burn always with this hard gemlike flame, to maintain this ecstasy is success in life. . . . Not to discriminate every moment some passionate attitude in those about us, and in the brilliancy of their gifts some tragic dividing of forces on their ways, is, on this short day of frost and sun, to sleep before evening.

So wrote Pater, calling an art-for-art's-sake muezzin to the faithful from the topmost turret of the ivory tower. By leaving out the more affected "any stirring of the senses, strange dyes, strange colours, and curious odours, or work of the artist's hands, or the face of one's friend" it becomes one of the great passages of Mandarin writing, and as a text concentrates as much on the moment in personal relations, on the ethical moment as on the sensual one. Henry James spent his life in "discriminating passionate attitudes and tragic divisions in those about him" as thoroughly as Wilde investigated his own moods or Moore and Yeats and Joyce waited for "some tone on the hills or the sea". Pater, when he realised its implications, suppressed the passage which is but the philosophy of the refractory pupil of Socrates, Aristippus of Cyrene, who believed happiness to be the sum of particular pleasures and golden moments and not, as Epicurus, a prolonged intermediary state between ecstasy and pain.

The artistic fault of the Cyrenaic philosophy is a tendency to fake these golden moments, inevitable when they are regarded as the only ones worth living for; the artist becomes like the medium who has to produce a psychic experience to earn her money, and the result is that he leans too heavily on the moment, and so produces that effect of satiety which runs, for instance, through the translations of Mackail. Similarly if we examine the kind of poetry that we read and appreciate when we are unhappy, we soon find that it is not the best kind or, if the best, that we appreciate it for the wrong reasons, we over-emphasize it to make it support a weight which it was not intended to bear. The perfectionists, the art-for-art's-sakers, finding or believing life to be intolerable except for art's perfection, by the very violence of their homage can render art imperfect. This was the danger of Firbank's growing seriousness, it is a danger which besets all lyric poets, dandies and ephemerids although it is a danger which by emotional awareness and technical discipline they can often avoid.

At the moment Dandyism in its extreme form, Perfectionism, is on the increase, for Perfectionists, like the hermits of the Thebaid, take refuge from the world in private salvation. I have known many perfectionists, all of whom are remarkable for the intense stripping process which they carry out. Their lives are balloons from which more and more ballast has to be cast; they never have more than one suitcase, wear no pyjamas or underclothes, travel constantly and are the mystics of our time "pressés

de trouver le lieu et la formule". An element of guilt and expia-
tion in their activity awakens distrust in the complacent herd and
certainly perfection has a bleaching, deathwishful quality. But it
is so seldom attained, that a little respect for it would do no harm
to its detractors.

It will be seen then that dandyism, despite its roots in the
status quo and its tendency to pessimism, is a tenable position—
since any position which can be shown to produce good writing is
tenable—for as long as the writer can count on a natural consti-
tutional gaiety to inform his lyricism. When that disappears as in
Housman, the wit becomes bitter, the lyricism morbid. It is therefore suitable to young writers or to those with plenty of money.
They have their roots in manure but the orchid blooms the richer
for it, until ultimately the bloom dies down, and the manure is
left. Tibullus, Rochester, Watteau and Leopardi—the greatest per-
fectionist of them all—died before this could happen. Congreve
retired; Walpole and Beckford became ancestor-worshipping and
reactionary antiquarians, only Horace and Degas, obedient always
to the discipline of their art and intellectually agile, arrogant and
tough, remained perfectionists to the last. Had he lived, Firbank
would not have written worse, he would have written differently.

[NOTE: The debt of Firbank to Beardsley's *Under the Hill* is not here sufficiently stressed. It is the archetype of sophisticated butterfly impressionism
in our tongue. Firbank perhaps was never quite so witty, vicious or well-in-
formed as the adolescent of genius, however he was more radiantly preposterous,
a humourist of wider calibre.]

CHAPTER VI

A BEAST IN VIEW

I HAVE TAKEN FIRBANK AS THE TYPE OF THE WRITER DANDY
but what has been said of him is also true of the early Eliot and
the early Huxley. Eliot is the purest of the three, for a lyric poet
works in a more distilled medium than narrative prose.

> Let us go then, you and I,
> When the evening is spread out against the sky,
> Let us go, through certain half-deserted streets . . .

I have often wondered what it must have felt like to discover
these opening lines of *Prufrock* in *Blast* or the *Catholic Anthology*
in 1914-15 with the Rupert Brooke poems, Kitchener's Army and
Business as Usual everywhere. Would we have recognised that
new, sane, melancholy, light-hearted and fastidious voice?

> There will be time, there will be time
> To prepare a face to meet the faces that you meet;
> There will be time to murder and create.

Surely we would have noticed it, would have "lingered in the
chambers of the sea" and experienced that exquisite sensation,
the apprehension of the first sure masterful flight of a great contemporary writer. But how few of us did!

What can one learn from Eliot? Not to be ashamed of bor-
rowing and to assimilate what we borrow. Yet his influence on
young writers is disconcerting; Auden, I think, is the one young

poet to survive it. The reason I believe is that Eliot, the purest artist and most austere critic in England to-day, is yet a writer whose background is unfamiliar—the least like anyone else's. He is an American expatriate who is escaping from a far more refined and cultivated, though perfectly barren society, than any he can find here—in other words, he is not running away from a rough America to a cultured England but from an overpolite and civilised humanism to the bellyworld of post-war London. As a result his poetry is a struggle to break down inhibitions in himself by which the coarser Englishman is not troubled and his solution, the Anglo-Catholic church, one that makes small appeal to his imitators.

Yet in spite of this he is a master; he has created for us a world of his own. There are places where I miss Firbank, in Knightsbridge or Rome, going over some Balkan palace or in an autumnal cathedral city; there are remarks one overhears or whole scenes between simple, fatuous, complacent people when one recognises that the artist who could best have done them justice is no more. But there exists a whole mood for whose expression we must thank Eliot, the mood of dissatisfaction and despondency, of barrenness and futility—the noonday devil, the afternoon impotence which is curiously unpoetical and which no one else has been able so adequately to render into verse.

The idea of futility is an important concept in the twenties and dominates the poetry of Eliot (up to *Ash Wednesday*), the novels of Huxley (to *Point Counter Point*) and much of the work of Lawrence, Hemingway, and Joyce. It is an extension of the ivory tower attitude which arises from a disbelief in action and in the putting of moral slogans into action, engendered by the Great War. Thus Henry James and the authors who were killed in the war had no such experience, it was left to those who survived beyond 1917 to make the discovery.

> Behold, behold, the goal in sight
> Spread thy fans and wing thy flight

sings Janus, in Dryden's *Secular Masque,* and Venus adds:

> Calms appear when storms are past
> Love will have his hour at last,

but the chorus is not taken in:

> All, all of a piece throughout:
> Thy chase had a beast in view;
> Thy wars brought nothing about;
> Thy lovers were all untrue.
> 'Tis well an old age is out,
> And time to begin a new.

And that might well have been the device of the writers of the early twenties.

I have said that futilitarianism is an extension of the philosophy of the Ivory Tower because no writer of that group pretended that art was futile; it is the men of action who do that. Behind the concept of futility is a passionate belief in art, coupled with a contempt for the subjects about which art is made. This puts too great a strain on technique, for even Flaubert, in *Bouvard and Pecuchet,* that Baedeker of futility, has not been able to avoid unintentionally boring the reader. But the novelists of the 1920's were not Flaubert's equal in construction. They knew that they had been "had" and they were in a hurry to tell the world about it. Those who had been fooled most were the young men who had fought and survived the war; the literature of that time in consequence is predominantly masculine, revolving round a theme which may be called "The Clever Young Man and the Dirty Deal". When I search for the most representative work of the period, I am inclined to choose *Petrouchka,* for though pre-war the ballet expresses the situation with clarity. The people at the fair are the audience whom Petrouchka, the introspective young masochist, wishes to win over; the Magician who controls him is Fate, that cruel deity of the Housman poems or the Vile Old Man, the general, the father too old to fight, gleefully sacrificing his son. Petrouchka's problem is how to keep alive, and have a

Characteristics of the Clever Young Men and their Dirty Deals

Author	Man	Place of Education	Nature of Predicament	Solution
Douglas	Denis, *South Wind*	Oxford	Inability to seduce a woman. Rival, young scientist. Father, Keith	Acquires virility and self-respect instead by assisting drunken pseudo-father to sober up.
Huxley	Denis, *Crome Yellow*	Oxford	Inability to seduce a woman. Rivals, painter and rich young peer. Father, Scogan	Flight to London ("and what on earth was he going to do in London when he got there?")
Huxley	Chelifer, Gumbril, Quarles	Oxford	Inability to seduce a woman. Rivals, all their friends. Father, Cardan, etc.	Expatriation (Mantua) the picture gallery and the reading-room.
Eliot	Alfred Prufrock	?	General indecision and fear of experience. Rival, Sweeney. Runs away from women.	Polite resignation
Joyce	Stephen Dedalus	Clongowes	Superiority to vulgar surroundings, yet at mercy of them. Rival, Buck Mulligan. Father, Bloom.	"Silence, exile and cunning." Expatriation, discovery of pseudo-father (Bloom)
Hemingway	Jake *The Sun Also Rises*.	?	War wound, hence inability to seduce a woman, general aroma of diffused alcoholism. Rivals, boxer, bullfighter, etc.	Trout-fishing, drink, the Catholic Church

successful love affair and his rival, the Moor, is the hated man of action, the accomplished womaniser who has not been to Balliol and has nothing of Hamlet in him, but in whom vulgarity triumphs. This situation or relationship has a way of turning up in many books.

The father-chorus in these books is not malignant, rather is it wistful and friendly, in some books of the period he is a priest. The lesson we can learn from this school is the danger of allowing those literary vices, cleverness and self-pity, to come up too often for air. It was, however, the clever young men who were the first to see the vanity of the war and the greater vanity of the peace. They could not settle down to boring jobs and unprofitable careers with pre-war patience and their cleverness seemed a liability rather than an asset. Besides women did not like it. Nor were they yet sure whether they liked women, for they were still romantic enough to be appalled by the distinction between love and lust and to find the inevitable transition degrading.

Such a state of war between intellect and the senses, unless a genuine truce is made between them, can only end unhappily. Either the senses conquer the mind and we get the erudite sensualist, the Keith of *South Wind,* the Cardan of *Those Barren Leaves* with their consciousness of wasted opportunities, or the mind is triumphant and we have what Huxley became, a moralist and a puritan. I have considered him in his early works as a dandy for it is only in them that he is an artist and in them that the irony and lyricism are unadulterated. *Leda, Limbo, Crome Yellow* and the stories of *Little Mexican* belong to this period, *Antic Hay* begins another.

I quote him often because he is the most typical of a generation, typical in his promise, his erudition, his cynicism and in his peculiar brand of prolific sterility.

CHAPTER VII

THE NEW MANDARINS

⁂

IT IS AS DIFFICULT TO FORETELL THE WEATHER IN A LANGUAGE as in the skies, and as urgent. In our case the problem is to find out what sort of writing at this moment at the end of the thirties is likely to last. We have seen that there are two styles which it is convenient to describe as the realist, or vernacular, the style of rebels, journalists, common sense-addicts and unromantic observers of human destiny—and the Mandarin, the artificial style of men of letters or of those in authority who make letters their spare-time occupation.

The lyrical or dandy style matures with age into the Mandarin.

As in party government, there is an interaction between these two styles; each will seem in or out of office at a given moment; when one style is in abeyance it will receive new blood and be thrust forward, when the other is at the height of its success, it will wither away. The panjandrums of the nineteenth century, Ruskin, Arnold, Pater, Meredith, Henry James, Swinburne, Conrad, give way to the realists, Gissing, Butler, Moore, Maugham, Bennett, Wells, and Shaw. It was now their turn to be driven from the temple. It was in 1906, I think, that the disheartened Conservative party, after being trounced in the general election, were elated by an attack made on their victors by young F. E. Smith. In the same year, in the pages of a dull review, another gifted young man, also a dark horse, was attacking the successful literary doctrine of the day, and the day's most eminent critic.

45

The study of Sir Thomas Browne, Mr. Gosse says, "encouraged John-son, and with him a whole school of rhetorical writers in the eighteenth century, to avoid circumlocution by the invention of superfluous words, learned but pedantic, in which darkness was concentrated without being dispelled". Such is Mr. Gosse's account of the influence of Browne and Johnson upon the later eighteenth century writers of prose. But to dis-miss Johnson's influence as something altogether deplorable, is surely to misunderstand the whole drift of the great revolution which he brought about in English letters. The characteristics of the pre-Johnsonian prose style—the style which Dryden first established and Swift brought to perfection—are obvious enough. Its advantages are those of clarity and force; but its faults, which, of course, are unimportant in the work of a great master, become glaring in that of the second-rate practitioner. The prose of Locke, for instance, or of Bishop Butler, suffers, in spite of its clarity and vigour, from grave defects. It is very flat and very loose; it has no formal beauty, no elegance, no balance, no trace of the deliberation of art. Johnson, there can be no doubt, determined to remedy these evils by giving a new mould to the texture of English prose; and he went back for a model to Sir Thomas Browne. . . . With the *Christian Morals* to guide him, Dr. Johnson set about the transformation of the prose of his time. He decorated, he pruned, he balanced; he hung garlands; he draped robes; and he ended by converting the Doric order of Swift into the Co-rinthian order of Gibbon. . . . Attacks of this kind—attacks upon the elaboration and classicism of Browne's style are difficult to reply to, be-cause they must seem, to anyone who holds a contrary opinion, to betray such a total lack of sympathy with the subject as to make argument almost impossible. . . . The truth is that there is a great gulf fixed between those who naturally dislike the ornate, and those who naturally love it. There is no remedy; and to attempt to ignore this fact only emphasises it the more. . . . Browne's "brushwork" is certainly unequalled in Eng-lish literature, except by the very greatest masters of sophisticated art, such as Pope and Shakespeare; it is the inspiration of sheer technique.

It was not till 1918, however, that the author, Lytton Strachey, became well known with *Eminent Victorians*.

Eminent Victorians is a revolutionary book. Through what at first sight seemed only biographical essays—on Arnold, Florence Nightingale, General Gordon and Cardinal Manning, dead for half a century—the author contrived to attack and undermine all that was most cherished in the morality of to-day. The public-school system, public service, philanthropy, the army, the empire, the Church, all were questioned in these sleek periods and skulking behind them, authority itself, the nature of the will, the hypocrisy by which good men climb and cling to power were in their turn examined and exposed. *Eminent Victorians* is the work of a great anarch, a revolutionary text-book on bourgeois society written in the language through which the bourgeois ear could be lulled and beguiled, the Mandarin style. And the bourgeois responded with fascination to the music, like seals to the Eriskay love-lilt. At first the suave tones brought nothing but pleasure: this was the civilisation they had been fighting to save: here were the restored humanities, the accent of the "studious cloisters of Trinity": too late they understood that four Victorian idols had been knocked off their pedestals in such a way that they have never been replaced, or deemed in any manner replaceable. And after they had dismissed the book as "clever, but unsound", worse was to follow, a questioning of the values the Victorians stood for and all reflected from the eyes of their own demobilised and disillusioned children.

The trial of Oscar Wilde was responsible for a flight from æstheticism which had lasted twenty years. He had himself done much to discredit it by the vulgar and insincere element which he had introduced; his conviction was the climax. From that moment the philistine triumphed and although there were still poets and critics who loved beauty, who were in fact romantic, their romanticism was forced to be hearty. Hence the cult of beer and Sussex, of walking and simplicity which ended with Masefield, Brooke, Squire and Gould; hence the leanest years in the history of English verse and the manly criticism of Quiller-Couch and Walter Raleigh. It was left to Lytton Strachey to lay the ghost of Reading Gaol, to proclaim "un peu de faiblesse pour ce qui est beau—voilà mon défaut," and so make nonconformity again permissible.

With the success which his first two books gained him, Strachey's bitterness disappeared, he became a lion and settled down to a quiet life of private pleasure. His gifts appear as with all fine critics, when he is able to love and to admire and for this reason he is at his best when writing about the eighteenth century. As a critic he is admirable, as a biographer he is slightly vulgar. In his second book, *Queen Victoria,* his insurrectionary movement expired, he could not dislike Melbourne or Disraeli, or such a human bundle as his subject. By *Elizabeth and Essex* his style has become an elaborate experiment in cliché which, though rising to fine passages, contains not a little of the sniggering we have commented on in Firbank. It is his first book (*Eminent Victorians*) so admirably argued, and constructed, original, polished and daring, to which we can profitably return together with his essays and criticism. There is much to be learnt from his gifts, from his intellectual pride, his forceful phrasing, his love of beauty and gesture, his grasp of character; "he is not dead but sleepeth" and one day these gifts will be rescued from the neglect into which, by his spectacular success, they were too soon precipitated.

Another Mandarin to emerge from his retreat in 1918 was Pearsall-Smith, whose *Trivia* was the preliminary bombardment in a long attack which is not yet exhausted against puritanism in English letters. His anthology of English prose (1919) which omits Dryden and devotes only twelve pages to the eighteenth century from Addison to Lamb, concentrating entirely on fine writing and the purple patch, continued the onslaught. He is with Professor Mackail the last of the old Mandarins, of the men of the eighties, and the most intransigent.

Meanwhile a new Mandarin was taking over the novel. In 1915 Virginia Woolf published *The Voyage Out.* This was followed by *Night and Day, Monday or Tuesday* (1921), *Jacob's Room* (1922), *Mrs. Dalloway* (1925), *To the Lighthouse* (1927) and *Orlando* (1928), one of the books in which, like *Elizabeth and Essex* or *Point Counter Point,* the new Mandarin movement of the twenties culminates.

Virginia Woolf seemed to have the worst defect of the Mandarin style, the ability to spin cocoons of language out of nothing. The history of her literary style has been that of a form at first simple, growing more and more elaborate, the content lagging far behind, then catching up, till, after the falseness of *Orlando,* she produced a masterpiece in *The Waves.*

Her early novels were not written in an elaborate style. Her most significant early book is *Monday or Tuesday* (1921) and demonstrates the rule that Mandarin prose is the product of those who in their youth were poets. In short it is romantic prose. Not all poets were romantic prose writers (e.g. Dryden) but most romantic prose writers have attempted poetry.

The development of Virginia Woolf is the development of this lyrical feeling away from E. M. Forster, with his artlessness and simple, poetical, colloquial style, into patterns of her own. The reveries of a central character came more and more to dominate her books. In *The Waves* she abandoned the convention of the central figure and described a group of friends, as children, as young people and finally in late middle age. In a series of tableaux are contrasted the mystery of childhood, the promise of youth, the brilliance of maturity and the complex, unmarketable richness of age. If *The Years* seems an impressionist gallery with many canvases, landscapes, portraits, and conversation pieces, then *The Waves* is a group of five or six huge panels which celebrate the dignity of human life and the passage of time. It is one of the books which comes nearest to stating the mystery of life and so, in a sense, nearest to solving it.

In *Mr. Bennett and Mrs. Brown,* Virginia Woolf attacked Bennett, Wells and Galsworthy for their materialism, for the doctrine of realism which they had made all powerful in the 1900's.

For Mandarin prose is romantic prose and realism is the doctrine of the vernacular opposed to it. Thus among the new Mandarins of the twenties were several who began as poets; besides Virginia Woolf and Lytton Strachey, it included the work of the

Sitwells with their flowery periods and predilection for highly coloured and sophisticated settings.

But the greatest Mandarin was Proust who has become so familiar as almost to rank as an English writer. He exhibits, beyond all others, the defect of the Mandarin style; the failure of the writer's intellectual or emotional content to fill the elaborate frame which his talent plans for it. The honeycombs continue to develop but fewer and fewer pollen-bags are emptied into them. There are many great passages where the complexity is worthy of the emotion expended on it, where very subtle and difficult truths are presented in language that could only express them if difficult and subtle.

Notwithstanding, now that the element of novelty and cult-snobbery has worn off, much of Proust, as of his master Ruskin, must stand condemned. He is often repetitive and feeble; the emotions of envy, jealousy, lust, and snobbishness around which his book is built, though they generate an enormous impetus, are incapable of sustaining it through twenty or thirty volumes; Swann's jealousy of Odette is enough without Proust's jealousy of Albertine, Saint-Loup's of Rachel and Charlus's of Morel and if the emotions repeat themselves, so also do the stories, the situations, the comments, parentheses and clichés. Proust will remain a great writer, but his titles to fame may have to be reconsidered. His hatred and contempt for the life of action suited the war-weary and disillusioned generation he wrote for, his own snobbery offered them both a philosophy and a remunerative career, he believed also in art for art's sake. He was in no sense a new writer although it was the illusion of novelty which contributed so much to his success. His models are pre-war, his artists are taken from the *haute bourgeoisie*, they are members, like his politicians and men of science, of the terrifying class which ruled in France and which corresponded to the Forsytes in England; his nobility are of the same period, so are his operas, his dinner-parties; it is the world of the Dreyfus Case, the Victorian world. He was modern enough to attack the values of this world but he had nothing to put in their place, for their values were his own, those of the narrator of the book who spends his life in going to parties and watching snobs behave but is never a snob himself.

In short, although he is preoccupied with time, his world is static because in all the movements of his book there is no movement of ideas. "Everything changes", he seems to say, "and I am the historian of that change", but what in fact he declares is that nothing changes except the small social set which he admired in his youth and which fell to pieces. How did they change? They grew older and went out less or got mixed up in anti-social love affairs or lost their money or died—but nothing else changed for him. There was a new face with an old title in a box at the opera —but the title and the box are always there, coveted and prized by the ruling class of six or seven countries; there are no new ideas, no revolution in wisdom, no reversals of taste, nobody to declare that they never want to see an opera again.

Proust was a reactionary writer so steeped in the lore of the high society which he envied in the nineties and with such a nostalgia for the emotions of his own childhood, he was so much the introspective masochist that he admitted no change in his world beyond the inescapable evidences of old age that confronted him. The aim of his book was how to revive his past and he discovered that by remembering everything that had happened, and by relying on intuitive visions produced by familiar smells and noises, such a revival was possible. And where he failed to revive it, his style, that blend of unselective curiosity with interminable qualification, would carry on like a lumbering, over-crowded, escaped tram that nobody can stop.

Proust lives rather through his extrovert satirical scenes, his balls and dinner-parties, the great ironical spectacle of the vanity of human wishes displayed by the Baron de Charlus and the Duchesse de Guermantes and through the delightful pictures which he provides of the countryside and his neighbours, the plain of Chartres, the coast, the quiet streets which Swann climbed in the Faubourg St. Germain. Where his egocentric masturbatory

self-analysis begins to function and his anxiety neurosis about his
grandmother or Albertine, love or jealousy, comes into play, then
all is tedious and unreal, like that asthma which his psychiatrist
said he was unwilling to cure since something more unpleasant
would be bound to take its place.

There are two more of these new Mandarins worth examining.
We have seen that Aldous Huxley is a writer particularly accessible
to the spirit of his time and by the middle twenties his period of
dandyism was over. The influence of Mallarmé and Prufrock
waned and he set himself to moralise on the flux around him.
Witty, serious, observant, well-read, sensitive and intelligent, there
can have been few young writers as gifted as Huxley—as can be
seen from his early stories, *Happily Ever-After, Richard Greenow,
Little Mexican, Young Archimedes* or *The Gioconda Smile*.

Yet he had the misfortune to suffer from what he considered,
quoting Buddha, to be the deadliest of mortal sins, unawareness,
for he was both unaware of his own nature as a writer and of the
temptations into which he was falling. His nature was a very
English one, that of the divided man, the lover of beauty and
pleasure dominated by the puritan conscience. At first his dichot-
omy is apparent in his treatment of love. Love means everything
to him but sex—and sex, although he is obsessed by it, is disgusting. The conflict is extended to become a warfare between the
senses on one side and the intellect, generously moralising in the
moment of victory, on the other until Huxley the intellectual
pulls the lower self along like a man pulling a dog by a leash;
there are glimpses of other dogs, lamp-posts, green grass, trousers
and tree-trunks; then comes a jerk, "eyes look your last" and a
scientific platitude.

It is a question whether anyone so at war with himself can be a
novelist, for to the novelist a complete integration is necessary;
the proper medium for the split-man is the *Journal Intime* or the
Dialogue. Ends and Means owes its success to being a complete
break with the novel for as a novelist, apart from being at war

with himself, Huxley was hampered by his inability to create character or see a character except in an intellectual way.

The greatness of a novelist like Tolstoy is that he creates characters who being real creations are able to think and behave unlike themselves, to be false to type. Proust also had some of this greatness, and in English, Thackeray. But weaker novelists can only sling a few traits on to the characters they are depicting and then hold them there. "You can't miss So-and-so", they explain, "he stammers and now look, here he comes—'What's your name?' 'S-s-s-so-and-s-s-s-s-so.' There you see, what did I tell you!" Nearly all English novels are written to this prescription. Huxley suffers from the intellectual's difficulty of communicating with the people around him except through the intellect. In consequence the only people he can write about at length are those with whom he can carry on an intellectual discussion.

But the consequences of Huxley's *artistic* unawareness are more serious. He is a defaulting financier of the written word, and nobody since Chesterton has so squandered his gifts. A contract to produce two books a year forced him to vitiate that keen sense of words with which he started and as he had less to say, so, by a process which we have noticed, he took longer in which to say it. For such a writer who had to turn out 200,000 words a year, the Mandarin style was indispensable.

By dinner-time it was already a Story—*the latest addition* to Mary Amberley's *repertory*. The *latest*, and as good, it seemed to Antony's *critically attentive ear* as the *finest classics of the collection*. Ever since *he received her invitation,* he now realized, *his curiosity had been tinged* with a *certain vindictive hope* that she would have *altered for the worse, either relatively in his own* knowledgeable *eyes, or else absolutely* by reason of the *passage of these twelve long years*; would have degenerated from what she was, or what he had imagined her to be, at the time when he had loved her. Discreditably enough, *as he now admitted to himself, it was with a touch of disappointment* that he had found her *hardly changed from the Mary Amberley of his memories.* She was forty-three. *But her body was almost as slim as ever, and she moved with*

all the old swift agility. With *something more than the old agility indeed*; for he had noticed that she was now agile on purpose, that she
acted the part of one who is *carried away by a youthful impulse* to break
into quick and violent motion—acted it, moreover, in circumstances
where the impulse could not, if natural, possibly have been felt.

                •   •   •   •   •   •   •

After a lonely dinner—for Helen was keeping her room on *the plea
of a headache*—Gerry went up to sit with Mrs. Amberley. He was *particularly charming that evening*, and so *affectionately solicitous that Mary
forgot* all her *accumulated grounds* of complaint and *fell in love* with
him *all over again*, and for *another set of reasons*—not because he was
so *handsome, so easily and insolently dominating*, such a ruthless and
accomplished lover, but because he was *kind, thoughtful, and affectionate*, was everything, *in a word*, she had previously known he wasn't.

I quote these as examples of Huxley's writing, of the muse's
revenge, but they also show the influence of Proust in all its
flatulence. Thus, although the clichés I have italicised are examples
of the lack of distinction in Huxley's writing, as is the use of unnecessary adverbs or the dogged repetition, the determination to hit
the nail on the head and then hit it on the head and then hit it on
the head, that vulgarity with which we are familiar yet there is
also here the Proustian note: ". . . either relatively . . . or else
absolutely . . . what she was, or what he had imagined her to
be, etc." It is fake analysis and fatigued introspection, a frequent
combination in Mandarinism at its worst.

The last and strangest arrival among these new Mandarins was
Joyce. *Work in Progress* is a Mandarin book which demands and
demands in vain, complete leisure, the widest education and devoted patience from the reader who wishes to understand it. It
could not be more remote from colloquial English, from the
spoken word. But on his way there Joyce had experimented with
both styles. Thus *Dubliners* and *A Portrait of the Artist* are in reformed or anti-Mandarin, and belong to the early years of Joyce's
Irish rebellion against the academic pundits and the literature of
the ruling class, while the value of *Ulysses* and its importance to

this analysis of the trends in English prose lies in the mixture of styles to be found there. In *Ulysses*, Joyce, a sensitive stylist, is trying to make his mind up as to the side he will take in the battle of the books. Thus we have in the passages where Stephen Dedalus holds the stage the Anglo-Irish lyrical mixture that we find in the *Portrait of the Artist*. But whenever Bloom is on the scene the language becomes the demotic journalese in vogue where people like Bloom foregather, and corresponds to the French of Celine who in his *Voyage au Bout de la Nuit* creates a Bloom-like character. In the two long reveries, that of Mrs. Bloom and the Cyclopean Nameless One, the style is petty bourgeois, almost proletarian; in the Lying-in hospital and the strange penultimate chapter highly Mandarin.

The quality common to the Mandarins was inflation either of language or imagination or of both and it was this inflation which made inevitable a reaction against them. For their success was enormous. In the history of literature there can have been few books more talked and written about; few names more mentioned than those of Proust, Joyce, Lytton Strachey, Virginia Woolf, the Sitwells and Paul Valéry. Their moment was propitious. After the post-war disillusion they offered a religion of beauty, a cult of words, of meanings understood only by the initiated at a time when people were craving such initiations.

The world had lived too long under martial law to desire a socialised form of art for human beings in the mass had proved but a union of slaughterers. There was more hope and interest in extreme individuality. This romantic restatement of the individual was of value to the younger generation since it enabled them to inflate their own lives and gave them a depth and importance which they otherwise lacked. Soon the universities were flooded with emotional dud cheques, stumers on the bank of experience forged in the name of Swann or Dedalus, Monsieur Teste or Mrs. Dalloway. Proustians developed a wool-winding technique in friendship, an indefatigable egotism in affairs of the heart, combined with a lively social ambition. Valérians made it clear that everything was a little more difficult than it seemed and then more difficult again. The Dedalus young men were defeatist, proud and twisted, their rudeness was justified by the impact of some ancestral curse; the Waste Landers were more miserable still while the young Huxleys found relief in epigrams and bawdy erudition.

> "Oh yes, decidedly
> Having a sense of humour and a past
> One will amuse oneself, decidedly . . ."

The Gidian immoralists were perverse and moody, the Stracheyites wore fringes and hooted with a dying pejorative fall, the Virginians were impulsive, the Mansfieldians very simple and "back-to-childhood", the Sitwellians went to the ballet in white ties and began their sentences with lingering sibilance: "I must say I do definitely think . . ." It was the golden age of Bloomsbury under the last long shadow of the Ivory Tower, a romantic, affected, and defeatist epoch; action was discredited, it had caused the war; "And as for goodness—listen to Freud. Truth? but what about Einstein? History? Have you read the *Decline of the West*? Nothing remains but beauty. Have you read Waley's *170 Chinese Poems*? Beauty—and, of course, one's intellectual integrity and personal relations."

I have not dealt at length with these authors because I am assuming that the reader for whom this is written, the artist in his search for a relative immortality, will know the most important book about them: Edmund Wilson's *Axel's Castle* (Scribner's, 1931) which includes essays on Yeats, Valéry, Eliot, Proust, Joyce and Gertrude Stein. His summing up is against them, in so far as it is against their cult of the individual which he feels they have carried to such lengths as to exhaust it for a long time to come but it is a summing up which also states everything that can be said in their favour when allowance for what I have termed "inflation" has been made. Here is the last paragraph:

The writers with whom I have here been concerned have not only, then, given us works of literature which, for intensity, brilliance, and

boldness as well as for an architectural genius, an intellectual mastery
of their materials, rare among their Romantic predecessors, are probably
comparable to the work of any time. Though it is true that they have
tended to overemphasise the importance of the individual, that they
have been preoccupied with introspection sometimes almost to the point
of insanity, that they have endeavoured to discourage their readers, not
only with politics, but with action of any kind—they have yet succeeded
in effecting in literature a revolution analogous to that which has taken
place in science and philosophy: they have broken out of the old mech-
anistic routine, they have disintegrated the old materialism, and they
have revealed to the imagination a new flexibility and freedom. And
though we are aware in them of things that are dying—the whole belle-
lettreistic tradition of Renaissance culture perhaps, compelled to special-
ise more and more, more and more driven in on itself, as industrialism
and democratic education have come to press it closer and closer—they
none the less break down the walls of the present and wake us to the
hope and exaltation of the untried, unsuspected possibilities of human
thought and art.

On this verdict we will leave them.

CHAPTER VIII

THE NEW VERNACULAR

>|<

THE MASS ATTACK ON THE NEW MANDARINS WAS LAUNCHED IN
the late twenties. By that time these had squandered their cultural
inheritance for their inflationary period coincided with the Boom
and their adversaries were to come into their own with the Slump.
In spite of their apparent success and publicity, the three great
Mandarin books of 1928, *Orlando, Elizabeth and Essex, Point
Counter Point,* were disappointing; they were not, except in America, popular successes and met also with considerable highbrow
opposition.

This opposition may be said to have formed in three quarters.
One quarter was that of the old realists, the remainder of those
young men who had rejected Pater, Swinburne, Meredith and
James. Of these Moore was too ill-read to be a good critic, Bennett too successful for he was anxious to conceal by his indiscriminate welcome to novelty the poverty of his own exhausted
impulse; the opinion of Galsworthy, Shaw, Wells, Kipling was
no longer of value in matters of art. It remained for Somerset
Maugham, after his long excursion as a playwright, to return as
the champion of "lucidity, euphony, simplicity, and the story with
a beginning, a middle and an end", the doctrines of his French
masters.

The second quarter was Paris which held in the attack on the
new Mandarins the line taken by Dublin against their predecessors
thirty years before. It was here that conspirators met in Sylvia

Beach's little bookshop where *Ulysses* lay stacked like dynamite in a revolutionary cellar and then scattered down the Rue de l'Odéon on the missions assigned to them. Here Gertrude Stein had launched her attacks on English culture by rinsing the English vocabulary, by a process of constant repetition, of all accretions of meaning and association. The prose style of Ezra Pound was hardly academic, and Joyce also, till he became the mandarin of *Work in Progress,* remained a king over the water for those who were discontented with the court of Bloomsbury. James Joyce, ambered in the Rue de Grenelle, and Gertrude Stein were the exiled royalties round whom centred the plots against Virginia Woolf and Lytton Strachey.

Any estimate of Miss Stein must largely depend on the pleasure derivable from her creations, but she applied to the writing of English as early as 1909 (*Three Lives*) a method which was to have far-reaching results. It was a simplification, an attack on order and meaning in favour of sound but of sound which in itself generated a new precision. Two young men were to be influenced by it, Sherwood Anderson and Ernest Hemingway, who each took Gertrude Stein's method and added to it his own quality of readability. The paper *Transition* was the court gazette of these kings in exile.

The third quarter in which opposition to the Mandarins arose was that of their contemporaries, Lawrence and Lewis. Lawrence, as the early lyricism of his pre-war books evaporated, became a master of the colloquial style. Though his work is marred by carelessness, repetition and want of ear and a tendency to preach and rant which ill-health accentuated, it is always vigorous, thoughtful and alive, the enemy of elaboration and artifice, of moral hypocrisy and verbal falseness. The poems in *Pansies* and *Nettles* are examples of the vernacular style at its best, as is the satire in his later books and stories such as *Lady Chatterley.* Around Lawrence centred Middleton Murry and his wife, Katharine Mansfield, who said in her diary that the greatest pleasure she had received from her stories was that they had given pleas-

ure to the printer who set them up and also several younger
writers of whom Richard Aldington, who also had one foot in
Paris, and Robert Graves were the most important. A friend of
Lawrence, though more influenced by George Moore, was David
Garnett whose *Lady Into Fox* and *Sailor's Return* were excellent
anti-Mandarin books, combining something of the dandyism of
Eliot and Firbank with a rustic basis, a fantasy logically worked
out in language as simple as Defoe's.

The most dangerous enemy of the new Mandarins was Wyndham Lewis who after his realistic novel *Tarr* (1918) was preparing his onslaught on the citadels of literary culture; on the one
hand Stein's simplicity and Joyce's complexity were to be attacked,
with Hemingway, Faulkner and all other derivatives, while in
England Bloomsbury was to tremble, Lawrence to be chastised for
his worship of the black sun of the solar plexus and the Sitwells
to be exterminated by an assassination five hundred pages long.
Roy Campbell, in *The Georgiad,* brought up the rear. Since Lewis'
style is that of a painter turned writer, it is difficult of analysis,
being strongly marked by the visual quality of his imagination.
His early books are full of fine onsets and satires and descriptions
written in a technique of his own while his later ones are more
colloquial or what he would call 'informal.'

To estimate his work is not easy. *The Art of Being Ruled, Time
and Western Man, The Childermass, The Enemy* and *The Apes of
God* contain some of the most vigorous satire, original description and profound criticism produced by the twentieth century;
Lewis was unique in being a philosophical critic, who, attacking
the modern conception of "time", was able to illustrate the workings of that conception by ranging up and down the whole of contemporary literature from the best poetry to the best seller, the best
seller to the lowest kind of journalism or jazz.

As a constructive critic however he has little to offer, a belief
in reason as opposed to metaphysical or sexual mysticism, a belief
in western civilisation, in the physical world, in the comic aspect
of love, in the external approach to things (describing people

via their personal appearance) and in the value of humour and satire. All this is not negligible, but it is not on a scale with the world he has set out to destroy or with his machinery of destruction.

What Lewis believes in most is himself and the measure he applies to his contemporaries is how far they differ from that yardstick and how far they stand in his way. His criticism also suffers from a lack of proportion. He will attack a writer on philosophical, or moral grounds and then as violently for the most superficial and frivolous of errors or he will turn from rending an important writer to maul an obscure and inconsiderable hack. He is like a maddened elephant which, careering through a village, sometimes leans against a house and carelessly demolishes the most compact masonry, trumpeting defiance to the inhabitants within, sometimes pursues a dog or a chicken or stops to uproot a shrub or bang a piece of corrugated iron. His writing can be redundant and slovenly, his dialogue is often dull, his novels begin with scenes worthy of a great master and gradually lose themselves in unplanned verbosity. His last volume of criticism, *Men Without Art*, while containing brilliant glimpses of his mind, is unexpectedly trivial and often bullying and unfair. His later books are ragged and his style has become somewhat unbuttoned. From an article of his in the Fascist quarterly, *British Union*, one gets the impression that it is because he is writing now for a new class of reader, the petty bourgeois, the philistine small tradesman, the Fascist under-dog.

What is necessary for Lewis is that some of his admirers or he himself should make an omnibus Lewis, an anthology of his best thought and finest passages, applying to his work the selection and compression which in the spate of his original creation have been wanting.

To go further it is necessary to bring the production chart up to date and I have added after some of the more extreme examples the letters (M) or (V) according as to whether they are written in the Mandarin, or Vernacular or Colloquial style.

1923. Mansfield, *The Dove's Nest* (V) ; Huxley, *Antic Hay* (M) ; Firbank, *The Flower Beneath the Foot* (Dandy) ; Hemingway, *In Our Time* (V) ; Willa Cather, *A Lost Lady;* Elizabeth Bowen, *Encounters;* Eliot, *The Waste Land.*

1924. Mansfield, *Something Childish* (V) ; Huxley, *Little Mexican;* Firbank, *Prancing Nigger;* Forster, *Passage to India;* Garnett, *Man in the Zoo* (V) ; Edith Sitwell, *The Sleeping Beauty* (M) ; Osbert Sitwell, *Triple Fugue* (M).

1925. Huxley, *Those Barren Leaves* (M) ; Dreiser, *American Tragedy* (V) ; Eliot, *Poems* (M) ; Compton-Burnett, *Pastors and Masters;* Garnett, *Sailor's Return* (V) ; Fitzgerald, *The Great Gatsby;* Loos, *Gentlemen Prefer Blondes* (V) ; Woolf, *Mrs. Dalloway* (M) ; Day Lewis, *Beechen Vigil;* Noel Coward, *The Vortex* (V) ; Geoffrey Scott, *Portrait of Zelide* (M).

1926. Huxley, *Two or Three Graces* (M) ; Hemingway, *Torrents of Spring* (V) ; Quennell, *Poems* (M) ; Lawrence, *Plumed Serpent;* Baring, *Daphne Adeane* (V) ; Cather, *My Mortal Enemy* (V) ; Fowler, *Modern English Usage;* V. Woolf, *To the Lighthouse* (M) ; Maugham, *The Casuarina Tree* (V).

1927. Bowen, *The Hotel* (M) ; Lehmann, *Dusty Answer* (M) ; Hemingway, *The Sun Also Rises* (V), *Men Without Women* (V) ; Lewis, *The Wild Body, Time and Western Man, The Lion and the Fox;* Mackenzie, *Vestal Fires;* Wilder, *Bridge of San Luis Rey* (M) ; Westcott, *The Grandmothers* (M).

1928. Sassoon, *Memoirs of a Fox-hunting Man;* Woolf, *Orlando* (M) ; Lawrence, *Lady Chatterley's Lover* (V) ; Nicolson, *Some People;* Edwards, *Winter Sonata* (V) ; Waugh, *Decline and Fall* (V) ; Isherwood, *All the Conspirators* (V) ; Lewis, *The Childermass;* Mackenzie, *Extraordinary Women;* Strachey, *Elizabeth and Essex* (M) ; Huxley, *Point Counter Point* (M) ; E. Sackville-West, *Mandrake Over the Water-Carrier* (M).

1929. Compton-Burnett, *Brothers and Sisters;* H. Green, *Living* (V) ; W. Faulkner, *The Sound and the Fury* (M) ; Hemingway, *Farewell to Arms* (V) ; Lawrence, *Pansies* (V) ; Joyce, *Fragments of Work in Progress* (M) ; Quennell, *Baudelaire and the Symbolists* (M) ; Graves, *Goodbye to All That* (V) ; Aldington, *Death of a Hero* (V).

1930. Kafka, *The Castle*; Dashiell Hammett, *Maltese Falcon* (V); O. Sitwell, *Dumb Animal* (M); Maugham, *Cakes and Ale* (V), *The Gentleman in the Parlour*; W. H. Auden, *Poems*; T. S. Eliot, *Ash Wednesday* (M); Evelyn Waugh, *Vile Bodies* (V); Spender, *Twenty Poems*; Lewis, *The Apes of God*.

1931. V. Woolf, *The Waves* (M); Roy Campbell, *The Georgiad* (V); A. Powell, *Afternoon Men* (V); Edmund Wilson, *Axel's Castle*.

1932. W. H. Auden, *The Orators*.

There are, we know, many kinds of vernacular; the colloquial language of Hemingway is different from the colloquial language of Maurice Baring yet each believes in informality and simplicity, they never use a word that they would not in conversation—words like "nay", "notwithstanding", "pullulating", "mephitic", "sublunary", "Babylon", "lest", "corpulent", "futurity", "ecstasy", etc.

The outstanding writer of the new vernacular is Hemingway and he was aided by the talkies as were realists a generation before by journalism. The talking picture popularised the vocabulary with which Hemingway wrote and enabled him to use slang words in the knowledge that they were getting every day less obscure, he surf-rode into fame on the wave of popular American culture. Here, taken from *Death in the Afternoon*, is a spat between him and a Mandarin which is in itself a defence of the new style:

Mr. Aldous Huxley writing in an essay entitled *Foreheads Villainous Low* commences: "In [naming a book by this writer] Mr. H. ventures, once, to name an Old Master. There is a phrase, quite admirably expressive" [here Mr. Huxley inserts a compliment], "a single phrase, no more, about 'the bitter nail-holes' of Mantegna's Christ; then quickly, quickly, appalled by his own temerity, the author passes on (as Mrs. Gaskell might hastily have passed on, if she had somehow been betrayed into mentioning a water-closet) passes on, shamefacedly, to speak once more of Lower Things."

"There was a time, not so long ago, when the stupid and uneducated aspired to be thought intelligent and cultured. The current of aspiration has changed its direction. It is not at all uncommon now to find intelligent and cultured people doing their best to feign stupidity and to conceal the fact that they have received an education"—and more; more in Mr. Huxley's best educated vein which is a highly educated vein indeed. What about that, you say? Mr. Huxley scores there, all right, all right. What have you to say to that? Let me answer truly. On reading that in Mr. Huxley's book I obtained a copy of the volume he refers to and looked through it and could not find the quotation he mentions. It may be there, but I did not have the patience nor the interest to find it, since the book was finished, and nothing to be done. It sounds very much like the sort of thing one tries to remove in going over the manuscript. I believe it is more than a question of the simulation or avoidance of the appearance of culture. When writing a novel a writer should create living people; people, not characters. A *character* is a caricature. If a writer can make people live there may be no great characters in his book, but it is possible that his book will remain as a whole; as an entity; as a novel. If the people the writer is making talk of old masters; of music; of modern painting; of letters; or of science; then they should talk of those subjects in the novel. If they do not talk of those subjects and the writer makes them talk of them he is a faker, and if he talks about them himself to show how much he knows, then he is showing off. No matter how good a phrase or a simile he may have, if he puts it in where it is not absolutely necessary and irreplaceable, he is spoiling his work for egotism. Prose is architecture, not interior decoration, and the Baroque is over. For a writer to put his own intellectual musings, which he might sell for a low price as essays, into the mouths of artificially constructed characters, which are more remunerative when issued as people in a novel, is good economics, perhaps, but does not make literature. People in a novel, not skilfully constructed *characters*, must be projected from the writer's assimilated experience, from his knowledge, from his head, from his heart, and from all there is of him. If he ever has luck as well as seriousness and gets them out entire they will have more than one dimension and they will last a long time. A good writer should know as near everything as possible. Naturally he will not. A great enough writer seems to be born with knowledge. But he really is not; he has only been born with a quicker ratio to the passage of time than other men and without conscious application, and with an intelligence to accept or reject what is already presented as knowledge. There are some things which cannot be learned quickly, and time, which is all we have, must be paid heavily for their acquiring.

They are the very simplest things and because it takes a man's life to know them the little new that each man gets from life is very costly and the only heritage he has to leave. Every novel which is truly written contributes to the total of knowledge which is there at the disposal of the next writer who comes, but the next writer must pay, always, a certain nominal percentage in experience to be able to understand and assimilate what is available as his birthright and what he must, in turn, take his departure from. If a writer of prose knows enough about what he is writing about he may omit things that he knows and the reader, if the writer is writing truly enough, will have a feeling of those things as strongly as though the writer had stated them. The dignity of movement of an iceberg is due to only one-eighth of it being above water. A writer who omits things because he does not know them only makes hollow places in his writing. A writer who appreciates the seriousness of writing so little that he is anxious to make people see he is formally educated, cultured or well-bred, is merely a popinjay. And this too, remember: a serious writer is not to be confounded with a solemn writer. A serious writer may be a hawk or a buzzard or even a popinjay, but a solemn writer is always a bloody owl.

The passage is an excellent example of Hemingway's style, notice the clumsy, facetious get-away, the admirable relation in the central passage between the language used and the thought to be conveyed, the polemical anti-climax at the end and notice also the slovenliness of such a phrase as "if the writer of prose knows enough about what he is writing about he may omit things that he knows". Like most writers of the thirties Hemingway seems terrified to blot a line.

Hemingway's difficulties as a writer arise from the limitations of realism. His style, derived from Huck Finn, Stein, Anderson with perhaps a dash of Firbank, is the antithesis of fine writing. It is a style in which the body talks rather than the mind, one admirable for rendering emotions; love, fear, joy of battle, despair, sexual appetite, but impoverished for intellectual purposes. Hemingway is fortunate in possessing a physique which is at home in the world of boxing, bull-fighting and big game shooting, fields closed to most writers and especially to Mandarins; he is supreme in the domain of violence and his opportunity will be to write the great book (and there have been no signs of one so far), about the Spanish war. Hemingway's tragedy as an artist is that he has not had the versatility to run away fast enough from his imitators. The talkies that facilitated his success brought on a flood of talkie-novels, the trick of being tough, the knack of writing entirely in dialogue interrupted only by a few sentimental landscapes caught on and with each bad copy the prestige of the original was affected. A Picasso would have done something different; Hemingway could only indulge in invective against his critics—and do it again. His colleagues in American realism, Dos Passos, O'Hara, Caldwell, have found the same difficulties and the Hemingway style is now confined to sporting journalists on the daily papers, advertising men with literary ambitions, cinema critics and the writers of thrillers. The first you-man sentence' of the *Portrait of the Artist*, "when you wet the bed first it is warm, then it gets cold", a sentence intended to represent the simple body-conscious needs of early childhood, after dominating fiction for years, would seem to have had its day.

Lewis has attacked Hemingway for being a "dumb ox", for choosing stupid inarticulate heroes who are the passive victims of circumstance rather than active and intelligent masters of their fate. Yet at the period at which Hemingway wrote his best books it was necessary to be a dumb ox. It was the only way to escape from Chelsea's Apes of God and from Bloomsbury's Sacred Geese.

The most resolute and coherent of the opponents of fine writing has been Somerset Maugham although his hostility arises, he tells us, from his incapacity.

I discovered my limitations and it seemed to me that the only sensible thing was to aim at what excellence I could within them. I knew that I had no lyrical quality, I had a small vocabulary and no efforts that I could make to enlarge it much, availed me. I had little gift of metaphors; the original and striking simile seldom occurred to me. Poetic flights and the great imaginative sweep were beyond my powers. . . . I knew that I should never write as well as I could wish, but I thought with pains I could arrive at writing as well as my natural defects allowed. On taking thought it seemed to me that I must aim at lucidity, simplicity and euphony. I have put these three qualities in the order of the importance I assigned to them.

Maugham (I am quoting from *The Summing Up,* though some of the arguments there are to be found in earlier books) then goes on to criticise Ruskin and Sir Thomas Browne with justice and to attack the influence of King James's Bible on English prose.

Ever since, English prose has had to struggle against the tendency to luxuriance. When from time to time the spirit of the language has reasserted itself, as it did with Dryden and the writers of Queen Anne, it was only to be submerged once more by the pomposities of Gibbon and Dr. Johnson. When English prose recovered simplicity with Hazlitt, the Shelley of the letters, and Charles Lamb at his best, it lost it again with de Quincey, Carlyle, Meredith, and Walter Pater. . . .

For to write good prose is an affair of good manners. It is, unlike verse, a civil art. . . . Poetry is baroque. I cannot but feel that the prose writers of the baroque period, the authors of King James' bible, Sir Thomas Browne, Glanville, were poets who had lost their way. Prose is a rococo art. It needs taste rather than power, decorum rather than inspiration and vigour rather than grandeur. . . . It is not an accident that the best prose was written when rococo, with its elegance and moderation, attained its greatest excellence. For rococo was evolved when baroque had become declamatory, and the world, tired of the stupendous, asked for restraint. It was the natural expression of persons who valued a civilised life. Humour, tolerance, and horse-sense made the great tragic issues that had preoccupied the first half of the seventeenth century seem excessive. The world was a more comfortable place to live in and perhaps for the first time in centuries the cultivated classes could sit back and enjoy their leisure. It has been said that good prose should resemble the conversation of a well-bred man. Conversation is only possible when men's minds are free from pressing anxieties. Their lives must be reasonably secure and they must have no grave concern about their souls. They must attach importance to the refinements of civilisation. They must value courtesy; they must pay attention to their persons (and have we not also been told that good prose should be like the clothes of a well-dressed man, appropriate but unobtrusive?). They must fear to bore, they must be neither flippant, nor solemn, but always apt; and they must look upon "enthusiasm" with a critical glance. This is a soil very suitable for prose. It is not to be wondered at that it gave a fitting opportunity for the appearance of the best writer of prose that our modern world has seen, Voltaire. . . . The writers of English, perhaps owing to the poetic nature of the language, have seldom reached the excellence that seems to have come so naturally to him. . . . If you could write lucidly, simply, euphoniously and yet with liveliness you would write perfectly; you would write like Voltaire.

I have quoted this passage because it is a typical defence of vernacular prose, as also of much literary wish-fulfilment. Maugham thinks with pleasure of the civilised and wealthy society of the eighteenth century, he has made his own life wealthy and civilised and therefore would like to believe that the prose of the eighteenth century is the best. But supposing a new age of "great tragic issues" is now in being, then a prose of humour, tolerance, and horse-sense will seem frivolous and archaic! And what writer could have been more lucid and simple, more admired by Maugham than Swift who living in the heart of that courteous and cultivated age contrived to go mad in it? Nor is the prose of Blake so negligible. Incidentally the defects of the colloquial style are well illustrated in this passage. The vocabulary is flat. "Sit back and enjoy", "pressing anxieties", "reasonably secure", "grave concern", "critical glance", "fitting opportunity", "it is not to be wondered at", while not yet officially clichés, are phrases so tarnished as to be on the way to them. They come from the vocabulary of political journalism; from the atmosphere where words deteriorate faster than in any other and the defect of the colloquial style, the breathlessness, the agitated dullness of the sentence which is too short for both eye and ear, becomes apparent. The phrases rattle like peas being shelled into a tin, the full stops bring the reader up short, the effect, owing to the absence of any relative clauses, is of reading a list of aphorisms and the best aphorists, even La Rochefou-

cauld, can be read only for a few pages. Again, the language of
the Bible is more plain than complicated; its bad influence on
English style has been in the direction of archaistic simplicity and
is apparent in a writer like Kipling. It is no accident, as Maugham
would say, that he goes on to praise American literature, ignorant,
he claims, of the Authorised Version and to flatter American
writers, galvanised by their journalism.

This concludes the case for the vernacular style. There remains
one other argument often heard in its favour. "If culture is to survive it must survive through the masses; if it cannot be made
acceptable to them there is no one else who will be prepared to
guarantee it, since the liberal capitalist society who protected it
will not be in a position to do so after another slump and a war.
Much that is subtle in literature and life will have to be sacrificed
if they are to survive at all; consequently it is necessary for literature to approach its future custodians in a language they will
understand."

The old world is a sinking ship, to get a place in the boats that
are pushing off from it not money nor leisure, the essayist's elegance nor the pedant's erudition will avail; the sailors are not
impressed by courtesy or attention to one's person, nor even by
good clothes and the conversation of a well-bred man; we cannot
take our armchair with us. Nothing will admit us but realism and
sincerity, an honest appeal in downright English. As far back as
1847 Tennyson said that the two great social questions impending
in England were the "housing and education of the poor man
before making him our master, and the higher education of
women" and as the time for making him our master grows nearer,
so his education becomes more necessary since on it depend the
cultural values which he will choose to preserve.

For this reason left-wing writers have tended to write in the
colloquial style while the Mandarins, the wizards and prose charmers remain as supporters of the existing dispensation. In England
the ablest exponents of the colloquial style among the younger

writers are Christopher Isherwood and George Orwell, both left-wing and both, at the present level of current English, superlatively readable. Here is an experiment:

The first sound in the mornings was the clumping of the mill-girls' clogs down the cobbled street. Earlier than that, I suppose, there were factory whistles which I was never awake to hear. There were generally four of us in the bedroom, and a beastly place it was, with that defiled impermanent look of rooms that are not serving their rightful purpose. One afternoon, early in October, I was invited to black coffee at Fritz Wendel's flat. Fritz always invited you to "black coffee" with emphasis on the black. He was very proud of his coffee. People used to say it was the strongest in Berlin. Fritz himself was dressed in his usual coffee-party costume—a thick white yachting sweater and very light blue yachting trousers. You know how it is there early in Havana, with the bums still asleep against the walls of the buildings; before even the ice wagons come by with ice for the bars? Well we came across the square from the dock to the Pearl of San Francisco to get coffee. My bed was in the right-hand corner on the side nearest the door. There was another bed across the foot of it and jammed hard against it (it had to be in that position to allow the door to open), so that I had to sleep with my legs doubled up; if I straightened them out I kicked the occupant of the other bed in the small of the back. He was an elderly man named Mr. Reilly. He greeted me with his full-lipped luscious smile.

" 'Lo, Chris!''

"Hullo, Fritz. How are you?"

"Fine." He bent over the coffee-machine, his sleek black hair unplastering itself from the scalp and falling in richly scented locks over his eyes. "This darn thing doesn't go," he added.

We sat down and one of them came over.

"Well," he said.

"I can't do it," I told him. "I'd like to do it as a favour. But I told you last night I couldn't."

"You can name your own price."

"It isn't that. I can't do it. That's all. How's business?" I asked.

"Lousy and terrible." Fritz grinned richly.

Luckily he had to go to work at five in the morning so I could uncoil my legs and have a couple of hours proper sleep after he was gone.

This passage is formed by adding to the first three sentences of Orwell's *Road to Wigan Pier* the first five sentences of Isherwood's *Sally Bowles* and then the first two sentences of Hemingway's *To Have and Have Not.* I have woven the beginning of the three stories a little further. Next three sentences by Orwell, then dialogue by Isherwood to "added", by Hemingway to "That's all", by Isherwood to "richly" and last sentence by Orwell again. The reader can now go on with whichever book he likes best, Orwell and his bed, Fritz and his coffee, or Harry Morgan and Havana. As Pearsall-Smith says of modern writers: "The diction, the run of phrase of each of them seems quite undistinguishable from that of the others, each of whose pages might have been written by any one of his fellows."

This, then, is the penalty of writing for the masses. As the writer goes out to meet them half-way he is joined by other writers going out to meet them half-way and they merge into the same creature—the talkie journalist, the advertising, lecturing, popular novelist.

The process is complicated by the fact that the masses, whom a cultured writer may generously write for, are at the moment over-lapped by the middle-class best-seller-making public and so a venal element is introduced.

According to Gide, a good writer should navigate against the current; the practitioners in the new vernacular are swimming with it; the familiarities of the advertisements in the morning paper, the matey leaders in the *Daily Express,* the blather of the film critics, the wisecracks of newsreel commentators, the know-all autobiographies of political reporters, the thrillers and 'teccies, the personal confessions, the *I was a so-and-so,* and *Storm over such-and-such,* the gossip-writers who play Jesus at twenty-five pounds a week, the straight-from-the-shoulder men, the middle-brow novelists of the shove-halfpenny school, are all swimming with it too. For a moment the canoe of an Orwell or an Isherwood bobs up, then it is hustled away by floating rubbish, and a spate of newspaper pulp.

It is interesting to notice the conflict between the two ways of writing in Auden. In the ballads he has lately been writing, excellent of their kind, he has attempted to reduce poetry to a record of simple and universal experience expressed in colloquial language.

> O plunge your hands in water
> Plunge them in up to the wrist
> Stare, stare in the basin
> And wonder what you've missed.

> The glacier knocks in the cupboard
> The desert sighs in the bed,
> And the crack in the tea-cup opens
> A lane to the land of the dead.

At the same time the bulk of his poetry has always remained private and esoteric.

CHAPTER IX

THE COOL ELEMENT OF PROSE

❧❧

IT IS NOW TIME TO EXPRESS AN OPINION ON THE BATTLE between the styles. I do not say that one is better than the other; there is much to admire in both; what I have claimed is a relationship between them, a perpetual action and reaction; the realists had it their way in the years before the war; from 1918 to 1928, the period of Joyce, Proust, Valéry, Strachey, Woolf, the Sitwells, and Aldous Huxley, the new Mandarins ruled supreme, while from 1928 to 1938 the new realists have predominated. The deflationary activities of the Cambridge critics (Richards, Leavis) have replaced the inflationism of Bloomsbury. But we have now had ten years of this new realism; ten years in which it has grown more popular and more tyrannical. Its vocabulary, never rich, has been worn away by the attrition of success; its exponents have been wearied by the enormity of their imitators.

It is possible to bring forward other causes for the silence or the deterioration of a writer than the weaknesses of his literary creed and the other causes are as likely to be correct. All we can say of the realists of the last ten years, is that nothing in their technique seems to have insured them against the disastrously short term of the writer's life. Realism, simplicity, the colloquial style, would appear to have triumphed everywhere at the moment —yet where are their triumphant professors? With the exception of Isherwood among the young and Maugham among the old their prestige is already fading. The movement has passed out of their

73

hands and sunk to a wider and more anonymous strata, to the offices, the studios and the novelist's week-end cottages where is produced the great bulk of present-day commercial writing.

I have discussed the situation with Isherwood, whom I regard as a hope of English fiction and I have suggested how dangerous that fatal readability of his might become. The first person singular of the German stories, Herr Christoph, or Herr Issyvoo, is the most persuasive of literary salesmen—one moment's reading with him and one is tobogganing through the book, another second and one has bought it—but he is persuasive because he is so insinuatingly bland and anonymous, nothing rouses him, nothing shocks him. While secretly despising us he could not at the same time be more tolerant; his manners are charming and he is somehow on our side against the characters—confidential as, when playing with children, one child older or less animal than the rest, will suddenly attach itself to the grown-ups and discuss its former playmates.

Now for this a price has to be paid; Herr Issyvoo is not a dumb ox, for he is not condemned to the solidarity with his characters and with their background to which Hemingway is bound by his conception of art, but he is much less subtle, intelligent and articulate than he might be. In the little knitted skein from the three books it will be remembered that not only was the language almost identical and the pace the same but the three "I's" of Isherwood, Orwell and Hemingway were also interchangeable; three colourless reporters.

In Isherwood's earlier *The Memorial* however, there is no first person. The hero is a character who is more favoured than the others, and in the Berlin diary (*New Writing*, No. 3) the first person singular, unhampered by the conventions of fiction, at once postulates a higher level of culture and intelligence, and possesses a richer vocabulary. In conversation, Isherwood, while admitting the limitations of the style he had adopted, expressed his belief in construction as the way out of the difficulty. The writer must conform to the language which is understood by the greatest num-

ber of people, to the vernacular, but his talent as a novelist will
appear in the exactness of his observation, the justice of his situations and in the construction of his book. It is an interesting
theory, for construction has for long been the weak point in modern novels. It is the construction that renders outstanding *The
Memorial, Passage to India,* and *Cakes and Ale.*

But will the construction, however rigid and faultless, of future
books, if they are written in what will by then be an even more
impoverished realist vocabulary, contribute enough to set those
books apart from the copies made by the ever-growing school of
imitators? At present it is impossible to tell; the path is beset by
dangers; it is fortunate that Isherwood, who possesses the mastery
of form, the imaginative content of a true novelist, is able to see
them.

The most convincing attack on the realism of the thirties was
made by Pearsall-Smith in his pamphlet on *Fine Writing* (reprinted in *Reperusals,* 1936). A Mandarin of the generation of
the eighties, an admirer of Pater and Jowett and a friend of Henry
James, he represents not a reaction against the new realism, but the
old Adam, the precious original sinner, against whom the later
realists took action. He, in return, attacks their austerity:

May it be accounted for by the fact that the spirit of Puritanism,
having been banished from the province of moral conduct, has found a
refuge among the arts? Do these critics of the art of writing, like certain critics of other arts, occupy themselves with the craft of literary
composition because they think it wrong? . . . I shall make to our
modern critics, especially of the Cambridge school, a few suggestions
which are not amiable, and are perhaps unfair. The disconcerting fact
may first be pointed out that if you write badly about good writing,
however profound may be your convictions or emphatic your expression
of them, your style has a tiresome trick of whispering, "Don't listen,"
in your reader's ears. And it is possible also to suggest that the promul-
gation of new-fangled æsthetic dogmas in unwieldy sentences may be
accounted for—not perhaps unspitefully—by a certain deficiency in
æsthetic sensibility; as being due to a lack of that delicate, unreasoned,

prompt delight in all the varied and subtle manifestations in which beauty may enchant us.

He goes on to suggest that economic causes are also responsible:

Are not the authors who earn their livings by their pens, and those who, by what some regard as a social injustice, have been more or less freed from this necessity—are not these two classes of authors in a sort of natural opposition to each other? He who writes at his leisure, with the desire to master his difficult art, can hardly help envying the profits of the money-making authors, since his own work at least till years, and often many years, have passed, has no appreciable market value. Unsaleability seems to be the hall-mark, in modern times, of quality in writing.

Puritanism in other people we admire as austerity in ourselves, yet there is much truth in Pearsall-Smith's accusation. Writing is a more impure art than music or painting. It is an art, but it is also the medium in which many millions of inartistic people express themselves, describe their work, sell their goods, justify their conduct, propagate their ideas. It is the vehicle of all business and propaganda. Since it is hard to paint or to compose without a certain affection for painting or music, the commercial element— advertisers, illustrators, are recognisable, and in a minority, nor do music and painting appeal to the scientific temperament.

But writing does. It is an art in which the few who practise it for its own sake are being always resented and jostled through its many galleries by the majority who do not. And the deadliest of these are the scientific investigators, clever young men who have themselves failed as artists and who bring only a passionate sterility and a dark, wide-focusing resentment to their examination of creative art. The aim of much of this destructive criticism, though not as yet publicly avowed, is entirely to eliminate the individual style, to banish imaginative beauty and formal art from writing. Prose will not only be as unassuming as good clothes, but as uniform as bad ones. For there is no use in Maugham arguing that a writer to be distinct from others must heighten his colloquial modern style by reading Newman and Hazlitt; he is by now, if he is like any other modern writer, moving too fast and such authors will seem to him, if he has the patience to read them, so occupied with unreal problems and so contaminated by a leisurely attitude to life as to be hardly less archaic than their stylistic rivals, Lamb, Ruskin, Pater, Matthew Arnold. The remedy is proposed too late.

The one way by which a cure can be undertaken is to persuade such writers to re-read their own books or those contemporary books which, up to a year ago, they most admired. Then, however jauntily they may protest—"Well, it was what the public wanted at the time—it was in me and it had to come out; it means no more to me now than my old toe-nails—and, hell, who wants to read the same book twice, anyway," a doubt will have arisen.

On the other hand Maugham expresses a truth when he says that much writing of the kind he dislikes is the work of "Poets who have lost their way". The defect of Mandarin writing is not that it is poetical or imaginative prose, but that much of it is not prose, but bad poetry. It is a fact of importance that the prose of true poets is firm and muscular. Landor, Coleridge, Shelley, Donne, Shakespeare, Milton, Dryden, Blake, Hopkins, Yeats, Eliot, Gray, Cowper, to name but a few, could write admirable prose—for poetry is a more precise art than prose and to write it implies qualities which prove valuable in the "other harmony".

The poetry of prose writers on the other hand is unworthy of them and very often they will have become prose writers only after the failure of a slim volume of verse. Since the decay of the Romantic Movement poetry has gone through a bad patch and severe discipline has been necessary to those who write it; consequently others who start out with only facility, sensibility and a lyrical outlook, rather than undergo the hardships of the training, have allowed their poetical feeling to relax in prose. The result has been to inflate and romanticise prose in its turn and thus to bring about a philistine, puritan and pedestrian reaction. The Tough Guy, of whose company we are now growing tired, is the inevitable offspring of the androgynous Orlando. There is no reason

why prose should not be poetical provided that the poetry in it is
assimilated to the medium and that its rhythms follow the structure of prose and not of verse—it is the undisciplined, undigested,
unassimilated poetry written often in unconscious blank verse and
bearing no relation to the construction, if any, of the book, which
has discredited "fine writing".

At the moment the vernacular is triumphant. Damon Runyon
sweeps the land. The You-men are everywhere victorious.

That is the situation. Is there any hope? Is there a possibility of
a new kind of prose developing out of a synthesis of Orlando and
the Tough Guy? Will the strong writers of the colloquial school
heighten the form of their work or can the Formalists deepen their
content? We must look to the poets for a lead, for there are signs
that from them is coming a revival of imaginative prose. I like to
detect a foreshadowing of it in Landor's description of the lioness
with her young, which appears, like an oasis, in Richard's *Principles of Literary Criticism*.

On perceiving the countryman, she drew up her feet gently, and
squared her mouth, and rounded her eyes, slumberous with content, and
they looked, he said, like sea-grottoes, obscurely green, interminably
deep, at once awakening fear and stilling and suppressing it.

Such a phrase belongs to the real texture of prose, a texture now
rarely seen, where syntax and a rich vocabulary are woven in a
pattern to match the thought of the maker.

I know that I am I, living in a small way in a temperate zone, blam-
ing father, jealous of son, confined to a few acts often repeated, easily
attracted to a limited class of physique, yet envying the simple life of
the gut, desiring the certainty of the breast or prison, happiest sawing
wood, only knowledge of the real disturbances in the general law of
the dream; the quick blood fretting against the slowness of the hope;
a unit of life, needing water and salt, that looks for a sign.

.   .   .   .

From the immense bat-shadow of home; from the removal of landmarks, from appeals for love and from the comfortable words of the
devil, from all opinions and personal ties; from pity and shame; and

from the wish to instruct . . . in the moment of vision; in the hour
of applause; in the place of defeat; and in the hour of desertion, O
Holmes, Deliver us.

. . . .

These two quotations from *The Orators* (W. H. Auden; Faber,
1932) show imaginative prose coming to life again by way of a
young poet influenced by Rimbaud and the Prayer Book. And
when the language comes to life, it ceases to be an imitation. The
prose of Spender is also unusual and in his critical book, *The
Destructive Element*, he makes a study of that great Mandarin,
Henry James, which must affect the values of any contemporary
who reads it, since he has restated for his generation the relationship between writing and ethics. The revival of the poetical drama
and the Group Theater gives writers like Eliot, Auden, Isherwood,
and MacNeice opportunities for declamatory and non-commercial
prose.

Other glimpses of a revival in imaginative writing may be
found in George Barker's *Janus* (Faber, 1935), Hugh Sykes-
Davies' *Petron* (Dent), David Jones' *In Parenthesis* (Faber),
Djuna Barnes' *Night Wood* (Faber), Henry Miller's *Tropic of
Cancer* (Obelisk Press), and Henry Green's remarkable novel
Living (Dent).[1]

One further question is raised by Maugham. "I have never had
much patience", he states, "with the writers who claim from the
reader an effort to understand their meaning." This is an abject
surrender for it is part of the tragedy of modern literature that the
author, anxious to avoid mystifying the reader, is afraid to demand
of him any exertions. "Don't be afraid of me," he exclaims, "I
write exactly as I talk—no, better still—exactly as you talk."
Imagine Cézanne painting or Beethoven composing "exactly as he
talked"! The only way to write is to consider the reader to be the

[1] Readers who find the lioness quotation stirs them, like the memory of
something of which they have been long deprived, may amuse themselves by
searching for this quality in modern prose, this combination of imagination and
accuracy into magic, and they will be fortunate if they can discover a single
example.

author's equal; to treat him otherwise is to set a value on illiteracy and so all that results from Maugham's condescension to a reader from whom he expects no effort, is a latent hostility to him as of some great chef waiting on a hungry Australian. As Richards says of the poet: "It is hard and, in fact, impossible, to deny him his natural and necessary resources on the ground that a majority of his readers will not understand. This is not his fault but the fault of the social structure."

At the present time for a book to be produced with any hope of lasting half a generation, of outliving a dog or a car, of surviving the lease of a house or the life of a bottle of champagne, it must be written against the current, in a prose that makes demands both on the resources of our language and the intelligence of the reader. From the Mandarins it must borrow art and patience, the striving for perfection, the horror of clichés, the creative delight in the material, in the possibilities of the long sentence and the splendour and subtlety of the composed phrase.

From the Mandarins, on the other hand, the new writer will take warning not to capitalise indolence and egotism nor to burden a sober and delicate language with exhibitionism. There will be no false hesitation and woolly profundities, no mystifying, no Proustian onanism. He will distrust the armchair clowns, the easy philosophers, the prose charmers. He will not show off his small defects, his preferences or his belongings, his cat, his pipe, his carpet slippers, bad memory, clumsiness with machinery, absent-mindedness, propensity for losing things, or his ignorance of business and of everything which might make the reader think he wrote for money. There will be no whimsy, no allusiveness, archaism, pedantic usages, no false colloquialisms, or sham lyrical outbursts; there will be no "verily" and "verity", no "when all is said and done", no "to my way of thinking", "hardly of my own choosing", "I may be very stupid but", and no "If it be a sin to be half in love with the old days then I must aver", there will be no false relationship between art and experience; none of those dodges by which the sedentary man of letters is enabled to write

about women, fighting, dancing, drink, by switching over to a
prepared set of literary substitutes called Venus, Mars, Bacchus,
and Terpsichore. References to infinity, to the remoteness of the
stars and planets, the littleness of man, the charm of dead civilisations, to Babylon and Troy, "on whose mouldering citadel lies
the lizard like a thing of green bronze" will be suspect. The
adventurers "among their books", the explorer who never leaves
his desk, will be required to live within their imagination's
income.

From the realists, the puritans, the colloquial writers and talkie-
novelists there is also much that he will take and much that he
will leave. The cursive style, the agreeable manners, the precise
and poetical impact of Forster's diction, the lucidity of Maugham,
last of the great professional writers, the timing of Hemingway,
the smooth cutting edge of Isherwood, the indignation of Lawrence, the honesty of Orwell, these will be necessary and the touch
of those few journalists who give to every word in their limited
vocabulary its current topical value. But above all it is construction
that can be learnt from the realists, that discipline in the conception and execution of a book, that planning which gives simply-
written things the power to endure, the constant pruning without
which the imagination like a tea-rose reverts to the wilderness.

He will not borrow from the realists, or from their imitators,
the flatness of style, the homogeneity of outlook, the fear of eccentricity, the reporter's horror of distinction, the distrust of beauty,
the cult of a violence and starkness that is masochistic. Nor will
he adopt the victory mentality of those left-wing writers who
imagine themselves already to be the idols of a conquering pro-
letariat and who give their laws in simple matter-of-fact hard-
hitting English to a non-existent congregation. That time is not
yet; the artist to-day is in the position of a patient Mahomet towards whom the great art-hating mountain of the British public
must eventually sidle.

This would seem the state of our literature. The battle between
the schools I think has been proved to exist, but as with all civil

wars, there are places where and moments when the fight rages
with greater violence than at others. I have concentrated on those
writers in the forefront of that battle, and any criticism I have
made of them is intended only to relate them to it. Thus to call
Proust a bad influence is not to deny that he is a great writer, but
rather to consider his work in terms of what can be learnt from
it to-day. It is the privilege of living in the twentieth century that
one can take both sides in such controversies.

What I claim is that there continue action and reaction between
these styles, and that necessary though it were and victorious as it
may appear, the colloquial style of the last few years is doomed
and dying. Style, as I have tried to show, is a relationship between
a writer's mastery of form and his intellectual or emotional content. Mastery of form has lately been held, with some reason, to
conceal a poverty of content but this is not inevitably so and for
too long writers have had to prove their sincerity by going before
the public in sackcloth and ashes or rather in a fifty-shilling suit
and a celluloid collar. Now has come the moment when the pen-
ance is complete and when they may return to their old habit. It
is no more a question of taking sides about one way or another of
writing, but a question of timing, for the you-man writing of
he-men authors is going out and the form must be enriched again.
Our language is a sulky and inconstant beauty and at any given
moment it is important to know what liberties she will permit.
Now all seems favourable. Experiment and adventure are indicated,
the boom of the twenties has been paid for by the slump of the
thirties; let us try then to break the vicious circle by returning to
a controlled expenditure, a balanced literary budget, a reasoned
extravagance.

PART TWO

THE CHARLOCK'S SHADE

The Strongest Poison ever known
Came from Cæsar's Laurel Crown.
BLAKE.

CHAPTER X

THE BLIGHTED RYE

⚘⚘

WE HAVE SEEN HOW CLOSELY THE STYLE OF A BOOK MAY
affect its expectation of life, passing through a charnel house in
which we have observed the death and decomposition of many
works confident ten years ago of longevity, hailed as masterpieces
of their period and now equal in decay. A few only present an air
of health and claim some immunity from the venom of time. It
is necessary now to analyse the conditions which govern the high
rate of mortality among contemporary writers, to enter a region,
"where the thin harvest waves its wither'd ears . . ." a sombre
but, to those for whom it is not yet too late, a bracing territory.

> There thistles stretch their prickly arms afar,
> And to the ragged infant threaten war;
> There Poppies nodding, mock the hope of toil,
> There the blue Bugloss paints the sterile soil;
> Hardy and high, above the slender sheaf,
> The slimy Mallow waves her silky leaf;
> O'er the young shoot the Charlock throws a shade,
> And clasping Tares cling round the sickly blade;
> With mingled tints the rocky coasts abound,
> And a sad splendour vainly shines around.

Let the "thin harvest" be the achievement of young authors, the
"wither'd ears" their books, then the "militant thistles" represent
politics, the "nodding poppies" day-dreams, conversation, drink
and other narcotics, the "blue Bugloss" is the clarion call of jour-

nalism, the "slimy mallow" that of worldly success, the "charlock" is sex with its obsessions and the "clasping tares" are the ties of duty and domesticity. The "mingled tints" are the varieties of talent which appear; the "sad splendour" is that of their vanished promise. These enemies of literature, these parasites on genius we must examine in detail; they are blights from which no writer is immune.

Before making further use of Crabbe's description of the heath with its convenient symbols we must answer a question sometimes put by certain literary die-hards, old cats who sit purring over the mouseholes of talent in wait for what comes out. "Is this age", they pretend to ask, "really more unfavourable to writers than any other? Have not writers always had the greatest difficulty in surviving? Indeed, their path to-day seems made much easier than it was, to give an example, for myself!" The answer, if they wanted an answer, is yes. Yes, because a writer needs money more than in the ivory tower decade since he can no longer live in a cottage in the country meditating a blank verse historical drama and still get the best out of himself. Yes, because he is more tempted to-day than at any other time by those remunerative substitutes for good writing: journalism, reviewing, advertising, broadcasting and the cinema, but most of all because a writer to-day can have no confidence in posterity and therefore is inclined to lack the strongest inducement to good work: the desire for survival.

For it is clear that "posterity" even to Samuel Butler,[1] writing in the last century, meant the reading public of the next few hundred years while since then the uncertainties of fame have so increased that Maugham confines it to two generations. A writer must grow used to the idea that culture as we know it may dis-

[1] "All books die sooner or later but that will not hinder an author from trying to give his book as long a life as he can get for it. . . . Any man who wishes his work to stand will sacrifice a good deal of his immediate audience for the sake of being attractive to a much larger number of people later on. Briefly the world resolves itself into two great classes—those who hold that honour after death is better worth having than any honour a man can get and know anything about, and those who doubt this; to my mind those who hold this and hold it firmly, are the only people worth thinking about."

appear and remain lost for ever or till it is excavated, a thousand years hence, from a new Herculaneum. Horace's boast of immortality, his *"non omnis moriar"*, neither anticipated the hostility of the church nor the ignorance of the Dark Ages. Of his two thousand years of posthumous life, a thousand slid by in a coma. One has but to consider the dearth of writers in Italy and Germany, the extinction of the cultural activity of the Weimar republic or the war waged by those countries against the intelligentsia of Spain to perceive how ephemeral are the securest literary reputations, the most flourishing movements. At any moment the schools of Athens may be closed, the libraries burnt, the teachers exterminated, the language suppressed. Any posthumous fame or the existence of any posterity capable of appreciating the arts we care for, can be guaranteed only by fighting for it and for many who fight, there will be no stake in the future but a name on a war-memorial.

The love of posthumous fame is a common psychological substitute for the love of perfection, even as the love of perfection may prove a projection into the world of art of a sense of guilt. Thus Astrologers find this love of perfection in those born under the sign of Virgo; it is to the artist as virginity to the nun and this love of purification they declare confined to those born between the end of August and the end of September. A writer should not be too conscious of such abstractions as perfection and posterity, "the cackle of the unborn about the grave", he should be above a flirtation with time, determined only to restore to the world in a form worthy of his powers something of what he has taken out of it. He must be a helping writer, who tells us what he sees through his periscope or there will be no writers and no readers left.

Otherwise Butler has stated the problem clearly. What ruins young writers is over-production. The need for money is what causes over-production; therefore writers must have private incomes. As he put it "No gold, no holy ghost." Genius is independent of money, but the world will always destroy it if it can.

A writer, then, to avoid over-production, unless he acquires a
private income, must either learn to make more money from his
books or to earn money in other ways congenial to the writing of
them.

To make more money from a book it is necessary either to pot-
boil, to give way to the taste of the reading public at the expense
of the judgment of the author or to find technical ways of im-
proving sales. Other ways of earning money and still finding time
to write consist of journalism, teaching, advertising, the civil
service and the family business. Journalism will be discussed separately. Of the other remedies, teaching provides long holidays and
the work is not such as to make inroads on the creative imagination but not many people can teach or enjoy teaching and, in spite
of the long holidays, the work seems to make any enlargement
of the writer's experience awkward and unwelcome. Of the dons
at Oxford and Cambridge remarkably few attain literary eminence
and the best known among them are writers who have mixed in
the world outside the universities. This is even more true of
schoolmasters. Nor is the Civil Service the Parnassus which it
became in the nineties; its talent would seem to have run dry with
Humbert Wolfe. Since being a civil servant is a static, arid and
parasitic occupation, it is unlikely that anyone who is content with
it will possess the imagination that creates or the talent which will
mature and ripen.

Most unsatisfactory is advertising for there is something about
copy-writing which so resembles the composition of lyric poetry
as to replace the process. When in order to satisfy a corset manu-
facturer in search of a slogan, a writer has to think of the rousing
or the lapidary phrase, the assonance of vowels and consonants,
the condensation of thought, the inflections of delicate meaning
at his disposal, he will be in no mood to write anything else. The
family business, if we have such a family and if it does no business, is the best way out.

An outside job is harmful to a writer in proportion as it ap-
proximates to his vocation. Thus reviewing poetry is the worst

profession for a poet, while broadcasting, advertising, journalism
or lecturing all pluck feathers from the blue bird of inspiration
and cast them on the wind. Living at home, on the other hand,
confines the writer's experience to the family circle; rich marriages
do not usually go with congenial tastes or a mutual love of the
literary life and patrons are capricious and hard to come by; besides, a relationship with one in these days is open to imputation.

It is curious that while the brief-flowering and quick extinction
of modern talent is everywhere so apparent, yet little should have
been written on the subject. Our two sages, Pearsall-Smith and
Maugham, croak their warnings but there is no sign that they are
regarded.

As soon as any glimmering of talent, any freshness or originality,
makes its appearance, it is immediately noted and exploited [Pearsall-
Smith, *Prospects of Literature* (Hogarth Press, 1927)]. Editors of the
weekly and even of the daily papers seize upon it; they have acquired,
one may almost say of them, the habits of cannibals or ogres; they suck
the brains of young writers, and then replace them by a new bevy of
adolescent talent. Publishers also compete nowadays with editors in
killing the goose whose golden eggs they live on. As soon as a young
author makes a success his publisher urges him to repeat it at once;
other publishers are eager to win his patronage, and he is not infre-
quently offered a fixed income on the condition that he shall regularly
provide one or two volumes a year. It would be invidious to mention
names, but in following the careers of the more recent writers whose
first books have charmed me, I almost invariably find that their earliest
publications, or at least their earliest successes, are their best achievements; their promise ripens to no fulfilment; each subsequent work
tends to be a feeble replica and fainter echo of the first.

Maugham is more inclined to blame the talent that is so easily
exhausted, and which he calls "the natural creativity of youth".

One of the tragedies of the arts is the spectacle of the vast numbers
of persons who have been misled by this passing fertility to devote their
lives to the effort of creation. Their invention deserts them as they grow
older, and they are faced with the long years before them in which,

unfitted by now for a more humdrum calling, they harass their wearied brain to beat out material it is incapable of giving them. They are lucky when, with what bitterness we know, they can make a living in ways, like journalism or teaching, that are allied to the arts.

The causes are interlocking. The trouble is that authors are not paid enough. If three hundred pounds were the normal advance on a book instead of fifty, a writer could take his time over it and refuse other work; that it is not is due to the intermediate profits and expenses of book production, and to the indifference of the reading public which is growing more impatient with books as it becomes more dependent on magazines. "The Reader's Digest" and its fellows will soon read the books for him.

The torpor of the reading public conditions the publisher; parsimonious to authors who fail to dispel that torpor, he is exacting and impatient with those who have succeeded. When publishers vacillate (and as repressed sadists are supposed to become policemen or butchers so those with an irrational fear of life become publishers), the second villain, the editor, steps in—even Tennyson complained of him. "All the magazines and daily newspapers, which pounce upon everything they can get hold of, demoralize literature. This age gives an author no time to mature his work."

CHAPTER XI

THE BLUE BUGLOSS

ℜℰ

LET US NOW TACKLE THE PROBLEM OF JOURNALISM—DEADLI-
est of the weeds on Crabbe's Heath—in its relation to literature.
We have suggested that journalism must obtain its full impact on
the first reading while literature can achieve its effect on a second,
being intended for an interested and not an indifferent public.
Consequently the main difference between them is one of texture.
Journalism is loose, intimate, simple and striking; literature
formal and compact, not simple and not immediately striking
in its effects. Carelessness is not fatal to journalism nor are clichés,
for the eye rests lightly on them. But what is intended to be read
once can seldom be read more than once; a journalist has to accept
the fact that his work, by its very to-dayness, is excluded from any
share in to-morrow. Nothing dates like a sense of actuality than
which there is nothing in journalism more valuable. A writer who
takes up journalism abandons the slow tempo of literature for a
faster one and the change will do him harm. By degrees the flip-
pancy of journalism will become a habit and the pleasure of being
paid on the nail and more especially of being praised on the nail,
grow indispensable. And yet of the admirable journalism that has
appeared in the literary weeklies, how little bears reprinting, how
little even has been reprinted! The monthly and quarterly papers
approximate more to literature and permit subjects to be treated
at greater length, but they are few indeed! For brevity is all-impor-
tant; it is the two-thousand word look which betrays journalism,

which makes the reader hurry on when he opens a volume of criticism and finds it to consist of jerky and disjointed essays, "The Prose of Keats", "Beddoes Revisited", "The English Hexameter", "Hazlitt's Aunt", "After Expressionism What?", "Miss Austen's Nephew", all with the fatal asterisk directing the reader to the title of some book once reviewed.

There are certain people who benefit from journalism. They are easily recognised and fall into two classes. The first are amateur writers who through lack of a public or through not having to consider a public, are verbose and obscure, who have acquired so many mannerisms or private meanings for the words they use or who employ such leisurely constructions that an editor alone, since they will not listen to their friends, can impatiently cure them. The other class who benefit are those well-stored minds who suffer from psychological sloth, and who can only reveal their treasures in short articles for quick returns. But this class includes few young writers and these would soon succumb to the atmosphere breathed with such impunity by a Hazlitt or by a wise old literary stager.

There is one other fortunate class: those who are masters of a literary style which so resembles journalism that they can make the transition from one tempo to the other without effort. Readers of *Abinger Harvest* by E. M. Forster will have found that there is about those essays nothing ephemeral since they are in the language of E. M. Forster the novelist. His literary style is cursive and no concession has to be made. The styles overlap; the tempos coincide. This is also true of Lytton Strachey who imposed his literary style on his editors. There are several writers in the same position as Forster. The danger for them is that, if their journalism is literature so is their literature journalism and Hemingway, for example, appears unable to distinguish between them, which accounts for the unevenness of such books as *Green Hills of Africa* or *Death in the Afternoon*.

Maugham detects another evil in journalism besides the vulgarisation of a writer's style.

There is an impersonality in a newspaper that insensibly affects the writer. People who write much for the press seem to lose the faculty of seeing things for themselves; they see them from a generalised standpoint, vividly often, sometimes with hectic brightness, yet never with that idiosyncracy which may give only a partial picture of the facts, but is suffused by the personality of the observer. The press, in fact, kills the individuality of those who write for it.

Journalism for most writers means reviewing.

Let Walter Savage Shelleyblake be a young author. Let his book be called *Vernal Aires*. Soon will come the delicious summons from the literary editor of *The Blue Bugloss*. "Dear Shelleyblake, I was so interested to meet you the other night and have a chance to tell you what I think of *Vernal Aires*. I have been wondering if you would like to try your hand at a little reviewing for us. We are looking for someone to do the Nonesuch *Boswell*, and your name cropped up."

The Nonesuch *Boswell* alone is worth four guineas, and soon a signed review, "Expatriate from Auchinleck" by Walter Savage Shelleyblake, appears in the literary supplement of the *Blue Bugloss*. It is full of ideas and Mr. Vampire, the editor, bestows on it his praise. The next book which Shelleyblake reviews, on Erasmus Darwin, is not quite so good but his article "Swansong at Lichfield", is considered "extremely bright". Suddenly his name appears under a pile of tomes of travel; the secrets of Maya jungles, Kenya game-wardens and ricochetting American ladies are probed by him. In a year's time he will have qualified as a maid-of-all-work and be promoted to reviewing novels. It is promotion because the novel review is a regular feature, because more people read them and because publishers "care". If he is complimentary and quotable he will be immortalized on the dust wrapper and find his name in print on the advertisements. And eight or ten novels a fortnight, sold as review copies, add to his wage.

Certain facts must now be stated. However much Mr. Vampire admired *Vernal Aires* and however fond he is of Walter Shelleyblake, he is, before anything else, an editor. He is concerned with

The Blue Bugloss and whether each number is bright enough to paint the sterile soil. In so far as he is developing in Walter latent gifts—competence, a turn for satire, lucidity, polish—his interests coincide; but they can never be identical, and the use Walter makes of these gifts is not his own concern but Mr. Vampire's. The competition for the best books, the Nonesuch *Boswells,* is fierce; Mr. Vampire is often lucky to get one of them himself and so if Shelleyblake is anxious to write several thousand words on the influence of Horace on English poetry or the psychological reasons for the retirement of Congreve, he will have to go on being anxious and hurry up with his copy on *Backstairs and Petticoats* (a chronicle of famous Royal Mistresses), or six more autobiographies, headed by *Fifty Years Down Under.*

Myself a lazy, irresolute person, overvain and overmodest, unsure in my judgments and unable to finish what I have begun, I have profited from journalism, owing to the admirable manipulation of my manager and trainer. Yet even so I would say to Shelleyblake who clearly does not belong to the Hazlitt group, that any other way of making money would be better, that reviewing is a whole-time job with a half-time salary, a job in which the best in him is generally expended on the mediocre in others. A good review is only remembered for a fortnight; a reviewer has always to make his reputation afresh nor will he find time for private reading or writing, for he is too busy reading other people's books and this will disincline him to read when he is not working. The sight of his friends' books accumulating depresses him and he knows that, besides losing the time to write books of his own, he is also losing the energy and the application, frittering it away on tripe and discovering that it is his flashiest efforts which receive most praise.

There are not more than four or five posts in reviewing that carry with them money, freedom and dignity, whose holders can inherit the mantle of Arnold and Sainte-Beuve so that the most Shelleyblake can expect is that, by reading two books a day and writing for three papers, he may make about four hundred a year.

During this time he will incur the hostility of authors, the envy of other reviewers and the distrust of his friends against whose books he will seem invariably prejudiced; the public will view him with indifference or accept him as an eccentric on whom they will launch their views and their manuscripts while old friends will greet him with, "Are you writing anything now?"—"apart of course from your articles," they will add. "I read you—but I don't say I agree with you," will be another approach, to which, "I know you, but I don't say I like you," is the correct answer.

No, if Walter Shelleyblake must be a journalist, there is but one chance for him. He must declare war on his employers and so manoeuvre them that he never reviews a bad book, never reviews more than one at a time and never writes a review that cannot be reprinted, i.e. that is not of some length and on a subject of permanent value. He will know that the bad books he reads are like hours on a sundial, *vulnerant omnes, ultima necat,* all wound, the last one mortally, neither will he spend himself on cheap subjects, nor put down his whole view of life in a footnote, for he will write only about what interests him. And whatever happens to him (and there are no pensions for literary hacks), he must realise that he is not indispensable.

> Brightness falls from the air,
> Queens have died young and fair . . .

but not *The Blue Bugloss* and Mr. Vampire and his new young men will be perfectly able to get on without him.

CHAPTER XII

THE THISTLES

⁂

AT THE MOMENT POLITICS, THE THISTLES

> . . . that stretch their prickly arms afar,
> And to the ragged infant threaten war

are more dangerous to young writers than journalism. They are dangerous because writers now feel that politics are necessary to them, without having learnt yet how best to be political.

Indifference to politics among artists has always been associated with a feeling of impotence. Thus those great non-politicals, the ivory-tower dwellers, flourished helpless, under the second Empire or in the Paris of 1870 after defeat in the Franco-Prussian war. English writers, in the late Victorian age, were equally helpless; only Kipling, who celebrated the jingoism and imperialism of the ruling class and the materialism of the time and Shaw who attacked them, obtained a political foothold. The "nineties" were a reaction of artists against a political world which they abhorred but could not alter. William Morris alone of the Victorian writers, combined poetry with socialism, while Tennyson's conception of the role of the poet as the supreme Endorser of new achievement in material progress was so forbidding as to deter younger writers from taking any interest in such subjects. This widespread indifference to politics crystallised into a theory that politics were harmful, that they were not artistic material of the first order, that an artist could not be a politician. Politics belonged to that realm of action which Proust and Strachey had discredited. A belief in action indicated a belief in progress, a belief in progress was Victorian and ridiculous.

Yet if we look at writers through the ages we see that they have always been political. Greek poets were political, they championed democracy or defended oligarchs and tyrants according to their sentiment. Pindar was political as were Aeschylus and Euripides, Plato and Aristotle, Catullus and Cicero, Virgil and Horace. Dante was engrossed in politics as were most of the artists of the Renaissance. Nobody told Byron he would be a better writer if he did not attempt *The Vision of Judgment* or Wordsworth not to bother with *Toussaint l'Ouverture;* Swift was not considered to have cheapened himself by *The Drapier Letters* or *The Conduct of the Allies,* nor Dryden to have let down poetry by *Absalom and Achitophel.* To deny politics to a writer is to deny him part of his humanity. But even from a list of political writers we can deduce that there are periods in the history of a country when writers are more political, or more writers are political than at others. They are not the periods of greatest political tension, they are those in which authors can do most, can be listened to, can be important, can influence people, and get their own way. Thus Roman poets ceased to be political after the Empire because they were powerless. A writer during the age of Augustus could not play the part of Catullus or Cicero. Writers flourish in a state of political flux, on the eve of the crisis, rather than in the crisis itself; it is before a war or a revolution that they are listened to and come into their own and it was because they were disillusioned at their impotence during the war that so many became indifferent to political issues after the peace.

It is clear that we are living now in a transition period as suited to political writing as were the days of Ship Money or the reign of Queen Anne. Writers can still change history by their pleading, and one who is not political neglects the vital intellectual issues of his time and disdains his material. He is not powerless, like the Symbolists of 1870, the æsthetes of the eighties and nineties, the

beer-and-chivalry addicts of the nineteen hundreds or the demobilised Georgian poet on his chicken farm. He is not a victim of
his time but a person who can alter it, though if he does not, he may
soon find himself victimised. By ignoring the present he condones
the future. He has to be political to integrate himself and he must
go on being political to protect himself. To-day the forces of life
and progress are ranging on one side, those of reaction and death
on the other. We are having to choose between democracy and
fascism, and fascism is the enemy of art. It is not a question of
relative freedom; there are no artists in Fascist countries. We are
not dealing with an Augustus who will discover his Horace and
his Virgil, but with Attila or Hulaku, destroyers of European culture whose poets can contribute only battle-cries and sentimental
drinking songs. Capitalism in decline, as in our own country, is
not much wiser as a patron than fascism. Stagnation, fear, violence
and opportunism the characteristics of capitalism preparing for the
fray, are no background for a writer and there is a seediness, an
ebb of life, a philosophy of taking rather than giving, a bitterness and brutality about right-wing writers now which was absent
in those of other days, in seventeenth-century Churchmen or
eighteenth-century Tories. There is no longer a Prince Rupert, a
Doctor Johnson, a Wellington, Disraeli, or Newman, on the reactionary side.

We have seen that writers are politically-minded when they are
able to accomplish something; that these periods are those of
change, on the eve of revolutions and civil wars and before the
resort to arms takes matters out of their control and we have seen
that we are in such a period now, and that unless writers do all
they can it will be too late; war will break out and the moment
be past when the eloquence of the artist can influence the destiny
of humanity.

If political writing is no more than the exercise of the instinct
of self-preservation, there can be no reason for classing "politics"
among the weeds that stifle writers. But there are dangers about

being political of which writers are unaware and so seldom avoid.
Thus being political is apt to become a whole time job;

> To-day the expending of powers
> On the flat ephemeral pamphlet and the boring meeting,

writes Auden, though copies of his pamphlets are excessively rare.
Canvassing, making speeches, and pamphleteering are not the best
medium for sensitive writers. They involve much time and trouble
and can be better performed by someone else. To command a
listening senate, however, is a secret ambition of many writers and
it is easy to justify it—to be "thankful that my words can be any
comfort to these poor men", etc. The truth is that oratory is a
coarser art than writing and that to become addicted to it is to
substitute the ruses of the platform for the integrity of the pen.
Neither is a writer improved by sitting on committees and cultivating the chairmanities.

Another effect of becoming too political is that such activity
leads to disillusion. Thus writers become disheartened by the vulgarity of politicians. They find it hard to realise that the militants
and executives of a movement may be narrow-minded, envious,
ambitious and ungrateful, yet their cause remain fundamentally
just and right. Their political judgment is often unsound for they
refuse to allow for the slow motions of public opinion; they are
disheartened by personal rebuffs and bored by drudgery. Defeat-
ism is their occupational disease.

Politicians, on their side, can be unappreciative. Their favourite
arts are those which are enjoyed in relaxation: light music or
Mickey Mouse, the Oxford Book of English Verse, Edgar Wallace,
Wodehouse, Webb. They do not like art to be exacting and difficult; they may envy the artists who collaborate with them because
they do not understand their success, but with their idealism and
their tender consciences they seem to them priggish and patronising. The enmities of highbrow and lowbrow, man of action and
man of thought, classical side and modern side are not yet buried

and reappear, over the ephemeral pamphlet or at the boring meeting, in unexpected forms.

In what way then should a writer be political? How can he make best use of his weapons?

Firstly, by satire. This is a satirical age and among the vast reading public the power of an artist to awaken ridicule has never been so great. To make the enemies of freedom look silly, to write like Low's cartoons or like

> I met murder on the way,
> He wore the mask of Castlereagh,

is the duty of any who can.

Then, if he is intelligent, he can analyse situations, draw attention to tendencies, expose contradictions and help his more active colleagues by cultivating lucidity, profundity and detachment. And lastly, he can help to contribute the idealism without which any movement fails. He must, in his serious writing, avoid propaganda and the presence in his work of lumps of unassimilated political material.[1] Like the termites who chew up the food for the fighters his rôle is to digest the experience they bring him. For this reason the poets are the best political writers for they have the best diges-

---

[1] It is objectionable because it introduces into the form a lower level of workmanship, that of the pamphlet or the tract, and an imperfect fusion with the creative process. Propaganda is betrayed by an air of naïveté, as in, "To-morrow he would canvas as he had never canvassed before," and "I had met the insidious power of Ann and defeated it, and now there was a splendid synthesis forming inside me," or "He was an admirable man and I felt warmed and happy when I looked at him. At Oxford he got up and stretched. I think he had read every word of the *Daily Worker* in the eighty minutes since we had left Paddington." Those are from a very young author. Here is an example from Upward:

" 'There will be a time of harshness and bitter struggle, but out of it will come flowers; splendour and joy will come back to the world. And life will be better than it has ever been in the world's history.'

" 'How soon can I join the worker's movement?'

" '. . . You can join some time within the next few days.'

" 'I don't want to wait.' "

This passage in a thoughtful novel brings a whiff of the Salvation Army. Right-wing propaganda, however, can be detected by an appeal to the reader to be "realistic."

tions, and can absorb their material. A poem like *Locksley Hall*, which has been so distilled, remains an alive and contemporary piece of thought.

I must mix myself with action lest I wither in despair
What is that which I should turn to, lighting upon days like these?
Every door is barred with gold, and opens but to golden keys,
Every gate is thronged with suitors, all the markets overflow
I have but an angry fancy: what is that which I should do?

And so we find the best modern political writing in such a book as Spender's *Trial of a Judge* or a poem like Day Lewis's,

Yet living here,
As one between two massing powers I live,
Whom neutrality cannot save
Nor occupation cheer.

The novelists who feel their responsibilities are also searching for something deeper and more universal than superficial realism and are finding it in the allegory. A story of Isherwood's like *The Novaks*, shows how political reality can inform and deepen, can be informed and deepened, by private experiences; and Spender's *Cousins* and his *Burning Cactus* are also excellent illustrations. To strike deep and keep general should be the maxim of the political artist, and he should avoid describing any experience that he has not first integrated and made part of him. He must take pains with his vocabulary for political writing is honeycombed with clichés; having been deadened to their meaning by oratory, politicians have no feeling for words; a phrase which seems healthy at night will be on the sick-list by morning. There is a tendency for left-wing journalists to criticise left-wing poets for being obscure which is dangerous and stupid. The public are not expected to understand the formulas from which are evolved a new explosive or a geodetic aeroplane. The poet is a chemist and there is more pure revolutionary propaganda in a line of Blake than in all *The Rights of Man*.

But if he wishes to be respected by politicians, to be treated as an ally to whom a certain eccentricity is permitted, a writer must let them alone and refrain from taking sides in political quarrels. There is a general left-wing position which has never been defined but which permits a working agreement with the parties, as they now stand, and which is well suited to a writer. To abandon this general position is safe for a militant journalist; for an artist, it may lead to a damaging retreat. There is so much side-choosing, heresy-hunting, witch-burning and shadow cabinet-making among the parties of the left, so much victory mentality among people for whom victory is most uncertain, that caution in a writer should be welcome. It is no time to quarrel with our own side.

I will conclude this excursion among the Thistles by quoting two points of view of left-wing writers, both communists, Upward and Stephen Spender. Upward, I find, is too logical for the times, his pronouncement on the only possible way for a writer to live is reminiscent of Tolstoy's socialist analysis of art which proved that Hugo's *Les Misérables* and Harriet Stowe's *Uncle Tom's Cabin* were the two great books of the nineteenth century. Spender lacks the narrowness and aridity of Marxist critics.

A writer to-day who wishes to produce the best work that he is capable of producing, must first of all become a socialist in his practical life, must go over to the progressive side of the class conflict. . . . He must be told frankly that joining the workers' movement does mean giving less time to imaginative writing, but that unless he joins it his writing will become increasingly false, worthless as literature. Going over to socialism may prevent him, but failing to go over *must* prevent him from writing a good book (*The Mind in Chains*).

What is meant by "going over"? Upward thinks it must mean the abandonment of the bourgeois life and immersion in the work of the socialist parties. I do not think so. I think a writer "goes over" when he has a moment of conviction that his future is bound up with that of the working classes. Once he has felt this his behaviour will inevitably alter. Often it will be recognised only by external symptoms, a disinclination to wear a hat or a stiff collar, an inability to be rude to waiters or taxi-drivers or to be polite to young men of his own age with rolled umbrellas, bowler hats and "Mayfair men" moustaches or to tolerate the repressive measures of his class. He is like a caterpillar whose skin dulls and whose appetite leaves it before becoming a chrysalis. Often a writer is unable to go over. He approaches the barrier, shies, and runs away. Such writers will externalise their feelings and satirise those who have made the transition, who have jumped off the slowly-moving train for the one which they believe leads towards life and the future. The angriest are the most frightened. But these fears can be surmounted by a moment of vision. It may be practical, a glimpse of the power of the writer in the socialist state or of his impotence in a capitalist one, going in perhaps, like Turgeniev, sixty-first at a fashionable dinner or it may be a mystical feeling of release and emancipation. It is too early yet to say whether writers have done anything for Spain, but it is clear that Spain has done an immense amount for writers, since many have had that experience there and have come back with their fear changed to love, isolation to union and indifference to action.

This is a time then when anyone who is anxious to avert a protracted world war will have to work very hard to undermine the whole system of armed alliances. If we hope to go on existing, if we want a dog's chance of the right to breathe, to go on being able to write, it seems that we have got to make some choice outside the private entanglements of our personal life. We have got to try somehow to understand that objective life moving down on us like a glacier, but which, after all, is essentially not a glacier but an historic process, the life of people like ourselves, and therefore our "proper study".

Ultimately, however interested the writer may be as a person, as an artist he has got to be indifferent to all but what is objectively true. The road the future will tread may be the road of Communism, but the road of the artist will always be some way infinitely more difficult than one which is laid down in front of him.

These two quotations are from Stephen Spender's *Destructive Element*, and express a point of view that is sometimes forgotten.

Political writing is dangerous writing, it deals not in words, but in words that affect lives, and is a weapon that should be entrusted only to those qualified to use it. Thus a burst of felicitous militancy with the pen may send three young men to be killed in Spain; for whose deaths the author is responsible. If human beings have any right they have the right to know what they are dying for. "Better live an hour as a lion than a lifetime as a lamb" is stencilled all over Italy—but supposing one is a lamb?

There is one last warning that must be given. In Blake's words, "The eagle never lost so much time as when it submitted to learn from the crow"—and if we look back at the political activities of artists, however necessary and satisfying they may have seemed at the time, now that time is past it is not by them they are remembered. Milton's poetry is read more than the *Areopagitica*. Marvell's pamphlets are read not at all, the political poems of Shelley and Byron are not preferred to their lyrics, the Houyhnhnms are more familiar to us than the *Conduct of the Allies*. *Robinson Crusoe* means more than the *True Born Englishman*, *The Lotus Eaters* than *Locksley Hall*. The writers who were most political in the last war are not the most famous. Zola too was more political than Flaubert, Lamartine than Baudelaire and the truth is that the value of political experience to a writer's art is indirect. Not Milton's polemical prose is the justification of his political life, but his character of Satan, his great assemblages in Hell. And this is true to-day, so that a writer whose stomach cannot assimilate with genius the starch and acid of contemporary politics, had better turn down his plate.

CHAPTER XIII

THE POPPIES

LET US NOW GLANCE AT THE POPPIES, AT THE DANGER WHICH is becoming known as "escapism". This is not a significant word, for in itself escaping cannot be right or wrong nor worthy of comment until we know from what danger the escapist is fleeing and whether flight is his best method of preservation. Escaping from a concentration camp or a burning building is admirable, escaping from responsibility, like the patient who wrote to his psychiatrist that he was "only happy when he had cast off every shred of human dignity" is sometimes not. We are all destroyed through that first escapist, Eve, and saved by the second who built an ark. The word is generally employed by realists to beat romantics with; thus it was "escapist" to live at Tossa or Torre Molinos till 1936, when the centre of actuality shifted, and Sir Peter Chalmers-Mitchell who had retired to end his days in the sun, found himself, for a few hours in Malaga, in the intenser glare of History.[1]

[1] Expatriation is often beneficial, as a stage in which the writer cuts adrift from irritating influences. It is a mistake to expect good work from expatriates for it is not what they do that matters but what they are not doing. It gives them a breathing-space in which to free themselves from commercialism, family and racial ties or from the "gentleman complex" which attacks public-school and university writers, just as the spectre of their "family business" haunts American ones. Only occasionally does a writer create a work out of his expatriation, Hemingway's *The Sun Also Rises* is such an exception. (Henry James was not an expatriate in so far as he repatriated himself as an Englishman —he exchanged American Society for international society and then settled down as an English man of letters.) It is important however to distinguish

It is vain to accuse people of escaping from contemporary reality. Time is not uniform for all of us, neither is our imagination's food nor our artistic material. We cannot all do our best work with the sun in our eyes. There is but one crime; to escape from our talent, to abort that growth which, ripening and maturing, must be the justification of the demands we make on society.

At present the realities are life and death, peace and war, fascism and democracy; we are in a world which may soon become unfit for human beings to live in. A writer must decide at what remove from this conflagration he can produce his best work and be careful to keep there. Often a writer who is escaping from his own talent, from the hound of heaven, will run into what appears to be reality and, like a fox bolting into a farm kitchen, will seek sanctuary from his pursuers in group activities outside. And after a time the hounds will be called off, the pursuit weaken —a signal that the Muses no longer wish to avail themselves of his potentialities. Thus among the hardest workers in political parties will be found, like Rimbaud at Harar, those whom the God has forsaken.

The old-fashioned boltholes of writers who do not wish to undertake the responsibility of creating a work of art are no longer so easy of access. Drink is available and there are still artists who drink to excess out of the consciousness of wasted ability, for drunkenness is a substitute for art; it is in itself a low form of creation. But it is not drink which is the temptation, since that is but a symptom of the desire for self-forgetfulness as is also the case with drugs which play small part in the literary life in England though among French writers opium has made such headway.

The harmless activities of day-dreaming and conversation are

---

between the flight of the expatriate which is an essential desire for simplification, for the cutting of ties, the writer "finding" himself in the hotel bedroom or the café on the harbour and the brisker trajectory of the travel addict, trying not to find but to lose himself in the intoxication of motion. "How narrow is the line", as Nicolson wrote of Byron's last journey, "which separates an adventure from an ordeal, and escape from exile."

more insidious. Daydreaming bears a specious resemblance to the workings of the creative imagination. It is in fact a substitute for it and one in which all difficulties are shelved, all problems ignored, a short cut ending in a blank wall. This is even more true of conversation; a good talker can talk away the substance of twenty books in as many evenings. He will describe the central idea of the book he means to write until it revolts him.

As journalism brings in quicker returns than literature so the profits of conversation are more immediate than those of journalism. By the silence which he commands, the luxury of his décor, and by the glow from the selected company who have been asked to meet him, a good talker is paid almost before he opens his mouth. The only happy talkers are dandies who extract pleasure from the very perishability of their material and who would not be able to tolerate the isolation of all other forms of composition; for most good talkers, when they have run down, are miserable; they know that they have betrayed themselves, that they have taken material which should have a life of its own, to dispense it in noises upon the air.

Than good conversation nothing is sooner forgotten and those who remember it do so unconsciously and reproduce it as their own. Coleridge, Swinburne, Wilde, Harry Melville, Vernon Lee —not much survives now of the conversation of these mighty-mouthed international geysers. They were at the mercy of a few indolent, forgetful, and envious listeners. If we try to record the spoken word of one of these chrysostoms it becomes apparent that thirty per cent of their talk is a series of reassuring and persuasive qualifications, a buttonholing of the listener; it is the ardour of the talker's wooing which convinces the audience of the splendour of his talk. This is not true of talkers of the old school like Bernard Berenson who use their golden tongues for denunciation, but modern conversationalists make too free a use of the glad eye. They are apologetic, not only because they monopolise and individualise in an age opposed to these things, but because they are taking part in a ceremony of self-wastage and their audience knows it.

Sometimes when in flight from the demands of talent, from the bite of the gadfly, writers will seek refuge in gentility, in ancestor-worship or by becoming members of an unliterary sporting class. They will breed bulldogs, hunt, shoot, attend race-meetings and try to lose contact with all other writers except those whose guilt is of equal standing. This instinct to hide themselves in a world where books are unheard of in no way resembles the artist's desire for "*luxe, calme, et volupté*", for a lavish, ostentatious life but is a particularly English affliction and it is no exaggeration to say that nearly every English author since Byron and Shelley has been hamstrung by respectability and been prevented by snobbery and moral cowardice from attaining his full dimensions. It is this blight of insular gentility which accounts for the difference between Dickens, Thackeray, Arnold, Tennyson, Pater and Tolstoy, Flaubert, Rimbaud, Baudelaire, Gide; it is the distinction between being a good fellow or growing up.

There remains one other major escape, religion. It is not so common now for writers to join a church. I know two Anglo-Catholic and one Roman Catholic convert among my contemporaries. All three are people of exceptional sensibility, poetically-minded writers for whom the ugliness of materialism is a source of horror. Are they escaping from their talent or from conditions which would have rendered impossible the use of it? We must wait and see. Religious faith involves the surrender of the intellect but not of the sensibility, which under its protection may long continue to develop. Yet for an intellectual, joining a church implies regression, it is a putting on of blinkers, a hiding under the skirts of one of the great reactionary political forces of the world and the poet drawn to the confessional by the smell of incense finds himself defending the garotte and Franco's Moors. Art becomes a means not an end to the churchman as to the politician. Churches are the retreat of artists with æsthetic appreciation, delicate humour, ethical sensibility and a sense of spiritual reality, who lack the enquiring mind, the constructive intellectual fearlessness which is the historic factor in western civilisation and which has now moved far onwards from religion.

But in vain we discuss the nature of the poppies which put writers to sleep or try to restrict their use. Since those who are escaping from their talent employ them, let us find out why they are escaping. Many are in flight for psychological reasons which belong to their childhood and with which this book is not competent to deal. But in authors who have dried up, who have put their hobby before their vocation, who now are doing well in the city or who collect first editions or old dust-wrappers, who run chicken-farms or set and solve Greek cross-word puzzles, who write detective stories or who have transferred their sensibility to cheese and old claret, there is one fact in common. They have all been promising.

Promise! Fatal word, half-bribe and half-threat, round whose exact meaning centred many tearful childhood interviews. "But you promised you wouldn't", "but *that* wasn't a promise", "Yes it was—you haven't kept your promise", till the meaning expands and the burden of the oath under which we grew up becomes the burden of expectation which we can never fulfil. "Blossom and blossom and promise of blossom, but never a fruit"—the cry first heard in the nursery is taken up by the schoolmaster, the friendly aunt, the doting grandmother, the inverted bachelor uncle. Dons with long reproachful faces will utter it and the friends of dons; the shapes and simulacrums which our parents have taken, the father-substitutes and mother-types which we have projected will accuse us and all await our ritual suicide. Whom the gods wish to destroy they first call promising.

Young writers if they are to mature require a period of between three and seven years in which to live down their promise. Promise is like the mediæval hangman who after settling the noose, pushed his victim off the platform and jumped on his back, his weight acting as a drop while his jockeying arms prevented the unfortunate from loosening the rope. When he judged him dead he dropped to the ground. Promise is that dark spider with which many writers are now wrestling in obscurity and silence. Occasionally they win and the load of other people's wish-fulfilments is cast off; they produce a book; more often after a struggle for breath they are stifled for ever. Let us listen in to them for a moment, poor wretches, on whom the executioner calls in the small hours.

Two o'clock. You won't accomplish anything now. Do you remember all the things you wanted to be? How Granny loved you! How we pinched and scraped to keep you at Oxford—and then those horrible bills! They killed Granny, you know, though we didn't tell you at the time. Now you're old enough to know. It wasn't that she minded the money—it was the thought you could ever do anything dishonourable. You did promise, you remember? That you could give all those bad cheques! Your father never got over it. Oh, we were all so proud of you. How could you, how could you, how could you!

Three o'clock. "We always hoped you'd write. A serious book, I mean. We can't count the kind of stuff you're doing now. I know a high academic degree is not always the true justification for three years here. There are many people whose careers after leaving college bring us more distinction than anything they achieve while they are up. We take a long view. But I think you'll agree we were very patient with you and I doubt if the stuff you are turning out now will prove we were right. Still we must be tolerant. I had hoped great things for you and I dare say I was rather silly. Anyhow I shall always be glad to hear from you.

Why didn't you write to him? He would so have loved a letter. He often spoke of you before he died. I may say he was deeply hurt at what he considered, rightly or wrongly, your ingratitude. He had been fond of you in spite of everything. If you'd even troubled to send him a postcard! Why didn't you? Why didn't you? Why didn't you?

Four o'clock. Teeth hurt? I don't envy you at forty. Just as you're going to sleep you give a kind of twitch all over and wake up! H'm—a kind of noise like a clock makes before it strikes goes off at the back of your nose? That's bad! Your heart seems to miss a beat and you sit right up in bed with a jerk? Your blood beats too fast? Your mind races along? You can't breathe properly? Your bladder troubles you? A kind of dull aching pain somewhere in the side? You think it must be the spleen? H'm—And a sharp searing pain in the aesophagus? That all? Oh yes—and a feeling like someone blowing up a balloon at the back of the nose? I wonder if you have some near relative or great friend whom I could talk to, just to check up on your family history. Your mother? Good. Well, Mr. Shelleyblake, if you don't mind waiting in here I think I'll try and get right through on the phone to her.

Five o'clock. *How old are you?* H'm, I see. Just about half-way. And you've done precisely what? H'm. Well, I must be off. Another patient. Sleep well, see you to-morrow, same time, same place.

. . . .

Sloth in writers is always a symptom of an acute inner conflict, especially that laziness which renders them incapable of doing the thing which they are most looking forward to. The conflict may or may not end in disaster, but their silence is better than the over-production which must so end and slothful writers such as Johnson, Coleridge, Greville, in spite of the nodding poppies of conversation, morphia and horse-racing, have more to their credit than Macaulay, Trollope or Scott. To accuse writers of being idle is a mark of envy or stupidity—La Fontaine slept continually and scarcely ever opened his mouth; Baudelaire, according to Dr. Laforgue, feared to perfect his work because he feared the incest with his mother which was his perfect fulfilment. Perfectionists are notoriously lazy and all true artistic indolence is deeply neurotic; a pain not a pleasure.

CHAPTER XIV

THE CHARLOCK'S SHADE

≥≤

SEX, THE CHARLOCK'S SHADE, IS NO MORE THE DANGER THAT
it was and seldom do we meet with a syphilitic Baudelaire,
squandering his fortune, and ruining his health for a coloured
mistress; the temptations of artists to-day are group-temptations
in which the Cynaras and the Jeanne Duvals play little part. However for a writer to be too fond of women is not uncommon and
the result may be found that they make crippling demands on his
time and his money, especially if they set their hearts on his
popular success. The charlock or wild mustard throws a more
baleful shade on the young shoot when it is the love that dare
not speak its name.

Many writers have been homosexual or gone through a homosexual period and, although from a literary standpoint it is en-
riching, they must grasp the limitations of homosexuality and plan
production accordingly. Thus a male homosexual if cut off by his
attitude from experience with women, will have a certain difficulty in depicting them. This is not of consequence if he is, for
example, a critic or a poet who works at that intense and sublimated level at which passion is general and the object of such
passion without importance. But many writers are neither poets
nor critics, and for novelists, short-story writers and playwrights,
difficulties arise. Thus homosexual novelists who are able to create
mother-types and social mother-types (hostesses) and occasionally
sister-types (heroines) have trouble with normal women and may
often make them out worse or better than they are. They are forced

to describe things they know little about because so much of life is concerned with them. Courtship, marriage, childbearing and adultery play a major part in existence, a knowledge of the relations between men and women is essential to a novelist, and a comparison of, say, *War and Peace* with novels written by less normal authors will show how few acquire it. The heroine of *War and Peace*, Natasha, is a delightful creature, but she is capable of leaving her hero and running away with a man whom she does not love, after a single meeting, because he looked at her in a certain way. But she remains delightful because Tolstoy continues to find her lovable for being human. If Natasha had been one of Proust's heroines he would have turned her into a monster, she would have been analysed till nothing remained of her but lust and self-interest.

Nor is Proust's system of giving the male characters in his life girls' names and putting them as girls into his novel satisfactory. Their real sex protrudes and they have no plausible relationships with other characters in the books (Albertine is unreal when she confronts Charlus or Swann or the Duchesse de Guermantes; there is an ambiguous cloud over her relations with the author), and they are incapable of childbearing, home-making, husband-cheering or any of the drabber functions of woman. There is no solution for these problems. Nothing, for example, will make the two amorous young girls in *The Importance of Being Earnest* either young or amorous. The homosexual writer, until we can change society, must construct his books so as to avoid situations where a knowledge of such women is required, just as stammerers avoid certain words and substitute others. Otherwise the equipment of the homosexual writer: combativeness, curiosity, egotism, intuition and adaptability, is greatly to be envied.

The clasping tares of domesticity represent the opposite danger, and these too have grown less formidable. The harried author who sits in a garret surrounded by screaming children, with duns at the door and a sick wife nagging from the bed, is a thing of the past. But there remains some substance in the vision. The initial difficulty is in the sensitive writer's inability to live alone. The more he is alone the more he falls in love, if he falls in love he is almost certain to marry, if he marries he is apt to take a house and have children, if he has a house and children he needs more money, must do uncongenial work and so deny himself the freedom which may have inspired him.

The homosexual is unable to treat of a section of the life of human beings but in return he is free from the limitations of that life. He is apt to have a private income, he renews himself by travel, he has time for old friends and for the making of new ones and as he grows old remains isolated, free from responsibilities and ties and if he has been able to break free from the parasitism which is the weakness of homosexuals, he is detached. If he has jointed the creative class, he is likely to become, like Gide, the "lonely old artist-man" that Henry James called himself.

In recent times the balance of literary success late in life is in favour of the childless writer. Children dissipate the longing for immortality which is the compensation of the childless writer's work. But it is not only a question of children or no children, there is a moment when the cult of home and happiness becomes harmful and domestic happiness one of those escapes from talent which we have deplored, for it replaces that necessary unhappiness without which writers perish. A writer is in danger of allowing his talent to dull who lets more than a year go past without finding himself in his rightful place of composition, the small single unluxurious "retreat" of the twentieth century, the hotel bedroom.

The fertility of the writer is often counterchecked by the happiness of the man. Each does not want the same thing and where their desires conflict, the writer-self will be the one to suffer. The "animal serenity", the "broad human touch" which Maugham envies in great writers, in Tolstoy and perhaps, in Thackeray and Dickens, can only be obtained by a series of experiences which have extinguished the lesser artists who have attempted them. As far as one can infer from observation it is a mistake for writers to marry young, especially for them to have children young; early marriage and paternity are a remedy for loneliness and unhappiness that set up a counter irritation. Writers choose wives, not for their money nor for their appreciation of art but for their beauty and a baby is even less capable of seeing the artist's point of view. As Tennyson put it—

> O love, we two shall go no longer
> To lands of summer across the sea;
> So dear a life your arms enfold
> Whose crying is a cry for gold.

Thus there would seem little to choose between the tares and the charlock. The homosexual avoids domesticity, he pays a price but pays it with his eyes open, the normal author walks into a trap. Most young writers are weak and know little about their weaknesses or their predicaments. They make a rush for the solution which promises them an immediate advantage and are not apprehensive of its after-effects. If they find the years when they come to London after the cosiness of the university unendurable then they marry the first person whom they can. They work hard to make money, grow torpid with domesticity and their writing falls off. After seven years or so they often divorce and their talent is given another chance which (it depends on how they marry again), may or may not be taken.

In general it may be assumed that a writer who is not prepared to be lonely in his youth must if he is to succeed face loneliness in his middle age. The hotel bedroom awaits him. If, as Dr. Johnson said, a man who is not married is only half a man, so a man who is very much married is only half a writer. Marriage can succeed for an artist only where there is enough money to save him from taking on uncongenial work and a wife who is intelligent and unselfish enough to understand and respect the working of the unfriendly cycle of the creative imagination. She will know at what point domestic happiness begins to cloy, where love, tidiness, rent, rates, clothes, entertaining and rings at the doorbell should stop and will recognise that there is no more sombre enemy of good art than the pram in the hall.

Some critics encourage a mystical belief in talent. They hold that in the nature of things it must come to fruition, that "if it is in you it's bound to come out", that true genius can neither be depressed by illness or poverty nor destroyed by success or failure. They go so far as to claim that people die at the right time, that Keats and Shelley had nothing more to say, that Marlowe or André Chénier met their violent deaths at the appropriate moment. This fatuous romantic fatalism is based on an optimistic nature and a refusal to face facts. If Milton had been drowned like *Lycidas,* there would have been people to say that he would never have written anything else. But talent is something which grows and which does not ripen except in the right kind of soil and climate. It can be neglected or cultivated and will flower or die down. To suppose that artists will muddle through without encouragement and without money because in the past there have been exceptions is to assume that salmon will find their way to the top of a river to spawn in spite of barrages and pollution. "If it's in you it's bound to come out" is a wish-fulfilment. More often it stays in and goes bad.

Fewer counsels and more money is what every artist must demand from society and it is the idiocy of society in refusing these demands, except to servile and indifferent performers, which is largely responsible for the present line up of artists against that society.[1] Capitalism is expelling the artist as Spain expelled her Jews or France her Huguenots and the effects will soon be apparent; the French nobles who had Voltaire flogged acted with similar foresight.

[1] I should like to see the custom introduced of readers who are pleased with a book sending the author some small cash token: anything between half-a-crown and a hundred pounds. Authors would then receive what their publishers give them as a flat rate and their "tips" from grateful readers in addition, in the same way that waiters receive a wage from their employers and also get what the customer leaves on the plate. Not more than a hundred pounds—that would be bad for my character—not less than half-a-crown—that would do no good to yours.

CHAPTER XV

THE SLIMY MALLOWS

ᴺᴷ

OF ALL THE ENEMIES OF LITERATURE, SUCCESS IS THE MOST insidious. The guides whom we have quoted, whose warnings come through to us from various parts of the field are unanimous against this danger. Pearsall-Smith quotes Trollope. "Success is a poison that should only be taken late in life and then only in small doses." Maugham writes,

> The common idea that success spoils people by making them vain, egotistic, and self-complacent is erroneous; on the contrary it makes them, for the most part, humble, tolerant, and kind. Failure makes people bitter and cruel. Success improves the character of a man, it does not always improve the character of an author.

Success for a writer is of three kinds, social, professional or popular. All three bring money but in none of them is money all important. Success is bad for a writer because it cuts him off from his roots, raises his standard of living and so leads to over-production, lowers his standard of criticism and encourages the germ of its opposite, failure.

Social success was the variety which most appealed to writers up to the Slump, for social success, besides gratifying the snobbery which is inherent in romantic natures, also provided them with delightful conditions, with the freedom and protection of large country houses.

There are writers for whom such success is beneficial, who find

there the material they need and the leisure to absorb it; their
public is also found among the world of fashion. Thus if Proust
had been a social failure, if Pope had never been asked to a ball
nor Henry James presented to a duchess, *The Rape of the Lock,
The Côté de Guermantes, The Ambassadors,* could never have
been written. It is clear that a social success benefits some writers
and is bad for others; it is because we envy it more than other
success that we denounce it so often. Writers are helped by it if
they are dandies or lyricists; if they have suffered from poverty to
the extent of being warped or weakened rather than braced or
steadied by it; if they are homosexuals who need a frame to expand on, a beanstalk to climb up or the kind of backing which
will impress and so free them from the domination of middle-
class parents; it is good for satirists and playwrights, priests and
poets. Congreve, Gay, Wilde were all the better for "being taken
up" for they were whisked away to the field best suited for the
flowering of their gifts, nor would Donne and Jeremy Taylor
have written great prose had they delivered their wonderful sermons to a slum parish. It must be remembered that in fashionable
society can be found warmhearted people of delicate sensibility
who form permanent friendships with artists which afford them
ease and encouragement for the rest of their lives and provide them
with sanctuary. Lady Suffolk's friendship with Pope, Lord Sheffield's
with Gibbon, Horace Walpole's for Gray, Lady Gregory's for
Yeats, Lady Cunard's for George Moore, acted as conservatories
where the artist's talents ripened at a suitable temperature, neither
forced too quickly, nor exposed to the rigours of the Grub Street
winter. That Milton or Blake or Keats or Hopkins did not require
such friendships does not discredit those who do.

> Blest be the great for those they take away
> And those they leave me. . . .

But apart from these especial intimacies or from such a comfortable greenhouse as Holland House, there is little to be derived
from an indiscriminating indulgence in fashionable society. That

society is hard-hearted, easily bored and will exact from a writer either a succession of masterpieces or a slavish industry in providing amusement at its own level, while he, in his turn acquires an appetite for external values, which, besides being hard to gratify, creates professional hostility and excludes him from a larger world in which he might be happily employed. The people for whom social success is most dangerous are the realists who have no place among such unreality, the militants whose weapons rust in that atmosphere or writers like Bennett who have already found their material, and can only deteriorate when transplanted.[1] The best that can happen for a writer is to be taken up very late or very early, when either old enough to take its measure, or so young that when dropped by society he has all life before him. Married writers in particular are tormented by the contrast between the world where they dine and the world in which they wake up for breakfast, nor are the relations between writers' wives and worldly hostesses renowned for cordiality.

Unfortunately the danger is past. Fashionable society is no longer a temptation as when it maintained a cultural standard. The singing birds nest no more in the great country houses; our Henry James and Robert Brownings of to-day are not met roaring for lunch in Belgrave Square. "Cliveden's proud alcove" has no Pope to sing in it. Maugham has shown that it is possible to possess and not be possessed by society; Forster that it is quite easy to do without it altogether, while Moore has summed it up: "Well-mannered people do not think sincerely, their minds are full of evasions and subterfuges . . . To be aristocratic in Art one must avoid polite society." A young writer must be careful not to pay the world more attention than it gives him, he may satirise it but

---

[1] Thus a writer not intended for social success was Swift, and it is interesting to notice what snobbish intoxication, what unpleasant vanity creep into the *Journal to Stella* at the height of his "swingboat" or fashionable period. Johnson's comment on Addison's marriage to Lady Warwick may also be considered: "The marriage if uncontradicted report can be credited, made no addition to his happiness, it neither found them nor made them equal. . . . It is certain that Addison has left behind him no encouragement of ambitious love."

is not advised to celebrate it, nor become its champion, for the moribund will turn on their defenders.[1]

Professional success, the regard of fellow-artists and would-be artists is a true delight, for it is absurd to assume that good writers cannot be famous in their lifetime. There have always been a few thousand judges of good literature, and these judges have recognised talent however unusual and uncontemporary, even as they have accorded to masterpieces of the past an appreciation independent of fashion. Thus nobody could be more forgotten than the poet Campbell yet the other day John Betjeman pointed out three lines from the Battle of the Baltic which he admired.

> . . . When each gun
> From its adamantine lips
> Spread a death-shade round the ships
> Like a hurricane eclipse
> Of the sun.

Yet Tennyson, according to Palgrave, singled out the "death shade" for praise when he was compiling the *Golden Treasury,* even as he admired Marvell's *To His Coy Mistress* or Cowper's *Poplars,* poems outside the general range of Victorian sensibility. These celebrators of the unfashionable best are the custodians of taste, the bodyguard of talent, like Maurice Baring who has kept alive, in *Have You Anything to Declare,* French poetry that would be lost to English readers were it not for his impartial ear. In similar fashion Strachey wrote about Racine, Pearsall-Smith about Sainte-Beuve and Madame de Sévigné, writers who tend to be ignored owing to the cult of more violent sensations, while Diderot, St. Evremond, Shenstone and Cowper have all of late received sensitive homage.

If a professional success is painful in that it arouses the envy of the ex-artists, a popular success is fatal. Much has been written on the subject; I will try to summarise.

---

[1] When suffering from social envy of other writers there is only one cure— to work. Whatever consideration they are enjoying may then come your way and in any case by working you are doing what they would most envy you.

Success is a kind of moving staircase, from which an artist, once on, has great difficulty in getting off, for whether he goes on writing well or not, he is carried upwards, encouraged by publicity, by fan-mail, by the tributes of critics and publishers and by the friendly clubmanship of his new companions. The fan-mail gives the writer a sense of a mission. "Well, if I have made them forget their troubles for a moment, my stuff may be some good." Publicity also seems innocuous since once a writer is "news" he continues to be so independently of his own wishes besides it helps to sell his books. As for the critics' habit of praising a first book and damning a second that can be put down to a personal grievance. "I regard every attack", a writer once told me, "as worth about sixpence a word."

A popular success may depend on the entertainment value of a writer or his political quality or his human touch. Those with the human touch never recover; their sense of mission grows overwhelming. Neither harsh reviews, the contempt of equals nor the indifference of superiors can affect those who have once tapped the great heart of suffering humanity and found out what a goldmine it is. Writers who have a political success may keep their heads, for they may soon experience a political disappointment.

I myself had that experience. I went three times to Spain. The first time I returned with enthusiasm and wrote an enthusiastic and popular article. The second time I came back less hopeful but still militant and fire-eating and my articles were still successful. The third time I returned with a hopeless premonition of defeat; all I was certain of was the weakness of the Aragon front, the dissension (which broke out in the May fighting) among the Catalans and the enormous difficulties which faced the Government in procuring food and materials for war. Knowing Spanish (unlike the other fire-eaters) I had the misfortune to receive many confidences from people who already showed a personal weariness of the war. I came back with a septic throat, and the feeling that we experience when we see a tired fox crossing a field with the hounds and the port-faced huntsmen pounding after it. I could either conceal this feeling and try to write another fire-eater, or say nothing at all, or tell the truth. I thought the readers of my paper had the right to know the truth as I saw it and so I wrote a depressing article, recording the points of view of different people I had met and adding my own reflections. It was the time when Malaga and Bilbao fell and the article made me immensely unpopular. I had been unpopular before for saying *Journey's End* was a bad play and for criticising the deification of Housman, but literary unpopularity was very different from the political kind, from being called a coward, a Fascist, a stabber-in-the-back, etc. and grateful to my escapism, I fled abroad. It is a mistake to exceed the artist's rôle and become political investigator.

The entertainer, on the other hand, suffers from no criticism whatever. No one has told P. G. Wodehouse which is his best book or his worst, what are his faults or how he should improve them. The fate of the entertainer is simply to go on till he wakes up one morning to find himself obscure.

For every admirer whom a writer gains by any means except the legitimate quality of his art he will gain an enemy. He will be an unconscious enemy, one who feels uneasiness at seeing the writer's name in the publisher's advertisements, who turns the other way from his picture in the Tube, one of those who voted against Aristides because he was tired of hearing him called "the just".

Every admirer is a potential enemy. No one can make us hate ourselves like an admirer—"de lire la secrète horreur du dévouement dans des yeux"—nor is the admiration ever pure. It may be *us* they wish to meet but it's themselves they want to talk about.

Popular success is a palace built for a writer by publishers, journalists, admirers, and professional reputation makers, in which a silent army of termites, rats, dry rot and death-watch beetles are tunnelling away, till, at the very moment of completion, it is ready to fall down. The one hope for a writer is that although his enemies are often unseen they are seldom unheard. He must listen for the death-watch, listen for the faint toc-toc, the critic's truth sharpened by envy, the embarrassed praise of a sincere friend, the silence of gifted contemporaries, the implications of the don in the manger, the visitor in the small hours. He must dismiss the builders and contractors, elude the fans with an assumed name and dark glasses, force his way off the moving staircase, subject every thing he writes to a supreme critical court. Would it amuse Horace or Milton or Swift or Leopardi? Could it be read to Flaubert? Would it be chosen by the Infallible Worm, by the discriminating palates of the dead?

To refuse all publicity which does not arise from the quality of his work, to beware of giving his name to causes, to ration his public appearances, to consider his standards and the curve of development which he feels latent within him, yet not to indulge in gestures which are hostile to success when it comes, must be the aim of a writer.

Failure is a poison like success. Where a choice is offered, prefer the alkaline.

There is a kind of behaviour which is particularly dangerous on the moving staircase—the attempt to ascend it in groups of four or five who lend a hand to each other and dislodge other climbers from the steps. It is natural that writers should make friends with their contemporaries of talent and express a mutual admiration but it leads inevitably to a succession of services rendered and however much the writers who help each other may deserve it, if they too frequently proclaim their gratitude they will arouse the envy of those who stand on their own feet, who succeed without collaboration. Words like "log-rolling" and "back-scratching" are soon whispered and the death-watch ticks the louder. Such writers must remember that they write for the reader—the most unloved person in the world. No jokes must be made which can't be explained to him, no relationships mentioned in which he is not asked to share. His capacity for being hurt, for feeling slighted and excluded, for imagining that he is being patronised, is infinite. And his capacity for revenge.

Success is most poisonous in America. According to Van Wyck

Brooks, "The blighted career, the arrested career, the diverted career are, with us, the rule. The chronic state of our literature is that of a youthful promise which is never redeemed." He calls American literature "one long list of spiritual casualties". Hemingway gives an account of the diseases of American authors which is worth comparing with our own analysis of spiritual tares.

We do not have great writers. Something happens to our good writers at a certain age.

You see we make our writers into something very strange, we destroy them in many ways. First economically. They make money. It is only by hazard that a writer makes money, although good books always make money eventually. Then our writers when they have made some money increase their standard of living and they are caught. They have to write to keep up their establishments, their wives, and so on, and they write slop. It is slop not on purpose but because it is hurried. Because they write when there is nothing to say or when there is no water in the well. Because they are ambitious. Then once they have betrayed themselves, they justify it and you get worse slop. Or else they read the critics. If they believe the critics when they say they are great then they must believe them when they say they are rotten and they lose confidence. At present we have two good writers who cannot write because they have lost confidence, through reading critics. If they wrote, sometimes it would be good and sometimes not so good and sometimes it would be quite bad, but the good would get out. But they have read the critics, and they must write masterpieces. The masterpieces the critics said they wrote. They weren't masterpieces of course. They were just quite good books. So now they cannot write at all. The critics have made them impotent.[1]

It is not authors only who are killed by criticism but critics as well; they seem, like scorpions, able to destroy themselves with their own venom. But Hemingway's point is well-made. The praise from a critic is inflated by hope as often as his censure is distorted by envy since his longing for perfection or his desire to be a John the Baptist may drive him prematurely to recognise a Messiah

[1] Scott Fitzgerald? Thornton Wilder? Glenway Westcott? John O'Hara?

and his disappointment thereby become correspondingly aggravated. Also, as Desmond MacCarthy has remarked, there comes a moment when every clever young man prefers to display his cleverness by exposing a writer's faults rather than proclaiming his virtues. That moment is most apt to occur in the early thirties which is a bad time all round both for creators and critics or it may occur when the critic is in his early thirties and the writer in his early forties. Butler said an author should write only for people between twenty and thirty as nobody read or changed their opinions after that. Those are the years when the artists are promising and the admirers full of admiration; by the time the artist has ceased to be promising and become a good writer, the admirer is a critic whose judgments are flavoured by his own self-hatred or who, taking the author as a symbol of his own youth, refers all his later books back to his earliest. When an admirer says, "Ah, yes! But if only he would write another *Prufrock*!" he means, "If only I was as young as when I first read *Prufrock*." The sour smell of the early thirties hangs over most literary controversy.

The shock, for an intelligent writer, of discovering for the first time that there are people younger than himself who think him stupid is severe. Especially if he is at an age (thirty-five to forty-two) when his self-confidence is easily shaken. The seventh lustre is such a period, a menopause for artists, a serious change of life. It is the transition from being a young writer, from being potentially Byron, Shelley, Keats, to becoming a stayer, a Wordsworth, a Coleridge, a Landor. It would seem that genius is of two kinds, one of which blazes up in youth and dies down, while the other matures, like Milton's or Goethe's, through long choosing, putting out new branches every seven years. The artist has to decide on the nature of his own or he may find himself exhausted by the sprint of youth and unfitted for the marathon of middle age. A great many writers die between those years; some like Hart Crane, Harry Crosby, Philip Heseltine commit suicide; others succumb to pneumonia and drink or have nervous breakdowns. Others become specialists in the arts or in hobbies verging on the arts. Writers turn painters or painters writers or renew themselves through someone from whom they can obtain self-confidence and encouragement and a vicarious youth. Eventually, though critics are unfriendly, creation difficult and the future monotonous or uncertain, a new position is established and the young writer of promise becomes a master in his prime, one who can pass into old age as a sage, a prophet or a venerated, carefree and disreputable figure.

But English criticism, unless it proceeds from the indiscriminate malice of rotting ambition, is unfair only in that it is overkind— for a critic is subject to temptations of his own. Through praising their books, he gets to know more and more authors personally and once he has met them finds it embarrassing to alter his opinion. Critics in England do not accept bribes but one day they discover that in a sense their whole life is an accepted bribe, a fabric of compromises based on personal relationships and then it is in vain to remember that, like James's old man of letters, "our doubt is our passion, and our passion is our task".

CHAPTER XVI

OUTLOOK UNSETTLED

⚘⚘

SUCH ARE THE DANGERS AND PRESENT TEMPTATIONS OF WRIT-
ers. What consolations can be offered them? What positive advice
will procure for a new book a decade of life and assure its author
a patent from oblivion for another ten years? We have seen that
realism, simplicity, the familiar attitude to the reader are likely to
grow stale, that imagination, formality, subtlety, controlled by an
awareness of the times we live in, are due to return. We can also
learn something of the forms which have vitality and are assured
of a future. Many writers who have no feeling for the live or the
dead form still attempt those which are doomed to failure. The
record of literature is that of great writers who perfect a form,
imitators who bring into disrepute that perfection, and a new artist
arising to perfect another.

Thus *Paradise Lost* dislocated the English language for a hundred years for it became impossible to write blank verse which was
not an imitation of Milton. Ultimately Cowper broke away and
after him Wordsworth and Tennyson. Since then poets have been
trying to escape from Tennyson by returning to the blank verse of
the Elizabethans. Coming after Milton, Pope was the first poet to
elude blank verse and bring to perfection a new form, the couplet,
and this couplet in its turn paralysed the poets of the eighteenth
century till it was adapted by Crabbe and Byron. Blake and Collins
meanwhile had broken free from the couplet and made possible
the rebellion of the romantics who can be said to have held their
own until *The Waste Land*.

A writer has to construct his shell, like the caddis worm, from the débris of the past, and, once there, despite the jostling of contemporaries, is safe till a younger generation dispossesses him or until the vicissitudes of taste crumble it about him. He may attempt a new form or he may revive an old one. But the revival, if it is to succeed, must not be too premature.

Which forms are available at the moment? The novel, the play, the poem, the article, the short story, the biography and the auto-biography seem the most fertile.

From the novel, dominant literary form of the last hundred years has emerged a succession of masterpieces. But there have been a number of bad novels and from them certain facts can be deduced. Firstly, that bad novels do not last; there is no point, therefore, in writing one unless it comes up to championship standard. And the novel is not a suitable form for young writers. The best novels (of Stendhal, Flaubert, Proust, James, etc.) are written from early middle age onwards. It is unsuitable because the construction of a long book is exacting for the young, whose novels generally begin well and go off and who lack staying power and because to write a novel an author must have experience of people as they are, and have resolved the contradictions in his own nature; he must be integrated, a machine for observation.

Young writers force upon real people the standards, motives and behaviour which appeal to them in books; they are split-men, at war with themselves, and uncertain of their philosophy. I know of admirable young novelists but their development was difficult, for they began as lyricists or satirists; even *Wuthering Heights* is not so much a novel as a lyric flight of sublimated eroticism. The satire of Evelyn Waugh in his early books was derived from his ignorance of life. He found cruel things funny because he did not understand them and he was able to communicate that fun. But the predicament of the humorist is that his sensibility, if it should go on developing, causes him to find things less and less amusing, "for all our wit and reading do but bring us to a truer sense of sorrow". The English humorist must therefore either cease to be funny and thereby lose his entertainment status or abandon his integrity and, æsthetically stunted, continue to give his public what it wants. For this reason humorists are not happy men. Like Beach-comber or Saki or Thurber they burn while Rome fiddles, or, like P. G. Wodehouse, repeat themselves with profitable resignation.

The short story and the long short story are more fruitful. The short story avoids routine, it is the most fluid and experimental of forms, as Elizabeth Bowen says,

> Peaks of common experience soar past an altitude line into poetry. There is also a level immediately below this, on which life is being more and more constantly lived, at which emotion crystallises, from which a fairly wide view is at command. This level the short story is likely to make its own.

The long short story is one of the most rewarding and yet neglected forms in literature whose abandonment is solely due to the animosity of publishers. While short stories can be published in magazines and then in book form and so be paid for twice, long short stories of from twenty to fifty thousand words can be published nowhere. Yet *The Aspern Papers, Sylvie, Candide, The Alien Corn, A Lost Lady,* and *Death in Venice* show to what perfection it can be brought, and *Sylvie* and *Daisy Miller* prove it an ideal medium for youthful creation.

The play is another form whose revival seems possible, the length is right for young authors, the technical difficulties can be solved by good advice. There are in particular two forms of drama which can be reclaimed by art: the English comedy and the revue. The prose comedy of manners is one of the finest creations of English literature, the perfection of our native dandyism. In Congreve the English language reaches the farthest point to which it can be pushed in the direction of stylised, colloquial, contemporary elegance. It is the polished, racy talk of men in periwigs, with muffs and long waistcoats. From that moment people were to shorten their wigs and subdue their clothing, to begin the retreat to bald heads, sock-suspenders and undistinguished diction. The tragedy of Congreve was that although a young man, his mission was to bring an old form to perfection and then see it into its grave.

We know very little about Congreve. His predicament was that he belonged to the past, the form he perfected, the comedy of manners belonged in spirit to the reign of Charles II, and was haunted by that prince of dandies Wilmot, Earl of Rochester. Rochester had already been taken by Etherege as the hero of his charming *Man of Mode* and it was his habit of joking confidentially, almost wistfully with his servant which, satirised here, established the favourite relationship of hard-up young master and wily, doting valet which has been a feature of the English comedy down to *Jeeves*. But what appealed to contemporary writers in Rochester was his mixture of gaiety and dignity, of the personal integrity of a man true to his own thought and feeling with the disregard of all law and convention of the nobleman and the rake. Such a hero is profoundly antipathetic to a bourgeois society, in which he is a kind of enviable outlaw; he can only exist round a court. His tradition retarded Congreve as much as that of Oscar Wilde and the nineties retarded many young writers of the 1920's. How typical of the most classical dandyism for instance, was his reserve. "He is comparatively reserved; but you find something in that restraint which is more agreeable than the utmost exertion of talent in others"—(Waller). Congreve must have felt an obsession for a man of an earlier generation so like what he himself would have wished to be, just as even Pope felt a certain nostalgia for the small-scale 'little England' quality of Charles II's court. The diction of his heroes closely resembles that which Etherege attributed to Rochester, one of Rochester's most favoured mistresses was a prominent member of Congreve's cast and Gosse mentions that Congreve bought a portrait of him. The Restoration comedy, after all, belonged to the Restoration yet by a paradox it attained perfection in the 1690's. *The Way of the World* appeared in 1700 and was a failure. There is a rumour that Congreve went on the stage in a fury and told the audience he would never write anything for them again. Certainly he must have been conscious that he had put the best of his genius into it. What he could not have been conscious of in his disappointment was that the audience of 1700 had changed; the merchants of the reign of Anne, the Whigs, the new middle-class would not stand for situations in which extravagant sons ruined selfish and bestial old fathers, duped their hum-drum creditors, seduced the wives of aldermen, made fun of country squires, got up in the afternoon and went out to see who they could pick up in the park after supper. London was becoming less and less like the Rome of Terence. It was a serious city. In the same year Addison's pompous *Cato* had a stupendous success.

There is room now for a revival of comedy. We have no dandyism of the Left. A play which is politically and socially true of its time and which yet achieves the elegance of *Love for Love* or the beginning of the *Importance of Being Earnest* would be secure of a future. Another likely form is the intelligent revue because short satirical sketches are easily written by young writers and because a revue which flattered the intelligence of the audience would present an element of surprise. Most creative writing to-day is Left in sentiment. It would gain by conquering those fields of comedy which are still feebly defended by Toryism in retreat, by dukes and butlers and people who think the word Epstein a joke in itself, by men of pleasure turned sour and baby blimps just cutting their water-wings.

The long article has a future, especially in the form of the critical essay, the analysis of times and tendencies, and the skilled "reportage". But articles which cannot be reprinted are not worth writing.

Poetry is highly explosive, but no poet since Eliot can but perceive the extreme difficulty of writing good poetry. The moment a poet forgets this, he will be superseded by a writer of prose. We have one poet of genius in Auden, who is able to write prolifically, carelessly, and exquisitely nor does he seem to have to pay any price for his inspiration. It is as if he worked under the influence of some mysterious drug which presents him with a private vision, a mastery of form and of vocabulary.

But poets have to keep in training. Poetry, to stand out, must be a double distillation of life that goes deeper than prose. It must be brandy as compared to wine, otherwise consumers will get their poetry from short stories and novels. This distillation of experience can be achieved only by a writer who maintains his sensibility and integrity at a high pitch and concentrates on the quality of his production. He must examine the meaning, weight, force, pace and implication of a word, he must calculate the impact of each line on the reader, know what concessions can be made to sound or sense, and deliver the finished poem only after a drastic trial. Otherwise prose will catch up on him. As things stand, inspiration is not enough, dreams have had their day, lucky shots miss the target. A poet, with the exception of mysterious water-fluent tea-drinking Auden, must be a highly-conscious technical expert. Poetry is an instrument of precision. That is why societies in return must respect him as they respect scientists or all who have made greater sacrifices in their interest than they themselves care to. The poet is susceptible to the temptations which we have described by reason of his sensibility and we must not bully him.

> "Popular, popular, unpopular,
> You're no poet," the critic cried.
> "Why?" said the poet. "You're unpopular!"
> Then they cried at the turn of the tide,
> "You're no poet!" "Why?" "You're popular!"
> Pop-gun: popular and unpopular.[1]

A lyric poet has the advantage over a prose-writer that he is entrusted with the experience of the ages; he is not a political conscript nor can he be accused of escapism if he confines himself to celebrating the changing seasons, memories of childhood, love or beauty. The tyranny of form to which he is subject is compensated by his free access to material. Literary history goes to prove that lyrical poetry is the medium which more than any other defies time. Didactic poetry becomes unreadable; epics are pillaged for

[1] Not Lawrence: Tennyson.

a few similes; plays quarried for the songs in them; novels and essays crumble or ossify; but ten minutes' extra thought on the choice of a word or the position of a stress may make in the lyric a difference of a thousand years. There is no age or period at which great lyric poetry cannot be written. It is possible to argue that Homer and Virgil to-day would have written in prose, that Shakespeare would have written novels—but Sappho, even after the international situation had been explained to her, would have remained true to verse.

One of the colophons of literature, one of those great writers who put full stop to a form of art, was Marcel Proust. The form whose consummation he brought about was the autobiographical novel. *The Way of All Flesh, Of Human Bondage, A Portrait of the Artist* preceded it; after 1922 they could not have been written, and such autobiographical novels as appear now are not by great writers. They are the green shoots which continue to put forth from a tree that has been cut down.

The result of the flight of all but the most obstinate from this dying form has been a return of emphasis to the autobiography which has an advantage over the novel in that it demands no fictional gifts from the writer and a disadvantage in that it permits no alibis; the characters are not imaginary and the hero is the one character with whom the author dare find fault. An interesting contribution was Harold Nicolson's *Some People*, which, disguised as short stories, is an autobiography where each episode represents a hurdle taken by the author on his way to maturity. Cowley's *Exile's Return* is another example of the planned autobiography (the one kind now worth writing), and in England I find it a temptation not to mention Orwell and Isherwood again. Closely related to reportage-autobiography is ideology-autobiography, in which an author looks back on himself in relation to the ideas of his time, a classic example of which is *The Education of Henry Adams*. There is room for many planned books of this sort by writers who can analyse themselves in relation to their environment and avoid padding, but all journalism must be kept out—

so must the ideology, for the faults of these books are already apparent.[1]

To write well and to go on writing well depends on our sense of reality. There is such a thing as literary health and so far we have considered only literary diseases. If a writer is not writing as well as he would like to or as often as he would wish, he should give himself an examination. Is he satisfied with his reality? Is he *"dans le vrai"*? If not, when and how has he departed from it? Reality is a shifting thing. I take it to mean the nature of things as they are and as they will be. It is life, and the future, however unpleasant and not death and the past, however desirable. What people want to happen is real if it can be willed to happen, and there are realities of the imagination—such as the belief in a future life or in a perfectible human society which transcend at times the physical realities of death and annihilation. But for a professional writer it involves the realities of his time, the ideas and the actions which are changing the world and shaping history. The most real thing for a writer is the life of the spirit, the growth or curve of vision within him of which he is the custodian, select- ing the experiences propitious to its development, protecting it from those unfavourable. When he fails to do this something seems to rot; he becomes angry, frightened, and unhappy, suffer- ing from what Swift called "that desiderium which of all things makes life most uneasy".

The spiritual reality of the artist may come into conflict with the historical reality of his time and true to his own reality, he may

[1] "A man scurried through the Chancellery. He moved too fast for me to get a glimpse of him—but I just discerned an ulster and a soft felt hat. 'That fel- low's scared' I muttered. 'You bet he is' said Jeff Post. 'It's Schuschnigg (Schacht—Stresemann)'. It was the only time I saw him till I followed his coffin down the Siegenallee". Or (ideological): "All that year Lenin was drinking café crèmes in Geneva. Trotsky was growing a beard, Kautsky was writing 'one step forward, two steps backward'; the Tennessee soapboilers' strike was repressed after twenty-nine days. Jauré's was fighting a municipal election but, obsessed with sex and education, my development was still experiencing a bourgeois time-lag of some two thousand years. I might have been talking with survivors of the 1905 revolution. I preferred to study Plato, Picasso and Proust".

even have to sacrifice himself by his opposition to the external world and so find that not life but premature death is required of him. There is no mysticism in this. We create the world in which we live; if that world becomes unfit for human life, it is because we tire of our responsibility. Genius is important in creating that world and therefore will be among the first things to suffer. There are destructive elements—war, plague, earthquake, cancer and the dictator's firing squad are among them—which take no account of the unfinished masterpiece or the child in the womb. They are real and their reality must never be under-estimated but there remains a reality of will and spirit by which within the unchanging limitations of time and death they can be controlled.[1]

Having satisfied himself of how he stands in relation to his time and whether his talent is receiving proper nourishment, an ailing writer will enquire about those other sources of creative happiness: health, sex, and money.

The health of a writer should not be too good, and perfect only in those periods of convalescence when he is not writing. Rude health, as the name implies, is averse to culture and demands either physical relief or direct action for its bursting energy. Action to the healthy man seems so desirable that literary creation is felt to be shaming and is postponed till action has engendered fatigue which is then transmitted to the reader. Also, in "this England where nobody is well", the healthy writer is communicating with a hostile audience. Most readers live in London; they are run-down, querulous, constipated, soot-ridden, stained with asphalt and nicotine and as a result of sitting all day on a chair in a box and eating too fast, slightly mad sufferers from indigestion. Except

[1] The Spanish poet Lorca was shot because he fell into the power of an element which detested spiritual reality. Yet Lorca fell into those hands because he lived in Granada. Had he lived in Barcelona or Madrid he would be alive to-day like Sender or Alberti. But he lived in reactionary Granada, a city of the past, of gipsies and bullfighters and priests, and he made his best poems about bullfighters and gipsies. That element in him which sought the past, which drew him to the mediævalism of Andalusia, contained the seed of his own death, placing him, who was no friend to priests or feudal chiefs, in a city where the past would one day come to life, and prove deadly.

on holiday an author should not be fitter than his public or too
well for reading and meditation. The relationship of an author
with his reader is the barometer of his æsthetic health. If he flatters or patronises, is hostile or pleading, then something is amiss
with him.

A preoccupation with sex is a substitute for artistic creation; a
writer works best at an interval from an unhappy love-affair, or
after his happiness has been secured by one more fortunate. So far
as we can generalise it would seem that the welling up of the
desire for artistic creation precedes a love-affair. Women are not
an inspiration of the artist but a consequence of that inspiration.
An artist, when his talent is uncoiling, has the desirability of any
object fulfilling its function but he also enjoys a certain clearhead-
edness. His habits become moderate, he drinks less because drink
has no longer a psychological appeal. He does not lack confidence,
he lives contentedly within his income and he sees love and friendship as delightful things but without their glamour. It is after
creation, in the elation of success, or the gloom of failure that love
becomes essential.

Solvency is an essential. A writer suffering from financial difficulties is good only for short-term work, and will leave all else
unfinished. And if he has too much money, unless he has had it
all his life, he will spend it, which is also a substitute for creation.
Every writer should, before embarking, find some way however
dishonest of procuring with the minimum of effort, about four
hundred a year. Otherwise he must become a popular success or
be miserable. Success he will take in his stride for fewer writers
are marred by it than are discouraged by failure. It is wholesome
magic.

> Gently dip, but not too deep
> For fear you make the golden beard to weep.

Failure on the other hand is infectious. The world is full of charming failures (for all charming people have something to conceal,
usually their total dependence on the appreciation of others) and

unless a writer is quite ruthless with these amiable footlers, they will drag him down with them. More dangerous are those who are not charming—the trapped foxes who bite the hand that would set them free and worst of all the Kibitzers, the embittered circle of scoffing onlookers—

> The common rout
> That, wandering loose about,
> Grow up and perish as the summer fly
> Heads without name, no more remembered.

It is by a blend of lively curiosity and intelligent selfishness that the artists who wish to mature late, who feel too old to die, the Goethes, Tolstoys, Voltaires, Titians and Verdis, reach a fruitful senescence. They cannot afford to associate with those who are burning themselves up or preparing for a tragedy or whom melancholy has marked for her own. Not for them the accident-prone, the friends in whom the desire for self-destruction keeps blistering out in broken legs or threatening them in anxiety-neuroses. Not for them the drumming finger, the close-cropt nail, the chewed glasses, the pause on the threshold, the wandering eye or the repeated "um" and "er".

We create the world in which we live and the artist plays a dominant rôle in that creation. By extension he can live in any world which he has created. At present, some artists are creating a militant others a pacifist world, and it is not artists only who are creating worlds, but capitalists and dictators. There is doubt about which world is best as there is doubt about which world will triumph. If a fascist world wins we may expect a black-out of art as under Attila. A communist world may make experiments in intolerance and then grow tired of them. Or nothing may happen during our lifetimes and a few drops of patronage still be wrung from a barren capitalism. Honours will be conferred on the adroit, smart luncheon parties given, medals awarded. Or a world revolution may establish conditions in which artists will through their own merit reach the public from whom they have been isolated.

Within his talent it is the duty of a writer to devote his energy to the search for truth, the truth that is always being clouded over by romantic words and ideas or obscured by actions and motives dictated by interest and fear. In the love of truth which leads to a knowledge of it lies not only the hope of humanity but its safety. Deep down we feel that, as every human being has a right to air and water, so has he a right to food, clothing, light, heat, work, education, love and leisure. Ultimately we know the world will be run, its resources exploited and its efforts synchronised on this assumption. A writer can help to liberate that knowledge and to unmask those pretenders which accompany all human plans for improvement: the love of power and money, the short-sighted acquisitive passions, the legacies of injustice and ignorance, the tiger instinct for fighting, the ape-like desire to go with the crowd. A writer must be a lie-detector who exposes the fallacies in words and ideals before half the world is killed for them. It may even be necessary for the poet to erect a bomb-proof ivory tower from which he can continue to celebrate the beauty which the rest of mankind will be too guilty, hungry, angry or arid to remember. There is room in the arts besides the militant novelists and journalists for the "necessary lovers", but the success worshippers, those for whom life is a Perpetual Party, a buffet where one swigs, if fortunate in the draw, for eighty years and then grudgingly makes room, are as out of favour as those who justify abuses as our christian burden "in this Vale of Tears". The artist of to-day must bear a wound—"cette blessure", according to Gide, "qu'il ne faut pas laisser se cicâtriser, mais qui doit demeurer toujours douleureuse et saignante, cette blessure au contact de l'affreux réalité." [1]

---

[1] "That wound which we must never allow to heal but which must always remain painful and bleeding, the gash made by contact with hideous reality."

PART THREE

A GEORGIAN BOYHOOD

Yet hark how through the peopled air
　　The busy murmur glows,
The insect youth are on the wing
Eager to taste the honied spring
　　And float amid the liquid noon.
Some lightly o'er the current swim
Some shew their gayly gilded trim
　　Quick-glancing to the sun.

GRAY.

"What sort of a thing is Tydeus?"
"Tydeus rose and set at Eton: he is only
Known here to be a scholar of Kings."
[West to Walpole: Walpole to West,
October, 1735.]

Altro dirti non vo'; ma la tua festa
Ch'anco tardi a venir non ti sia grave.

LEOPARDI.

CHAPTER XVII

CREDENTIALS

❧❧

UP TO THIS POINT THE FUNCTION OF THIS WORK HAS BEEN
entirely critical and performed with those privileges of the critic
which allow him to assume equality with those whom he criticises
and to take their books to pieces as if he were their equal in stature.
But this equality is a fiction, just as it is a fiction that a juryman
is superior to the temptations and stupidities of the prisoner he
judges or qualified to convict a company director on a point of
corporation law. A critic is a product of his time who may affect
impartiality but who while claiming authority over the reader projects his doubt and aspiration. Every critic writes as if he were
infallible, and pretends that he is the embodiment of impartial
intellectual sanity, a reasonable though omniscient pontiff. But
without his surplice the preacher of the loftiest sermon is only
human or subhuman, and now is the moment to step down from
the pulpit, to disrobe in the vestry. The autobiography which follows is intended to be such a disrobing; it is meant to be an analysis
of the grounding in life and art which the critic received, of the
ideas which formed him in youth; the education, the ideals, the
disappointments from which are drawn his experience, the fash-
ions he may unwittingly follow and the flaws he may conceal.

A critic is an instrument which registers certain observations;
before the reader can judge of their value he must know sufficient
of the accuracy of the instrument to allow for the margin of error.
We grow up among theories and illusions common to our class,

our race, our time. We absorb them unawares and their effect is incalculable. What are they? In this case, I am trying to find out, hoping that all I discover, however personal, may prove of use. To do so I have to refer to something which I find intolerable, the early aura of large houses, fallen fortunes and county families common to so many English autobiographers. If the reader can stomach this, I will try to make it up to him.

CHAPTER XVIII

THE BRANCHING OGHAM

I HAVE ALWAYS DISLIKED MYSELF AT ANY GIVEN MOMENT; THE total of such moments is my life.

The first occurred on the morning of the 10th of September 1903 when I was born at Coventry where my father had gone to look after a body referred to as "The Volunteers". My father was in the regular army. His father, Admiral Connolly, son of a General Connolly and nephew to various other veterans of the wars with France, belonged to a naval family long resident in Bath where he had married late in life the eldest daughter of the then Rector of Bath, Charles Kemble, who had restored the Abbey in the Victorian taste and who inhabited what is now the Spa Hotel. The Kembles of Overtown near Swindon were West Country squires who in the eighteenth century had gravitated to London and Bray and made a fortune in the tea trade. Charles Kemble had inherited the wealth of these nabobs and from his mother, a Miss Brooke, the estate of Cowbridge House, Malmesbury, which he had rebuilt in the baroque style with Italian workmen from the Great Exhibition. The vigorous, dominating millionaire Rector of Bath was said to be too Broad-Church in his views to be made a Bishop, for from Wadham he had joined the Clapham Sect. The Connollies, however, were a frugal, blue-eyed, long-lived, quiet, tidy, obstinate race of soldiers and sailors; the Admiral's uncle, Captain Mathew Connolly, had been a kind of arbiter of Bath elegance in the reign of George IV. There was something eight-

eenth-century about the Connollies, while the Kembles were emi-
nently Victorian. My grandfather, the Admiral, was born in 1816
and had done much of his sailing in the Mediterranean and the
Pacific on wooden ships of which he was a great defender against
the "ironclad". He was older than my grandmother, older than the
Rector, his father-in-law, and died in 1901 at his house in Marlborough Buildings, Bath with a great reputation for good looks
of the genial, bearded, crusty, open sort, charm, gallantry, temper
and bad language.

Meanwhile the Rector's fortune had vanished among his eleven
children, his rectory had become a public school, his country houses
all been sold. He left a book called *Memorials of a Closed Min-
istry* and a Victorian gothic church he had built at Stockwell. The
fifty thousand pounds he had contributed to the restoration of the
Abbey was a bitter memory to his grandchild, whose frequent
complaints about it to my mother afforded me at an early age a
grudge against society. I never had a chance! Both my great-grand-
father the Rector and my great-great uncle Mathew Connolly have
their monuments in the Abbey and windows commemorate my
great-uncle Brooke Kemble who was drowned off Tunis as a mid-
shipman, and other members of the family. That quiet corner
where are grouped in such incongruous harmony the Roman Bath,
the Gothic Abbey and the eighteenth-century Colonnade is not the
less sultry for enclosing my roots.

In 1900 when my father's regiment was on a visit to Ireland
he met and married my mother, the daughter of Colonel Edward
Vernon, D.L., J.P., of Clontarf Castle, outside Dublin. The Vernons of Clontarf were a branch of the Vernons of Haddon Hall
and Tonge who had come over to Ireland with the Duke of Or-
mond in the reign of Charles II by whom John Vernon, Paymaster-
General of the Royal Army, had been given Clontarf, then a castle
of the Templars. They were a fiery race, proud of their Anglo-
Norman descent, their sixty-three quarterings and their position
among the sporting Church-of-England "Ascendancy", the landlords of the Pale.

My earliest memory is of a chemist's shop in Bath with col-oured bottles in the window and a circular air-cushion with a hole in the middle. This mysterious rubber object excited me beyond words. What was it for? I never knew except that it must be for something quite unimaginably disgusting and horrible. I knew it and It knew it, and It knew that I knew it. It was vice made vis-ible. And It was for Me!

Then my father's regiment was sent to South Africa, and all my memories became exotic; arum lilies, loquats, eucalyptus, freezias, are the smells which seem to me divine essences, balms of Eden remembered from another life. The freezias grew wild in the grass and those long thin stems with their wayward creamy blossom, and their fragrance, so strangely fresh and yet sophisti-cated, were my first clue to the vast riches of the universe. I remem-ber also Cape Point, the walk to the sea through clumps of rushes and over white sand feathered with the tracks of lizard and all around me an indescribable irradiation of sun and wind and space and salt. And at Montagu there was an island in the mountain river on to which I used to be hoisted, clutching a stinking meer-cat's skin, lord of a rock on which a bird deposited the shells of crayfish, an Ithaca twelve feet long.

We lived at Wynberg; there were chameleons in the garden and squashed apricots; on Sundays the Regiment had church parades and there were smells of pine and eucalyptus paint blisters and hot tar. I had already grown accustomed to being an only child and enjoyed playing by myself. I had a dog called Wups, a cat called One-Eye and a crowd of other animals, some real and many imaginary. I derived enormous pleasure from animals and some-thing approaching ecstasy from the smells of flowers and fruit and from the arid subtropical scenery.

Already my life was a chain of ecstatic moments; I invented happy families of tops and fir-cones or made overtures to the sacred personages whom I learnt about from *Line upon Line*: Isaac on his way up the mountain to be sacrificed, the infant Samuel, the other children David and Benjamin. But my deepest concern was the apprehension of visual beauty. To stand among arum lilies, faintly scented, thick in texture and to break off their leaves or among the brittle lines of sweet pea or with my watering-can, by the rose-beds smelling of wet earth and to pour out the spraying water—these were experiences, like climbing a willow tree near the stables where the green and edible willow branches hung down like the reed curtains in Spanish doorways by which my existence was transformed! In vain Captain Scott shook hands with me on his last voyage to the South Pole, in vain I was shown the giant tortoises and the fleet at Simonstown or saw the Regiment parade on Minden Day—my relations, sadistic with One-Eye and Wups— æsthetic, with pale cones of silver fir and the gummy blue cups of eucalyptus, were all that concerned me.

I twice visited South Africa; at the age of five, and six. In between we went to Ireland and stayed at Clontarf, and then at Mitchelstown Castle in Cork which left a deep impression. This castle was an enormous eighteenth-century Gothic affair, which belonged with some thirty thousand acres to my great-aunt Anna, Countess of Kingston, who had once been besieged there by the Fenians; there was a lake in the grounds, and a wishing well. Now alas, not a stone remains. It was winter and there were icicles along the lake. I wore brown gloves on week-days and white ones on Sundays and held an icicle (the first I had seen) with its mysterious purposeful pointed whiteness, in my white glove. Of the rest of the visit I remember little. Lord Kingston descendant of Milton's Lycidas had long been dead, but my grandfather was there, terrifying. "Where is Grandpapa?" I asked my nurse one morning. "He's busy." "What's he doing?" "He's doing his duty." This answer, which would have covered the activities of all Irish landlords at that date, I took to mean that he was in the lavatory (Have you done your duty to-day?), and was more frightened of him than ever except when he would come in with his gun and a huge stiff dead grasshopper two feet long in his hand, waving it at me and saying "snipe, snipe."

This was my first visit to Ireland since babyhood and besides the love of the beautiful, it awoke in me a new passion. I became a snob. The discovery that I was an earl's great-nephew was important to me; I soon made another. My mother's favourite sister had married a rich man. Aunt Mab was very beautiful but she also had special smells, smells of furs and Edwardian luxe. Uncle Walter gave me a steam train and a watch for Christmas. Wherever we went with Aunt Mab there were presents and large houses and the appeal her wealth made to an imaginative child was irresistible. Bishopscourt, Loughananna, Rochestown, Marlay, the names of her houses (for she moved every six months) held a poetry for me. They went with security and romance, fires and potato cakes, footmen, horses and soft aquatinted Irish winter.

> Cold grew the foggy morn, the day was brief,
> Loose on the cherry hung the crimson leaf;
> All green was vanished save of pine and yew
> That still display'd their melancholy hue;
> Save the green holly with its berries red
> And the green moss upon the gravel spread.

      *   *   *

In 1910 I was sent home from Africa for good. My parents stayed on while I went with my nurse to join my father's mother and sister in Corsica where they had a villa. By now I was an æsthete. I adored my mother, but lived otherwise in a world of my own. Sunsets were my preoccupation. I saw all words, people, numbers and proper names in colours or notes of music and there was a different colour for every day of the week which I tried to paint but failed. I remember being often ill with fever, and the taste of the orange-leaf tea I was given to bring my temperature down. I added the flavour of this infusion to my ecstasies, with walks in the "maquis" and sessions by the garden tank where I sailed my prickly pear leaves in the evening.

Then there was the sea itself, though, like Petronius, I cared only for the sea-shore, for the beach by "Les Iles Sanguinaires" where transparent "Venus' slippers" were thrown up by the sea.

One evening I was taken out in a boat to see the French destroyers fire their torpedoes. The lurid Mediterranean sunset, the ships, the noise, the rolling, were not to my liking. I cried louder as each torpedo went off and from that evening I date a horror of battleships, bands playing, noises, displays of arms and all official functions.

I also discovered friendship in Corsica and fell in love with a child called Zenon, a Pole, three years older than myself. He had dark eyes, a fringe of brown hair and adored fighting. He made cardboard swords and shields for us on which he used to paint our coats of arms and we would hack at each other till our escutcheons were broken. From that moment I have seldom been heart-free and life without love for me has always seemed like an operation without an anæsthetic. I have been inclined to regard that condition as the justification of existence and one that takes priority over all other ideologies.

> Love the most generous passion of the mind,
> That cordial drop heaven in our cup has thrown
> To make the nauseous draught of life go down.

From Corsica we moved on to Tangier, where I was infatuated again, this time with a handsome bearded Moorish guide called Salem. We showered presents on each other and I still have a beautiful drum he gave me. Then we returned to Bath, where aged six I was sent to school as a day boy. It was the hot summer of 1910 and we wore dark blue cockades for the general election, except the dentist's son, who was a liberal. He seemed to me to smell quite different from the other boys. Oily.

I was now nearly seven and from this moment my character began to deteriorate. My grandmother spoilt me. I have since observed that it is a pleasure of grandparents to spoil their grandchildren. They revenge themselves in that way on their children for the insults they have suffered from them. My grandmother, lonely, religious and unselfish, was only playing her biological role. The tragedy was that I found it out and recognised my victim.

I remember being spoilt as an actual sensation, waking up early on Christmas morning and seeing the thrilling contours of my presents taking shape, the stocking bulging in the dark, afterwards unpacking the toy soldiers and setting them up in the new fort, going to church in my Eton jacket and suddenly, about three o'clock, being afflicted with a sensation of utter satiety and aggressive boredom. It was like eating—having been delicate and often feverish my appetite was most stimulated by invalid foods—the egg, the grape, the pat of butter, the cutlet, the tangerine, they were my highspots. In the winter afternoon I would play by the fire with mines of matchboxes fired by trains of torn paper in the grate, for I hated to leave the fire for a moment, then tea would be brought in, my grandmother would cut the buttered toast into fingers, ready to dip into the boiled eggs. Which tastes best? The first or the second? The first finger of toast or the last little triangle dug out from the bottom with a spoon? I don't know—but I do know one should never have a third egg, and I remember the unwilling sensation of not wanting to eat it yet hating to let it go and finally forcing myself to dispose of it, and then rounding on my grandmother—a vicious little golden-haired Caligula.

To this period I trace my worst faults. Indecision, for I found that by hesitating for a long time over two toys in a shop I would be given both and so was tempted to make two alternatives seem equally attractive; Ingratitude, for I grew so used to having what I wanted that I assumed it as a right; Laziness, for sloth is the especial vice of tyrants; the Impatience with boredom which is generated by devotion; the Cruelty which comes from a knowledge of power and the Giving way to moods for I learnt that sulking, crying, moping, and malingering were bluffs that paid.

The people I had been in love with before, my mother, my nurse Betty, Wups, One-Eye, Zenon, and Salem or Selim (the spelling varied) were people who loved me, but we loved as equals, conscious of each others' rights. Sufficiently provoked One-Eye would scratch, my mother rebuke, Betty spank, Zenon, Wups and Salem slink away. Now for the first time I learnt of unequal love.

I was not in love with my grandmother, she was in love with me, or perhaps so ignorant and helpless with children as to seem in love, and I took advantage. *Sic ego perire cœpi.*

At school I was popular for I had embarked on the career which was to occupy me for the next ten years of "trying to be funny". I was neither good nor bad at games; my favourite exercise was to take a short piece of pointed wood in my hand and meander for hours through the long summer grasses round the playing fields, calling at imaginary ports, tunnelling through the hay, chewing sorrel and following my faint tracks in the silver grass as a liner follows a trade route. Inside my desk a cardboard shoebox perforated with holes supported a brood of looper caterpillars. Who can forget that smell of caterpillars, the smell of wet cardboard, drying leaves and insect excrement, the odour of northern chilhood? It was on one of these long summer cruises, in a patch of cow-parsley, that I realised my own identity; in a flash it came to me that my name and myself were something apart, something that none of the other boys were or could be, Cyril Vernon Connolly, a kind of divine "I am that I am" which I should carry all through life and at last deposit on my grave, like a retriever with a bit of stick.

I was still in love, as I had been since I first saw in Little Arthur's History of England the picture of the Princes in the Tower —those two royal princes, so sweetly embracing, so soon to be smothered—what only child could look at them without a disturbance or read of Prince Arthur himself, walking trustfully beside the gaoler on his way to have his eyes put out? Indeed, like many children, I had fixations on the early Plantagenets. With their remote grandeur and their drooping black moustaches these sad bad Kings seemed like my great-uncles, huge brooding stylised figures who awoke a sense of guilt.

My great friend was a boy called Hubert Fitzroy Foley. I remember leaning out of the dormitory window with him to watch the fireworks on a summer night, while the rockets went off and we heard the inevitable Gilbert and Sullivan from the distant military band. That summer I seemed to be initiated into the secrets of preparatory school life. I came to know the smell of the class-rooms, of slates, chalk and escaping gas, and to fear the green baize door which separated the headmaster's part of the house from the boys. On the one side, silence, authority, the smell of savouries; on the other noise and freedom.

At night we made "tabernacles" by stretching the sheets up over the tops of the beds and I would lie in the evening sunshine playing flicking matches between the fingers of my right hand and my left or arching my hands into swan-like shapes that swooped up and down above my head. When I was ill there were cracks in the ceiling to map and explore and patterns in the wall-paper. I learnt the rhythm of the seasons: summer, which is the time for overdoing things, the recoil of creative autumn, the vibrant coma of winter and the lowering spring. I began to enjoy my work and to win prizes. I acted in a play and wrote facetious little Leacockian sketches. I declared a rebellion against the masters and returned a prize to one of them saying none of us would ever speak to them again. This was part of my insensitive teasing, but he took it seri-ously and looked hurt. I was so spoilt that I felt bored and dis-appointed with myself and tried to take it out on whom I dared. Otherwise I was a typical schoolboy, with a red cap, a belt with a snake (which I slept with under my pillow), a cricket bat, a knowledge of the tracks made by wapiti, skunk, raccoon and wolverine and a happy bitchiness which endeared me, as it was intended to, to my superiors. I went in brakes to watch matches and came home summertipsy in the dusk; I adored sausages and Sunday breakfasts, said my prayers, bickered with other boys on walks, cried "quis" and "ego", and was conceited and bright in the way in which so many small boys are, and which, alas, proves such a false dawn of intelligence.

I can never remember not being able to read and was already deep in "Natural History". I could reel off the habits of aardvarks, aye-ayes, and Tasmanian Devils, and I knew (from *The World of Wonders*) about the great Tun of Heidelberg, the deadly Upas Tree, and the Pitch Lake of Trinidad. I collected stamps, pressed

flowers in blotters and adored chess. For lighter reading there were
fairy stories and nonsense books. I enjoyed Burnand, Mark Twain
and Stephen Leacock but wept at the humiliations of *Vice Versa*
or the sufferings of the Yonghi Bonghi Bo. My thrill of the week
was to visit a little shop on Landsdowne Hill in the early dusk
of winter afternoon and receive a rolled-up bundle of "Comic
Papers"; *Chips* and *Comic Cuts*, the *Rainbow*, the *Gem* and the
Magnet—I hold them, as I did with everything, to my nose, the
smell is excruciating—damp paper, newsprint; I feel I shall burst.
Ahead of me stretches the evening with my grandmother; the gas
lit, the fire burning, the papers unrolled and untied, the peace and
security of the literary life though even then I am depressed by the
knowledge that nothing I shall find inside will come up to the
sensation of opening them. As with Leopardi's peasants, the eve
of the Festival will always bring me more happiness than the Feast
itself.

There was one other lesson I learnt, living with my grandmother. Hitherto I had been in exotic African surroundings or in
Ireland. But my grandmother was poor and we lived in "rooms";
sometimes they were by the seaside in the isle of Purbeck, where
balls bounced on the porphyry pavement, and a horse-drawn tum-
bril dragged the long-robed bathers far out into the string-coloured
sea; sometimes they were in London, sometimes in Bath—but they
were always middle-class. While listening to tales of the Admiral's
splendid dinner parties or of her childhood: the Rector's fine
horses galloping the twenty-four miles from his country house at
Malmesbury to his Palladian villa at Bath with its fourteen gardeners, the opulent safe Victorian saga, I yet was coming to know
the world of the realist novel, those fuggy rooms with plush sofas
and antimacassars, gas mantles, kettles on the hob, and their land-
ladies, overfamiliar women with common voices and ripe bosoms
sprayed with jet. I came into contact with the lower classes too,
for we used to visit one or two old servants to whom my grandmother had made pensions. One, Old Sally, who lived in an alco-
holic bed-ridden fug, distressed me particularly. Here were horrible

things: illness, poverty, old age, and I felt I must make every effort to avoid coming into further contact with them.

I now made the comparison, as many a small boy would:
England = Grannie, Lodgings, School, Poverty, Middle Class.
Ireland = Aunt Mab, Castles, Holidays, Riches, Upper Class.
Ireland, therefore, became desirable and England sordid. This division, however unreal it may seem, had importance for me, it conditioned my homeless insecure lonely childhood, and made me a social hybrid. I could not consider myself entirely upper class; yet I was not altogether upper middle. I had fallen between two standards of living. With the upper class I felt awkward, dowdy, introspective and a physical coward. With the middle class I felt critical, impatient and sparkling. This class distinction, the line between Kensington and Belgravia, is a source of anguish. To consider oneself born into one and yet be slowly conditioned to the other was as uncomfortable as having one shoulder too low.

Meanwhile my mother returned and tried to repair the damages to my character. She disapproved of the school in Bath where I was always ill. I had whooped my way through the coronation summer, I had come out in measles and german measles, and chicken pox and, after a recurrence of malaria, I was removed. My mother came down to see me while I was ill and brought a trunk of toys, all the composition animals whom I adored in the holidays, with their house of parliament and the cricket elevens. I was ashamed of them and refused to play, for already my solitary only-child world seemed disgraceful to my social school-world, even my mother's presence in it seemed incorrect. She took me away to Ireland and so Bath—that beautiful, relaxing town where the Abbey chimes played *The Harp that once through Tara's Halls* with morbid sweetness as we watched the county cricket matches, knew me no more.

Clontarf was a paradise for up in the musicians' gallery of its gothic hall was a pitch for the kind of cricket I played, bowling a marble with my left hand to my right hand which held a toy animal as bat. A book standing up was the wicket. When an animal was out another took its place. Animals that were solid like the elephant or streamlined like the seal, made the best bats; animals like the giraffe whose legs broke when they hit out, were less successful. Books were filled with their batting averages and my celluloid seal, besides being the best cricketer, was also a potent voice in my animals' parliament, and taken every night to bed with me.

My grandfather tried to give me real fielding practice on the lawn but I was frightened. There is a two-handed sword in the castle, reputed to have been used by Brian Boru in his battle there against the Danes, with which my grandfather and my great-uncle Granville Vernon would pretend to chop off my head. Their sombre jesting accentuated my cowardice, but I became interested in Brian Boru, and so was led to cultivate my "Irish" side. I wanted to learn Gaelic and I read history books from the nationalist standpoint. Shane O'Neill, Owen Roe O'Neill, Wolfe Tone, Lord Edward Fitzgerald were my heroes and I learnt to sing the Shan Van Vocht. The last intellectual to stay at Clontarf had been Handel, whose bedroom was my nursery, and I began to be considered "Queer". The introduction—"This is cousin Cyril [my nephew Cyril]. (*p*) He's supposed to be very clever. (*pp*) His grandmother's spoilt him," depressed me. I responded as usual by showing off and "trying to be funny."

I went on "trying to be funny" till I was seventeen. This grisly process was my defence mechanism. It was the shell I was secreting as a protection from the outside world: by making people laugh I became popular, and I ultimately became feared as well. "Go on, be funny!" some boy would command, and I would clown away or recite my poems and parodies, with their echoes of Mark Twain and Stephen Leacock. "Connolly's being funny," the word would go round and soon I would have collected a crowd. I revelled in this and would grow funnier and funnier till I passed quite naturally into tears. "Connolly's not funny now. He's gone too far," and the group would break up and leave me, except for some true friend who remained to puzzle over the psychology of the manic-depressive. "But you were being quite funny a moment ago." "Oh, Boo-Hoo-Hoo. I wish I was dead." "Oh, shut up, Connolly." "Oh, go away. I hate you." Then a master would come by and comfort me. I would be handed, still hysterical, to the matron, and the inevitable case-history would be gone over. (p) "It's his grandmother. (pp) She spoils him."

But I could not be so funny in Ireland. My wit was the opposite of the native sense of humour, my jokes, a combination of puns and personal remarks interlarded with the wisecracks of the day, ("Oh, go and eat soap" was a favourite) were beyond the Anglo-Irish, who saw only the humour of situations, and could not appreciate a *calembour*. They began to tease me about being English, which I gathered meant possessing a combination of snobbery, stupidity, and lack of humour and was a deadly insult. There were many stories of social triumphs at the expense of parvenu England —especially against unpopular viceroys, like Lord Aberdeen. The Anglo-Irish were a superior people. Better born, but less snobbish; cleverer than the English and fonder of horses; they were poorer no doubt but with a poverty that brought into relief their natural aristocracy. And, above all, they were loved (for "being Irish" meant belonging to the Protestant Landed Gentry) by about four million devoted bog-trotters, who served them as grooms, comic footmen, gardeners and huntsmen.

And the real Irish—what had happened to them? They were my first lost cause, and I worshipped them with passion, reciting the "Dead at Clonmacnois" to myself in a riot of grief.

> In a quiet watered land, a land of roses,
> Stands Saint Kieran's city fair
> And the warriors of Erin in their famous generations
> Slumber there.

> There beneath the dewy hillside sleep the noblest
> Of the Clan of Conn,
> Each below his stone with name in branching Ogham
> And the sacred knot thereon.

Many and many a son of Conn the Hundred Fighter
In the red earth lies at rest;
Many a blue eye of Clan Colman the turf covers,
Many a swan-white breast.

Even to-day such verses typify Ireland, the soft constipating
weather, the unreality of that green cul-de-sac turned away from
Europe where the revolutions lead backwards and the Present is
invariably the victim of the Past.

In the meanwhile what of Clan Colman? Great-Uncle Granville
obligingly made a list of chieftains for me. They were not all extinct; behind the Anglo-Norman families of the Pale, the Fitz-
geralds, de Burghs, Tristrams, Talbots, Vernons and Plunkets,
lurked the remnant of an older race—the O'Grady of Killybally-
owen, the O'Gorman, the O'Connor Don, the Magillicuddy of the
Reeks, the O'Reilly and the Fox! These were the legitimate rulers,
downtrodden heirs of Shane and Owen Roe. I begged Uncle Granville to point them out to me. To serve the O'Gorman! To speak
Gaelic, wear a saffron Irish kilt, and sing the Shan Van Vocht!

In the curragh of Kildare
And the boys will all be there

with the O'Connor Don! The parliament of animals became supporters of the movement and the great seal himself, a fine cricketer
and a generous stateman added the letters D.A.I. (Dublin and
Irish), after his name. I planned a restoration of the monarchy
and pestered my Uncle Granville about the claims of various families. Who should be considered the rightful king of Ireland, the
successor of Brian Boru? Naturally all Connollys, O'Connors, and
O'Connells, through Conn, the King of Connaught. That pointed
to Edward Conolly of Castletown. But his family had taken the
name Conolly and were really Pakenhams. Besides, his Gaelic
. . . ? The O'Briens were Uncle Granville's candidates for the
vacant throne. They had a Gaelic motto and were descended from
Brian Boru himself through the kings of Thomond. Lord Inchi-
quin had the best right to the crown of Tara. For my own part I

had no personal ambition, nothing to hope for from the Restoration.

> It was friends to die for
> That I would seek and find.

and my day-dreams ended in my being sacrificed for the new king, like little Arthur.

This Irish nationalism may seem an extraordinary phase but it must be remembered that there are still several million who believe in it. Gaelic is now compulsory in Ireland, and I believe Lord Cullen of Ashbourne even wore a saffron kilt in Richmond Park. Monarchy has lost ground there since 1912, but at that time the revolutionary movement was unknown to me. My own feelings were romantic and literary, in fact English.[1] Ireland represented glamour and luxury, and I tried to make a religion out of them. Of course, I was a failure with the Irish. I never could learn the Gaelic Alphabet, nor for that matter could I talk with an Irish brogue and the only Irish people I knew were the housekeeper at Clontarf and her husband.

All my cousins were healthy, destructive, normal children. I was lonely, romantic and affected and already the friction between extrovert and introvert was set up. I was extremely shy, for the effort to accommodate my inner life to my outer one was proving harder and harder. I was sentimental at night and facetious in the morning. Between morning and evening my personality would swing from one mood to the other as I watched my wisecracking morning self with its defiant battle-cry "Oh, go and eat soap," turn by degrees into the tearful Celtic dreamer who believed in ghosts and at night would go into a trance over a line of poetry. My appetite for Gaelic and ghosts waxed and waned with my craving for titles. There were evenings when I wanted to kill myself

[1] The surnames of my eight great-grandparents were Connolly, Hall, Kemble, Catley, Vernon, Bowles, Graves and Brinkley. The Vernons had no Irish blood, the Connollys, at any rate since the early eighteenth century, had never been there and now despite my early infatuation nothing infuriates me more than to be treated as an Irishman.

because I was not the O'Grady of Killballyowen. Why had not my father got a title? Why was I not the heir to Castletown? It was heartless, anguishing—why be born, why live at all if I could not have one? Nobody understood me. Nobody cared, and I would scream and scream with real tears and screams that grew more and more artificial as I had to raise my voice to carry to the dining-room. Nobody loved me, nobody understood me, nobody would give me what I wanted, there was an Elemental under the bed. I could die for all They cared. Wur! Wur! Wur! till at last my mother appeared in evening dress and would sit with me and stroke my head smelling of chocolates.

The fever I got from time to time was a recurrence of African malaria, and was just enough to cause anxiety—the anxiety enough to procure me privileges. Nobody could be quite certain that I was shamming. And in the morning, when my night fears had been discussed and I would come down to an atmosphere of sympathy it was "Oh, go and eat soap," or "Stick him with a fork."

Such were these early excesses that to-day I cannot listen to any discussion of titles or open a peerage without feeling sick, as from the smell of rubber steps and stale whisky on the stairway of a Channel boat. I shall never be able to breathe till they are abolished. Nor has "being understood" proved reassuring.

In the end I compromised on the brogue. I pretended that I had got rid of it except in moments of great excitement and I would even affect to lose my temper so as to try out a few phrases, though I was careful to do this when no Irish boys were in the room. My new history books taught me to abominate England for I read *Tales of a Grandfather* at the same time and it never occurred to me that the England I hated, the oppressor of the Celt and the Gael, the executioner of Fitzgerald, Emmet and Wolfe Tone, was made manifest in my grandfather, who owned a thousand acres of suburban Dublin, and a shoot in Kerry; that the Anglo-Irish were themselves a possessor class whose resentment against England was based on the fear that she might not always allow them to go on possessing.

CHAPTER XIX

WHITE SAMITE

❧❧

THE NEW SCHOOL MY PARENTS CHOSE FOR ME WAS ON THE
coast. At first I was miserable there and cried night after night.
My mother cried too at sending me and I have often wondered if
that incubator of persecution mania, the English private school, is
worth the money that is spent on it or the tears its pupils shed.
At an early age small boys are subjected to brutal partings and
long separations which undermine their love for their parents
before the natural period of conflict and are encouraged to look
down on them without knowing why. To owners of private schools
they are a business like any other, to masters a refuge for incompetence, in fact a private school has all the faults of a public
school without any of its compensations, without tradition, freedom, historical beauty, good teaching or communication between
pupil and teacher. It is one of the few tortures confined to the
ruling classes and from which the workers are still free. I have
never met anybody yet who could say he had been happy there.
It can only be that our parents are determined to get rid of us!

Yet St. Wulfric's where I now went was a well run and
vigorous example which did me a world of good. We called the
headmistress Flip and the headmaster Sambo. Flip, around whom
the whole system revolved, was able, ambitious, temperamental
and energetic. She wanted her venture to be a success, to have more
boys, to attract the sons of peers and to send them all to Eton. She
was an able instructress in French and History and we learnt with

her as fast as fear could teach us. Sambo seemed a cold, business-
like and dutiful consort. The morale of the school was high and
every year it won a shooting trophy and the Harrow History Prize
from all the other preparatory schools. Inside the chapel was a
chaplain, inside the gym a drill-sergeant and there were a virid
swimming-pool, a cadet corps, carpenter's shop and riding class.

The school was typical of England before the last war; it was
worldly and worshipped success, political and social; though Spartan, the death-rate was low, for it was well run and based on that
stoicism which characterised the English governing class and which
has since been under-estimated. "Character, character, character,"
was the message which emerged when we rattled the radiators or
the fence round the playing fields and it reverberated from the
rifles in the armoury, the bullets on the miniature range, the saw in
the carpenter's shop and the hoofs of the ponies on their trot to
the Downs.

> Not once or twice in our rough island's story
> The path of duty was the way to glory

was the lesson we had to learn and there were other sacred mes-
sages from the poets of private schools: Kipling or Newbolt.

Muscle-bound with character the alumni of St. Wulfric's would
pass on to the best public schools, cleaning up all houses with a
doubtful tone, reporting their best friends for homosexuality and
seeing them expelled, winning athletic distinctions—for the house
rather than themselves, for the school rather than the house and
prizes and scholarships and shooting competitions as well—and
then find their vocation in India, Burma, Nigeria and the Sudan,
administering with Roman justice those natives for whom the final
profligate overflow of Wulfrician character was all the time pre-
destined.

After I had spent one or two terms at St. Wulfric's, blue with
cold, haunting the radiators and the lavatories and waking up
every morning with the accumulated misery of the mornings before, the war broke out. My parents had taken a house in London

in Brompton Square and the holidays had become an oasis after St. Wulfric's austerity. In the big room at the top of the house with my grandfather's sea chest and the animal books by Ernest Thompson Seton, a fire and the view of the sea-green limes of the Brompton Oratory or in the drawing-room with its vine-clad balcony and rose-wood furniture from Cowbridge I could be happy. The square abounded with looper caterpillars, tight in the shallow earth wriggled the pupæ of the privet moth (in those that did not wriggle the icheumon was at work). On Sundays people made jokes about not going to church but went and the churches disgorged their top-hatted congregations into the Park from whence they strolled back, myself in top hat and Eton jacket moving in an Anglo-Irish phalanx and imagining I was Charles Hawtrey, through gates and squares and crescents aromatic with Sunday luncheons, the roast beef, the boredom, the security of 1913. At night my fear of the dark was still acute. I had to have night-lights and I had a terror of anything "going out"—I could not bear a dying fire or a guttering candle, or even a clock to run down—it seemed a kind of death-agony.

The rest of my time at St. Wulfric's was spent on a war-time basis. The school throve; it's *raison d'être* apparent in the lengthening Roll of Honour. Old boys came down in uniform and retired generals lectured to the corps while the boys stuck flags into maps, gave Woodbines to the wounded soldiers and learned to knit; doing without more and more, as Flip's organising genius found its expression.

The master who first took me in hand was Mr. Ellis. He was gruff and peppery with an egg-shaped bald head. He and Mr. Potter, the high-priest of the shooting trophies, were professional teachers, the rest makeshifts thrown up by the war. Ellis was pro-German; the Germans deserved to win the war, he thought, because of their superior efficiency. The boys respected his point of view; to them, a German victory would have seemed natural, a chastisement on England for neglecting duty and discipline, and not listening to "Lest we forget". He made me enthusiastic over algebra and as my enthusiasm grew I became good at it.

From that moment Daddy Ellis befriended me. He called me Tim Connolly and built up a personality for me as the Irish Rebel, treating me as an intelligent and humorous person, an opponent to respect. When the Germans conquered our decadent country through their discipline and the superiority of their general staff I should be one of the first elements to be shot.

My new personality appealed to me. I changed my handwriting and way of doing my hair, jumped first instead of last into the fetid plunge-bath, played football better and became an exhibit: the gay, generous, rebellious Irishman, with a whiff of Kipling's McTurk. Flip also admired the transformation and began to introduce me to parents as "our dangerous Irishman", "our little rebel". At that time I used to keep a favour chart in which, week by week, I would graph my position at her court. I remember my joy as the upward curve continued, and as I began to make friends, win prizes, enjoy riding and succeed again at trying to be funny. The favour charts I kept for several terms; one's favour began at the top and then went downwards as term wore on and tempers.

When angry Flip would slap our faces in front of the school or pull the hair behind our ears, till we cried. She would make satirical remarks at meals that pierced like a rapier and then put us through interviews in which we bellowed with repentance— "It wasn't very straight of you, was it, Tim? Don't you *want* to do me credit—don't you *want* to have character—or do you simply not care what I think of you as long as you can get a few cheap laughs from your friends and shirk all responsibility?" The example of brothers or cousins now in the trenches was then produced to shame us. On all the boys who went through this Elizabeth and Essex relationship she had a remarkable effect, hotting them up like little Alfa-Romeos for the Brooklands of life.

The one thing that would bring our favour back (for, woman-like, Flip treated the very being-out-of-favour as a crime in itself, punishing us for the timid looks and underdog manner by which we showed it) was a visit from our parents and many a letter was sent off begging for their aid. I was restored, after a low period during which I had been compared before the whole school to the tribe of Reuben because "unstable as water thou shalt not excel", by an enquiry for me from Lord Meath, the founder of Empire Day. Sometimes we could get back by clinging to friends who were still "in favour". It might drag them down or it might bring us up and the unhappiness of these little boys forced to choose between dropping a friend in his disgrace or risking disgrace themselves was most affecting.

I had two friends whose "favour" was as uncertain as my own, George Orwell, and Cecil Beaton. I was a stage rebel, Orwell a true one. Tall, pale, with his flaccid cheeks, large spatulate fingers, and supercilious voice, he was one of those boys who seem born old. He was incapable of courtship and when his favour went it sank for ever. He saw through St. Wulfric's, despised Sambo and hated Flip but was invaluable to them as scholarship fodder. We often walked together over the downs in our green jerseys and corduroy breeches discussing literature, and we both won, in consecutive years, the inevitable "Harrow History Prize". There was another prize for having the "best list" of books taken out of the library during the term, the kind which might have been invented only to create intellectual snobs and to satiate boys with the world's culture at a time when they were too young to understand it. The books were given out in the evening by Flip herself and a way by which it was sometimes possible to get back into "favour" was by taking out or returning one which caught her eye. Old boys who came down promptly enquired, "What sort of favour are *you* in?" and letters to those who had gone on always ended up, "I am (touch wood) still in good favour"—"I shall have to do something, I'm losing favour"—or "I am in the most awful favour"; unjust at the time as this feminine tyranny seemed it was a valuable foretaste of the world outside; even the nickname Flip suggested some primitive goddess of fortune. Thus, although I won the prize through heading my list with "Carlyle's *French Revolu-*

tion"—and Orwell won it next, we were both caught at last with two volumes of *Sinister Street* and our favour sank to zero.

We both wrote poetry. At sunset or late at night in the dark, I would be visited by the Muse. In an ecstasy of flushing and shivering, the tears welling up as I wrote, I would put down some lines to the Night Wind. The next morning they would be copied out. Although the process of composition always seemed an authentic visitation, the result was an imitation of Stevenson or Longfellow or my favourite, Robert W. Service. I would compare them with Orwell's and be critical of his, while he was polite about mine, then we would separate feeling ashamed of each other.

The remarkable thing about Orwell was that alone among the boys he was an intellectual and not a parrot for he thought for himself, read Shaw and Samuel Butler and rejected not only St. Wulfric's, but the war, the Empire, Kipling, Sussex, and Character. I remember a moment under a fig-tree in one of the inland boulevards of the seaside town, Orwell striding beside me and saying in his flat, ageless voice: "You know, Connolly, there's only one remedy for all diseases." I felt the usual guilty tremor when sex was mentioned and hazarded, "You mean going to the lavatory?" "No—I mean Death!" He was not a romantic, he had neither use for the blandishments of the drill sergeant who made us feel character was identical with boxing nor for the threats of the chaplain with his grizzled cheektufts and his gospel of a Jesus of character who detested immorality and swearing as much as he loved the Allies. "Of course, you realise, Connolly," said Orwell, "that, whoever wins this war, we shall emerge a second-rate nation."

Orwell proved to me that there existed an alternative to character, Intelligence. Beaton showed me another, Sensibility. He had a charming, dreamy face, enormous blue eyes with long lashes and wore his hair in a fringe. His voice was slow, affected and creamy. He was not good at games or work but he escaped persecution through good manners, and a baffling independence. We used to mow the lawn together behind an old pony, sit eating the gooseberries in the kitchen garden or pretend to polish brass in the chapel; from Orwell I learnt about literature, from Cecil I learnt about art. He occupied his spare time drawing and painting and his holidays in going to the theatre.

On Saturday nights, when the school was entertained in the big schoolroom by such talent as the place could offer, when Mr. Potter had shown lantern slides of *Scrooge* or Mr. Smedley, dressed up like a pirate at a P. & O. gala, had mouthed out what he called "Poethry"—there would be a hush, and Cecil would step forward and sing, "If you were the only girl in the World and I was the only boy." His voice was small but true, and when he sang these sentimental songs, imitating Violet Loraine or Beatrice Lillie, the eighty-odd Wulfricians felt there could be no other boy in the world for them, the beetling chaplain forgot hell-fire and masturbation, the Irish drill-sergeant his bayonet practice, the staff refrained from disapproving and for a moment the whole structure of character and duty tottered and even the principles of hanging on, muddling through, and building empires were called into question.

On other Saturday nights gramophone records were played; when we came to "I have a song to sing O, sing me your song O" I would open a book which I had bought in the Charing Cross Road, at the prepared place and read:

Far out at sea when the evening's dusk is falling you may often observe a dark-coloured bird with white under-plumage flit by just above the waves—another and another make their appearance, and you soon find out that a party of Manx Shearwaters have paid your vessel a passing call. They are nocturnal birds for the most part, spending the hours of daylight in their burrows, and coming out in the gloom to speed across the frowning waters in quest of food. There is something very exciting about the appearance of this singular bird. The noisy gulls which have been playing about all day drop slowly astern as the sun nears the west; the parties of Razorbills and Guillemots and Puffins have sped away to their distant breeding colonies; and the wide waste of waters seems unusually destitute and dreary as the night approaches, and the evening breeze fluttering in the sails, and through the rigging, is the only sound that breaks the oppressive stillness. But the hour of the Manx Shearwater's ghostly revelry has come, he holds high carnival over the waste of gray waters, flitting about in most erratic manner in his wild impetuous course, following the curve of every wave, dipping down into the hollows, where he is almost invisible, and then mounting the foamy crests, where you catch a brief glimpse of his hurried movements.

The combination of the music with this passage was intoxicating. The two blended into an experience of isolation and flight which induced the sacred shiver. The classroom disappeared, I was alone on the dark seas, there was a hush, a religious moment of suspense, and then the visitation—the Manx shearwaters appeared, held their high carnival, etc., and vanished. At length the schoolroom where each boy sat by his desk, his few possessions inside, his charted ink channels on top, returned to focus. This experience, which I repeated every Saturday, like a drug, was typical of the period. For those were the days when literature meant the romantic escape, the purple patch; when none of our teachers would have questioned the absolute beauty of such a line as "clothed in white Samite, mystic, wonderful!" We were still in the full Tennysonian afterglow and our beliefs, if the muse of St. Wulfric's could have voiced them, would have been somewhat as follows.

"There is a natural tradition in English poetry, my dear Tim, Chaucer begat Spenser, Spenser begat Shakespeare, Shakespeare begat Milton, Milton begat Keats, Coleridge, Shelley, Wordsworth, and they begat Tennyson who begat Longfellow, Stevenson, Kipling, Quiller-Couch and Sir Henry Newbolt. There are a few bad boys we do not speak about—Donne, Dryden, Pope, Blake, Byron, Browning, FitzGerald, who wrote *The Rubáiyát of Omar Khayyám*, and Oscar Wilde who was a criminal degenerate. Chaucer is mediæval but coarse, Spenser is the poet's poet, Shakespeare you will remember from your performance as the witch ('aroint thee, witch, the rumpfed runion cried her husbands to Aleppo gone the master of the tiger, but in a sieve I'll thither sail and like a rat without a tail I'll do I'll do and I'll do'). Precisely. Milton was a great poet, he wrote *L'Allegro, Il Penseroso* and *Paradise Lost*; Keats wrote *The Ode to a Nightingale*; and Tennyson wrote *The Lady of Shalott*—and what else? *Morte d'Arthur, Locksley Hall, In Memoriam, Break, Break, Break*, and *Crossing the Bar*. Longfellow wrote *Hiawatha*, Stevenson *Under the Wide and Starry Sky*, Kipling *Sussex* and *If* and *Gunga Din*, Quiller-Couch is a Good Influence and *Drake's Drum* and *Lyra Heroica* are by Sir Henry Newbolt.

"There are other good poems, *Chevy Chase, John Gilpin, The Armada, The Ancient Mariner, Grayselegy*. A poem is good either because it is funny (Ingoldsby Legends, Bab Ballads) or because it makes you want to cry. Some funny poems make you want to cry (the Jumblies, the Dong with a Luminous Nose); that is because you are not a healthy little boy. You need more Character. The best poems have the most beautiful lines in them; these lines can be detached, they are purple patches and are Useful in Examinations. Gray's *Elegy* is almost all Purple Patch and so is the *Ode to a Nightingale*, especially

> Magic casements, opening on the foam
> Of perilous seas, in faëry lands forlorn.

When you come to a purple patch you can tell it by an alarm clock going off, you feel a cold shiver, a lump in the throat, your eyes fill with tears and your hair stands on end. You can get these sensations for yourself when you write poems like your *Ode on the Death of Lord Kitchener* or *To the Night Wind*.

"Nobody wrote so many purple patches as Tennyson, and he had character too (*Bury the Great Duke, Charge of the Light Brigade, The Revenge*). Kipling is the only great poet alive to-day. Poetry is romantic, purple—a help in time of trouble—or else it is clever and funny, like Calverley—or has Character. (Life is real, Life is earnest, And the grave is NOT its goal.) It is also something to be ashamed of, like sex, and (except with the chaplain) religion."

My experience with the Manx shearwater fulfilled these conditions. It was prose, so could not become poetry and truly purple, till heightened by music. It was romantic; something out of the ordinary, remote, and false, for in real life I should hate tossing about the Hebrides in a small boat—and escapist, since I imagined myself away from my present surroundings, alone on the northern waters, and yet not alone, a Manx shearwater, playing with others of my kind. The twilight was "my" time of day (the time I felt most the poetical thrill), the waste of grey waters my weepy Celtic spiritual home. Because poetry was associated with emotional excess, night and unhappiness, I felt disgusted with it by day as by a friend in whom when drunk one has unwisely confided and I never exhibited the Manx shearwater even to Orwell.

It will be seen that the thread running through this autobiography is an analysis of romanticism, that romanticism in decline under whose shadow we grew up. Romanticism I would call the refusal to face certain truths about the world and ourselves, and the consequences of that refusal. It is a refusal which can be both splendid and necessary, this pretence that truth is beauty and beauty truth, that love is stronger than death, the soul immortal and the body divine—but in the hundred years that have elapsed since the romantic revival we have had too much of it. By the twentieth century the best work has been done and those of us who thought we were angels or devils have had a long struggle to free ourselves from such ideology. We have been the dupe of words and ideas, we have been unable to know when we are well off, we have expected too much from life, too many treats and we have precipitated crises to satisfy the appetite for sensation acquired in childhood; the womb world of the hot bath and the celluloid duck has been too near us. The romantic's artillery is always bracketing over the target of reality, falling short into cynicism or overreaching it into sentimental optimism so that, whatever the achievements of romanticism in the past, to be a romantic to-day, knowing what we know about the nature of man and his place in the universe, is the mark of a wilful astigmatism, a confession of cowardice and immaturity.

If but some of us lived in the world of romantic poetry, we all lived in the world of romantic love; there was no sentiment in *Maud* or *In Memoriam* that to us seemed exaggerated, we accepted "being half in love with easeful death" as a matter of course, like the psychology of the *Belle Dame Sans Merci*. Love was a recurrent ecstasy which drove us to make sacrifices for an object which might or might not be aware of them. Reciprocation killed love faster than anything, then came Ridicule; it was only Ignorance in the Beloved that could permit the emotion to last. The prosaic Sambo seemed to have a flair for detecting our romances and he would try to expel the Cyprian by taps on the head from his heavy silver pencil.

> Always I long to creep
> Into some still cavern deep,
> There to weep and weep, and weep
> My whole soul out to Thee.

Such was my ideal, and if it met with any opposition I would reply in the romantic's way with a spiteful poem.

The boy whom I loved for the last three years I was at St. Wulfric's was called Tony Watson. He was small, brown, wiry, good at games, untidy and silent, with a low brow, green eyes and a fringe of rough short hair. I describe him because he is a type that has recurred through my life and which gets me into trouble. It is that faunlike, extrovert creature with a streak of madness and cruelty, not clever, but narcissistic and quick to adapt itself to clever people. In appearance it is between colours with a small mouth, slanting eyes and lemon-yellow skin.

By the time I was twelve all four types to which I am susceptible had appeared. I do not know whether it is glands, numerology, the stars or mere environment which dispose one to these fierce sympathies, inherited as if from another life, but by now I recognise my kindred forms with some familiarity; the Faun, the Redhead, the Extreme Blonde and the Dark Friend.

The Fauns well know their fatal power which a series of conquests have made obvious and they derive a pleasure that I mistake for reciprocation, from the spectacle of its workings. Age is often unkind to these charmers and the world is apt to turn against them. With the other types my relations are happier. I supply them with vitality and intensive cultivation, they provide me with affection, balance, loyalty, good taste. The Extreme Blondes are quiet, intelligent, humorous, receptive; they have an impressive reserve against which I roll, like the Atlantic Ocean on the Cornish cliffs, confident that they will be able to withstand me. The Dark Friends are the most sympathetic, they have brown eyes and oval faces; they like my jokes and look after me when I am ill, but it is one of the hardships of romantic love that rarely is it bestowed on people like ourselves and the Dark Friends end by being Consolers. The Redheads have some of the quieting effect of the Extreme Blondes but they may suddenly become as deleterious as the Faun. They are a special type, not the dreamy, brown-eyed, long-faced auburn, nor the aggressive albino, but the gay, thin, dashing green-eyed variety.

Being an only child I romanticised sisterhood, I wanted an Electra and longed for a relationship with sister types of the same age. I liked health and equality in women, an implicit friendship. I desired the same for my imaginary brothers. The Dark Friends and the Extreme Blondes supplied this, the Redheads added an excitement which raised it to perfection. And then the exotic Faun would reappear and all peace of mind would vanish. As with other only children my desire for a brother or a sister was so strong that I came to see existence in terms of the couple; in whatever group I found myself I would inevitably end by sharing my life with one other, driven by an inner selection through a course of trial and error till after forming one of a group of four or five and then of a trio, I achieved my destiny as one half of a pair.

I christened this search for the *"dimidium animae meae"* the Pair System, and I was fascinated, when later I read the Symposium of Plato, to come across his theory that human beings had once been double and were for ever seeking the counterpart from whom they had been so rudely forced. We were all one half of a Siamese Twin.

> The brothered one, the not alone
> The brothered and the hated.

But it is a romantic theory and it is part of the romantic's misfortune that in the search for his affinity he is not guided by a community of interests but by those intimations which are the appeal of a mouth or an eye, an appeal which is not even private so that the spectacle is presented of half-a-dozen Platonic half-men trying to unite with the same indifferent alter ego. Love at first sight—and the first sight is the supreme consummation for romantics—is an intuition bred by habit of the person who can do us harm.

Yet Tony Watson let me down lightly. He was a wild little boy with plenty of character but not of the right kind. He taught me to smoke (which I hated); to rag in the corridors at night, fighting among the coats hanging from their pegs and to take part on the downs in gang warfare, which I adored. He moved in a fast set of hard-smoking and hard-swearing cronies from whom he protected me. Our unlikeness made us over-polite. He accepted my devotion, even to a poem beginning, "Watson, the silent, Watson, the dauntless" and showed me, in return, an extraordinary drawing, a Parthenon Frieze on sheets of paper stuck together that unfolded like a concertina, to reveal a long procession of soldiers —cavalry, infantry, artillery, wounded and dying, doctors, nurses, ghurkas, staff-officers and engineers on their way to the war.

For most of us the war was skin-deep. The *Titanic* had gone down, the passengers all singing, "Nearer my God to Thee"—that was terrible—and now the war: pins stuck in maps, the Kaiser dying of cancer of the throat, Kitchener drowned, ration cards, Business as Usual, a day when we were told of the Battle of Jutland and another when we heard that a terrible thing had happened, a revolution in Russia with a monster called Kerensky now in power. None of us, except perhaps Orwell, believed that England could lose the war or that we would grow up to fight in it nor were we old enough to understand the peril of our elder cousins or the tragedy when—like Uncle Granville's only son, they were killed on the first day of the Gallipoli slaughter. And meanwhile Watson's exact and bloodthirsty pageant grew fuller, a page at a time, till it stretched, by 1917, the whole length of the schoolroom.

Tony shared my love of animals and drew for me pictures of foxes in lonely postures barking to the moon. I had several excruciating moments with him. Once we vowed blood-brotherhood in the Albanian fashion. Tony cut a cross on each left hand and we held the bleeding scratches together. Another time, left in the bathroom alone, he came up to me, wrapped in his bath towel and pursed his lips for a kiss. My spinster modesty made me flinch. He turned away and never did it again while for weeks I lay awake angry and miserable. He slept in a dormitory called the Red Room; I was in a two-bedded one across the passage with the Dark Friend, his cousin, Frankie Wright. Tony would come over in the morning after a night of pillow fighting, gang reprisals and smoking on the roof, and get into my bed where my innocence hung round my neck like an albatross. Then the eight o'clock bell would ring and we would troop down to the ghastly plunge-bath. There was a smell of gooseflesh and slimy water. One by one, under the cold eye of Sambo and to the accompaniment of such comments as "Go on Marsden, you stink like a polecat", we dived or jumped in until it was the turn of the group of water-funks who shrank down the steps, groaning wer-wer-wer, while the sergeant-major waited to haul them out from the stagnant depths by a rope attached to a pole. When the last had been towed it was time to dress and go on the asphalt for "gym".

Year by year the air, the discipline, the teaching, the association with other boys and the driving will of Flip took effect on me. I grew strong and healthy and appeared to be normal for I became a good mixer, a gay little bit who was quick to spot whom to make up to in a group and how to do it. I knew how far to go in teasing and responding to teasing and became famous for my "repartee".

I had a theory that there was one repartee effective for every situation and spent weeks in elaborating it. At that time the magic phrase seemed, "Dear me, how very uninteresting!" If I had to choose one now it would be "This is a very bad moment for both of us." I kept a Funny Book which contained satirical poems and character sketches. I became good at history, that is to say I learnt dates easily, knew which battle was fought in the snow and who was "the little gentleman in black velvet." I read Dickens, Thackeray, Carlyle and Scott and got marks for them and for pleasure John Buchan. It was time for me to go up for a scholarship. I had crammed Watson energetically for the common entrance which he just managed to pass and when I saw him again in the holidays he was a dapper public schoolboy with his hair brushed back, a felt hat and a cane and we had nothing to say to each other.

My first attempt at a scholarship was at Wellington with Orwell. I hated every moment: the blue-suited prefects bustling about the dismal brick and slate, the Wellingtonias and rhododendrons, infertile flora of the Bagshot sand. It was winter and an old four-wheeler bore me from the examinations to my great-aunts with whom I was staying. The musical groaning of the wheels and springs in the winter stillness had a profound effect and I felt like Childe Roland, mystical and Celtic. Pines and heather, the whortle-bearing ridges, seemed to have a message for me, to be the background for some great event as I trundled over them after the afternoon paper. Orwell got a scholarship which he did not take. I failed but the experience was considered good practice.

A year later I went up for Eton, which was very different. Sambo took charge of us; he knew many people there and we had tea with old Wulfrician boys and masters. I had a moment on Windsor Bridge; it was summer, and, after the coast, the greenness of the lush Thames Valley was enervating and oppressive; everything seemed splendid and decadent, the huge stale elms, the boys in their many-coloured caps and blazers, the top hats, the strawberries and cream, the smell of wistaria. I looked over the bridge as a boy in an outrigger came gliding past, like a waterboatman. Two Etonians were standing on the bridge and I heard one remark, "Really that man Wilkinson's not at all a bad oar." The foppish drawl, the two boys with their hats on the back of their heads, the graceful sculler underneath, seemed the incarnation of elegance and maturity.

There was no doubt that this was the place for me, for all of it was, from the St. Wulfric's point of view, utterly and absorbingly evil. I got in twelfth on History and English as Orwell, after Wellington, had done the year before. In case there was no vacancy I went up for one more scholarship, this time at Charterhouse where we did the examination in a cellar during an air raid.

My last year at St. Wulfric's was rosy. I was in sixth form which had its own sitting-room, with Ned Northcote, the captain of the school (Extreme Blond), Frankie Wright (Dark Friend) and Nigel Kirkpatrick (Faunlike). We were about as civilised as little boys can grow to be. We were polite and we hardly ever caned anyone. We wrote to each other in the holidays, we got on with each other's parents, we went to theatres together and took tea at Rumpelmayer's. Ned was captain of the eleven and Nigel of the football team. I was head of the sixth.

My lack of character was now a permanent feature. I was *unreliable*. For that reason I was head of the sixth but not captain of the school; I occupied already the position I was so often to maintain in after life, that of the intellectual who is never given the job because he is "brilliant but unsound". I was also a physical coward, though I learnt how to conceal it, a natural captain of second elevens, and a moral coward by compensation, since, in an English community, moral cowardice is an asset.

Already I had accepted the theory that (1) Character is more important than intellect. (2) Intellect is usually found without character (Oscar Wilde). (3) Intellect, when found with character, is called Nous. (Intellect plus character = Nous plus gumption.) Character is desirable because it makes for success at school (winning colours and reporting best friend for homosexuality), prepares boys for the university and is the foundation of success

in business, politics, the army, the navy, the Indian and Egyptian
civil services, and the African Police. But my analysis of success
had disclosed another quality which seemed, in school life at any
rate, to go as far. It might be called Prettiness. In the matriarchy
of St. Wulfric's, it was not Character, but Character plus Prettiness
that succeeded; Colin and Nigel Kirkpatrick in their green kilts,
even the outlawed Tony Watson or Roy Brown with his fine treble
voice; they were the favoured of fortune, petted when others were
scolded, permitted to wait on parents and old boys at Sunday night
supper in their blue suits, introduced to the guests when they
brought the food into the room and in a position to stuff their
pockets with potato salad when they took it out.

Prettiness alone (Cecil) was suspect like intellect alone (Orwell) but prettiness that was good at games meant "Character"
and was safe. Since I was not pretty I worked hard to be charming
and the four of us grew so civilised that we became inseparable.
We were a little clique at the head of the school, a kind of "Souls"
of St. Wulfric's, gay, powerful, introspective and absorbed in each
other's impressions. We took to visiting in our cubicles at night.
One evening, after lights out, Ned Northcote, and Frankie Wright
were talking in mine when we heard the matron pass along.

> Stalk and sneak, stalk and sneak,
> Maud of the rubbery shoes.
> Sneak sneak every week,
> Maud of the rubbery shoes.
> Over the cubicle wings you go
> Hearing the Red Room whispering low . . .

I had once written to please Tony, and now it was my turn to be
caught.

Maud went into Northcote's cubicle. No sign of him. She called
out in a terrible voice, "Where's Northcote?" I answered from my
cubicle, "I think he went to the lavatory." We heard her go along
to open the door and lost our heads, like rabbits chased by a
ferret. Ned bolted the latch of my cubicle with a toothbrush, and
started to climb over the partition into his own. But Maud came

and rattled it. "Why is this door locked? Open it this instant." I was afraid to. Silence. At last, with white face, Frankie opened it and she burst in. There was an eternity of waiting while our crime was reported, and then the three of us were taken down and caned by Sambo in our pyjamas. The locked door was evidence which our being a trio instead of the usual compromised pair could not palliate. It was Oscar Wilde over again.

The caning was only the beginning; next day our sergeant's stripes were removed, we were turned out of sixth form and a period of miserable disfavour started from which there seemed no hope of escape. But my scholarship was needed, like Ned's bowling, for propaganda; gradually we were forgiven, and our disgrace forgotten except by ourselves. For we never felt quite the same, we grasped that since we were all completely innocent there must be a pitch of civilisation which once reached, brought down a Nemesis. Character was safest: we had seen the writing on the wall.

Before I went to Eton I had spent the Christmas of 1917 in Ireland, in my aunt's house at Rathfarnham. The Easter Rebellion had taken place since I was last there and to be pro-Irish, pro-Celt, pro-Gaelic was no longer a harmless eccentricity. I used to go riding with a groom over the Wicklow mountains and for the first time the Sinn Feiner of St. Wulfric's met his equal. Frank the groom was supposed to command a company of the Irish republican army whom he drilled in the glens of Kilmashogue and up by the Hell Fire Club. I afterwards pretended that I had been present at these parades but never met anyone with him except an old hermit. We went to the Abbey Theatre and saw Synge acted, and heard "God Save the King" hissed and to Clontarf for a pink-coated Christmas dinner at which everyone told hunting stories in the brogue. I felt dowdy, awkward, and English again.

Otherwise my holidays had been uneventful. My great moment at home had been the purchase of a bicycle with three speeds which I called the Green Dragon. I rode it over to where we lived at Crondall and a few days later was allowed to go away for a night by myself. My mother and my favourite Great-uncle Granville saw me off. I bicycled that day from Farnham to Winchester, stayed at the George and went over the school and the Cathedral. The hotel people thought I had run away from somewhere and were suspicious, for the sight of a tourist of thirteen booking a room and dining by himself, with a guidebook propped up was unusual. It was the first welling up of the passion for travel that was to dominate my spare time for the next twenty years.

I was still ignorant of anything which I had not read in a book but just before I went to Eton a concerted attack was made on my modesty. My father struggled to explain the facts of life and the chaplain at St. Wulfric's gave the boys who were leaving a seedy exhortation. Sambo was more precise. We were going into a world full of temptations, he said, especially the Etonians; we must report any boy at once who tried to get into our bed, never go for a walk with a boy from another house, never make friends with anyone more than a year and a half older (eventually it would be younger), and above all, not "play with ourselves". There was an old boy from St. Wulfric's who became so self-intoxicated that when he got to Oxford he had put, in a fit of remorse, his head under a train. That miserable youth, I afterwards learnt, had attended all the private schools in England.

Sambo gave a few examples of Wulfricians who had made good and mentioned cases where those who were doing well and were now heads of their houses, had been able to lend a helping hand to those floundering amid the sexual difficulties due to lack of character. The other boys leaving looked at me curiously, for I was warned to be careful, my literary temperament rendering me especially prone to "all that kind of poisonous nonsense" and I was told that the boy with "character" in my election at Eton who would, although not an old Wulfrician, keep an eye on me, was called Meynell. The Easter term over, we bade a tearful farewell to each other, Flip turned suddenly into a friend, and Nigel Kirkpatrick, Ned Northcote, Frankie Wright, promised to exchange letters with me from Marlborough, Repton and Radley. But it was three years before I wrote another letter.

CHAPTER XX

DARK AGES

☙❧

IF WE HAD WRITTEN, ALL OUR LETTERS WOULD HAVE TOLD THE same story. The lively aristocrats of the cubicles and the sixth-form room were reduced to serfdom, cultivated Greeks pitched into the Carthaginian slave market. We began to adapt ourselves to our new indignity; C. V. Connolly, Esq., K.S., New Buildings, Eton College, Windsor.

The seventy Eton scholars lived together in a house, part Victorian, part mediæval where they were governed by the Master in College who had under him the Captain of the School and nine other members of Sixth Form, who wore stick-up collars, could cane, and have fags. All boys were divided into elections according to the year in which they won their scholarship; the elections moved slowly up the school *en bloc* and each represented a generation.

Below the top twenty came another thirty boys or so who formed the bulk of college and then the bottom twenty about fifteen of whom were doing their compulsory year of fagging, and who, while all the others had rooms, lived in wooden cubicles in Chamber.

The whole school, ruled in theory by Sixth Form and the Captain of the School, was governed by Pop or the Eton Society, an oligarchy of two dozen boys who, except for two or three *ex officio* members, were self-elected and could wear coloured waistcoats, stick-up collars, etc., and cane boys from any house. The masters could not cane. They punished by lines, detentions, and "tickets" or chits of misbehaviour which had to be carried to the housemaster for signature. Serious offences or too many tickets, meant being complained of to the headmaster and might end in a birching.

This system makes Eton the most democratic of schools, for it is a school where all the prefects except the Sixth Form (who are only powerful in College) are self-elected. The boys get the government they deserve.

In practice Eton was not a democracy for the system was feudal. The masters represented the church, with the headmaster as Pope; the boys, with their hierarchy of colours and distinctions, were the rest of the population, while the prefects and athletes, the captains of houses and the members of "Pop" were the feudal overlords who punished offences at the request of the "church" and in return were tacitly allowed to break the same rules themselves. Thus a boy had two loyalties, to his tutor and to his fagmaster or feudal overlord. Sometimes the "church" could protect a young clerk, making the lot of a serious little boy more bearable, in other houses the housemaster was powerless, the "church" weak and unable to control the feudal barons. At other times there were struggles between master and boy which ended in Canossa.

On the whole the feudal system worked well. The boys elected to Pop, those who combined goodness at games with elegance, vitality and a certain mental alertness, were urbane and tolerant; it was among the house-barons that bullies and stupid types were to be found.

A fag in Chamber I was in the lowest ranks of serfdom. Though fagmasters were usually chivalrous to their own slaves, mine was not, nor had we privacy, for our spare time was at the mercy of our rulers, who could send us far into Windsor to buy them food and beat us if we made a mistake over it. I had not often been beaten at St. Wulfric's, at Eton it became a hideous experience for even the little boy who was "Captain of Chamber" could beat us, not with a cane but with a piece of rubber tubing. There was a "Chamber Pop" who also could beat one in a body for a breach of privilege.

I felt quite lost and friendless in this world and sought out Meynell, the boy selected by Sambo to keep an eye on me. An eye was a euphemism for here was the familiar blend of character and prettiness, a tousled wire-terrier of a boy, tough, humorous, a natural leader and political commissar. We were all unhappy and had such a feeling of persecution that we bullied each other to forget it. I was sixty-ninth in college order and among the most bullied boys in my election where Meynell was ringleader. He invented tortures as a perpetual inquest to see if we had "guts" and was much liked in the elections above him who considered him a "good influence".

Nobody would have believed that he could make me stand on a mantelpiece and dance while he brandished a red-hot poker between my feet and said: "What is your name?" "Connolly." "No —what is your real name? Go on. Say it." "Ugly." "All right, Ugly, you can come down." He was aided by a few boys who hoped that their sycophancy would save their skins and by another bully called Highworth. Highworth was not a torturer like Meynell, but a conceited, rakish, conventional boy who could not bear anyone to be eccentric or untidy. He should never have been in College, he was a natural Oppidan.[1]

I spent much of my spare time in School Library, sheltering among the poets. I had discovered the Celtic Twilight and in proportion as I was unhappy, I took it out on the *Lake Isle of Innisfree,* the *Little Waves of Breffny, Glencullen* and other escapist poems, to which I added the *Golden Journey to Samarcand.* I tried to make friends with one other bullied boy but he reciprocated too violently, showed me his own poems, and sniffed at the back of his nose. Instead I fell for a boy called Wilfrid, the faun type over again with green eyes, nectarine colouring who was quick to divine in the little black-gowned, dirty colleger a potential admirer, even as a beautiful orchid accepts the visits of some repulsive

---

[1] Oppidans were the thousand other boys not in College who paid the full fees. Oppidans could be brilliant scholars but they could never experience the advantages and disadvantages of the intensive intellectual forcing-house which College was.

beetle. He was an Oppidan, good at games and older than me. It was only possible to see him leaving his classroom about once a week or sometimes coming out of Chapel or at Absence when the whole of our Feudal society assembled in School Yard. If he was with anyone important he would cut me; if not he would make a joke or two at my expense while I grinned like a waiter. My day-dreams centred round him. I looked up his home address, found out about his family, and copied his initials on to bits of paper. It was something to be in love at last.

The beatings were torture. We were first conscious of impend-ing doom at Prayers when the eyes of Sixth Form would linger pointedly on us. They had supper in a room of their own and a special fag, "senior" who was excused ordinary duties, like other police spies, was sent from there to fetch the "wanted" man. From Upper Tea Room "Senior" set out on his thrilling errand, past the boys chatting outside their rooms. "Who's 'wanted'?" "Connolly." "What, again?" At last he reached the fags who were shivering with terror—for this was always an agonising quarter of an hour for them—in their distant stalls in Chamber. Those who were sitting in their tin baths paused with the sponge in the air—they might have to get out again to dress. The talkers ceased their chorus simultaneously, like frogs, even the favoured who were being tickled in their stalls by the Master in College stopped gig-gling and fear swept over the wooden partitions. "It's Connolly." "Connolly, you're 'wanted'." "Who by?" "Wrangham." "That's all right. He won't beat me, only tick me off. He's my fagmaster." "He's going to beat someone. He's got the chair out."

The chair was only put in the middle of the room when beatings were to take place and sometimes the fag was sent beforehand to get the canes with which he would himself be beaten.

The worst part was the suspense for we might make a mistake the day before and not be beaten for it till the following evening. Or we could get a day's grace by pleading a headache and getting "early bed leave" or by going out to the shooting range, the musical society or to a mysterious evening service, held once a

week to expedite the war which was much frequented by guilty
consciences, called Intercession. The huge chapel was dark and
deserted, the gas mantles plopped, the stained-glass windows glit-
tered, the headmastered droned the prayers from the altar. I too
was praying. "Please God may Wrangham not 'want' me, please
please God may Wrangham not 'want' me or may he forget about it
by to-morrow, and I will clean my teeth. And make me see Wilfrid.
Amen."

Often mass executions took place; it was not uncommon for all
the fags to be beaten at once. After a storm of accusation to which
it was wiser not to reply since no one, once the chair was out, had
been known to "get off", the flogging began. We knelt on the
chair bottoms outwards and gripped the bottom bar with our
hands, stretching towards it over the back. Looking round under
the chair we could see a monster rushing towards us with a cane in
his hand, his face upside down and distroted—the frowning mask
of the Captain of the School or the hideous little Wrangham. The
pain was acute. When it was over some other member of Sixth
Form would say "Good night"—it was wiser to answer.

These memories are associated for me with the smell of Sixth
Form supper and with the walk back through the spectators to the
bed that pulled down from the wall, with the knowing enquiries
of the vice-haunted virginal master in college, a Jesuit at these executions and the darkness that prisoners long for.

The Captain of the School, Marjoribanks, who afterwards committed suicide, was a passionate beater like his bloody-minded successors, Wrangham and Cliffe. Meynell began to receive anonymous notes which made certain suggestions and showed "character"
by taking them straight to his fagmaster. The Captain of the School
was told and the culprit was ordered to confess; nothing happened.
Then another note arrived. The sender, clearly very high in the
school, was never discovered, but in one satisfactory evening Marjoribanks had beaten all the lower half of college. Thirty-five of us
suffered. Another time we were all flogged because a boy dropped a
sponge out of a window which hit a master or we would be beaten

for "generality" which meant no specific charge except that of being "generally uppish".

The result of these persecutions, combined with Chamber beatings and bullyings, was to ruin my nerve. My work went off, and I received several "tickets" which I had to present my tutor, in itself a torture. To this day I cannot bear to be sent for or hear of anyone's wanting to see me about something without acute nervous dread.

My own election were broken under the strain of beatings at night and bullying by day; all we could hope for was to achieve peace with seniority and then become disciplinarians in our turn. But there was one ray of hope. The election now in power was a reactionary one which would be succeeded as it passed on by a gentler crowd, and our own senior election, the year above us, whom as yet we hardly knew contained heroic fighters for liberty and justice. It bristled with Pyms and Hampdens and the feudal system was powerless there.

I had another stroke of luck. After a "chamber pop beating" from Meynell and four other boys, he began a heart-to-heart— "Ugly, why are you so filthy, what is the matter with you?" After the tears which followed I succeeded in making him laugh, and revealed my capacity as a wit. I was able to expand it and soon I could make not only Meynell laugh, but Highworth: they began to leave me alone, bullying me only when they could not find anyone else, but even then sparing me, if I seemed unsuspecting and confident and did not smell of fear. At last I made them laugh at the expense of their victims and my sarcasm became useful. One evening in my second term, after the Armistice had been signed, Meynell asked me to call him Godfrey. From then I was safe, my prayers at "intercession" were answered. I had become a bully too.

Highworth's father and Meynell's and my own had all been professional soldiers who had employed the methods of the parade ground for the disciplining of their sons. We now became the rulers of Chamber, in which Godfrey Meynell was the Hitler, Highworth the Goering, and I the Goebbels, forming a Gestapo who bullied everyone we could and confiscated their private property.

After two terms of being bullied, I had with occasional relapses, a year of bullying until, owing to some bad tactics, I let both Godfrey and Highworth combine against me. Yet we were fond of each other and our triumvirate was racked with jealousy. Highworth was a big neat handsome boy, good at games, a fast bowler, fond of girls and dirty stories. Godfrey was untidy, lazy, yet energetic, sentimental and self-reproachful, a puritan with a saving grace of humour, a border baron half-converted to Christianity whose turbulent life fitted exactly into the pattern of Eton feudalism for he was an example of character and prettiness in authority; his courage was tremendous, to play football under his captaincy, on a losing side, was a sensation. For an hour and a quarter he blamed, praised and appealed to our feelings, leading rush after rush against boys bigger than himself, poaching any kicks he could get and limping off the field with his arm round my neck. "My God, you went badly to-day, Nolly—haven't you any guts—to think we lost to those bastards by three to one" and tears of rage would roll down his cheeks. "Next time we've got to win—we've just got to—understand, Flinchface?"

His personality dominated us because it was the strongest and because it was the incarnation of schoolboyness; the five hundred years of Eton life had gone to make it, the Gothic windows, the huge open fireplace, the table in the middle of Chamber round which our life centred, had been brought into being for him. He was emotional and as Captain of Chamber would "beat" me for untidiness, half miserable at having to flog his best friend, half pleased at fulfilling a Roman duty, only to suffer remorse at the condition of his own belongings. "God knows what I'm to do— I can't let you beat *me*—I haven't the authority—if I ask you to hit me as hard as you can I might lose my temper and knock you down. We'll have to make Wayne and Buckley tidy our stalls for us in future."

Godfrey's relaxation was reading Homer, he adored the Odyssey, for the Homeric world was one in which he was at home and the proverbs of "the wily Odysseus", to the disgust of the able but Philistine Highworth, were never off his lips. "Oh, bababababarbaba bababababarbaba," he would storm; "for God's sake stop spouting Greek—I can't understand a fellow with guts like you Godfrey wanting to quote that filthy Greek all the time—and as for you, Cyril, you're worse,—nine bloody beanrows will I have there and a hive for the honey bloody bee—my God it makes me crap."

Between two such personalities it seemed that I never would have a chance to develop, or find room to reach out to the sun, but I had two pieces of good fortune. Highworth always sexually precocious laid hands on a confirmation candidate in the confessional stage and was sent away for two terms and Godfrey got pneumonia. He was in the sick-room for a month and while he was ill his trampled satellites plucked up their courage. I made friends with three of them and when he came back, we presented a united front against further bullying. Godfrey himself was deeply altered by his illness, his mischievous restlessness left him; being ill for so long and perhaps discovering how little he was missed and how well people got on without him, how transitory was power, had changed his character. For the rest of his time at Eton (he left early for Sandhurst), he was hardworking and modest. He never recovered his leadership but became liked by all those who once had gone in fear of him. The border baron, the prince of the dark ages, had undergone a change of heart, a genuine conversion.

Godfrey afterwards joined his father's regiment, went out to India and had himself transferred to the Indian Army, for he disliked the social side of army life and wanted to be in closer contact with the men he loved. From there he went with his ghurkas to Waziristan, still reading Homer and was killed in action on the frontier, winning a posthumous V.C.

> Liquenda tellus et domus et placens
> Uxor . . .

Encased in the shell secreted by my cowardice, I have thought about his death on that untenable hillside, outnumbered, putting heart into his troops by assuring them that help would reach them, though well aware that help could not, and dying covered with wounds after fighting all day.

Such an end seems remote from the literary life, yet it was the end of one my own age, with whom for four years I had been shaken about like stones in a tin. To a parent passing through College there must have seemed nothing to choose between Godfrey and myself, two small boys in Eton jackets cooking their fag-master's sausages, both untidy, noisy, and mouse-coloured and yet in each a fate was at work; two characters, reacting differently to the same environment, were shaping their lives. The qualities I admire are intellectual honesty, generosity, courage, and beauty. Godfrey was brave. I was not.

Such was the reward of leadership, the destiny of character—not the position of business responsibility which St. Wulfric's had promised us but a premature and lonely death with the barren glory of a military honour.

*   *   *

The boys in my election with whom I now made friends were Charles Milligan, Kit Minns, and Jackie O'Dwyer. Charles became of morbid interest through being caught smoking which made him seem romantic and subversive. He was the Extreme Blond with delicate features and an air of neatness and languor. Minns, a peaceable Oriental-looking boy, surprised the Gestapo by refusing to be bullied. He was quiet and good-natured but when threats or force were employed he would not move. The Gestapo were puzzled; we felt like hunters up against a new animal for Minns was invincible, not through his badgerlike strength, but because he knew he was right. For the first time we felt guilty, aware that our bullying proceeded from a sense of inferiority deepened perhaps by sexual ignorance, and confined ourselves henceforth to the official victims.

O'Dwyer was nearly always in tears but he was affectionate, witty and genial and I secretly made friends with him. We arranged that if he publicly stood up to the Gestapo in my presence I would try to prevent him being punished. The moment came. Godfrey, as usual, was late in changing for afternoon school. "My God, I've lost my braces." He looked round, then marched up. "O'Dwyer, give me your braces." "No." "Take off your braces and give them me at once." "No." This was unheard of: Godfrey glowered at O'Dwyer, who stood rooted to the spot with the tears streaming down his face. After a silence, Godfrey turned away and claimed some braces elsewhere. Another serf was on the road to emancipation. Not unnaturally our election had a bad name though no one quite knew what was going on in it.

I was now fifteen, dirty, inky, miserable, untidy, a bad fag, a coward at games, lazy at work, unpopular with my masters and superiors, anxious to curry favour and yet to bully whom I dared. The rule of the election system was that we spoke only to the boys of our own year; we could be beaten for speaking first to a boy in an election above and were expected to enforce the same discipline on those below. All our election were most formal with the year that had arrived beneath us. I got a bad report and was described as "cynical and irreverent" *"tu ne cede malis"*, wrote Mr. Stone, *"sed contra audentior ito"*.

My parents were upset, heads were put together, and the blame was thrown on Orwell, who was supposed to be my "bad influence" though now I hardly ever saw him. We had been for walks on Sundays but we belonged to two different civilisations. He was immersed in *The Way of All Flesh* and the atheistic arguments of *Androcles and the Lion,* I in the Celtic Twilight and Lady Gregory's resurrected Gaelic legends. His election found us (Meynell excluded) brutish and savage. They were anxious to talk to their junior election and subvert in that way the reactionary "election" system but they did not know how to begin for we were hardly the material on which liberal opinions could be tested.

The moral leaders of my senior election, known as "the caucus",

were Denis Dannreuther, Roger Mynors, Robert Longden, Gibson
and Cazalet. Orwell was rather extreme and aloof, and Farlow,
the most original and vigorous member, too rough and cynical for
the lofty inner ring of whiggery. These two precocious boys were
bosom friends: Farlow a boisterous sceptic who applied "cui bono"
—"who benefits by it" as a criterion to the whole school system and
Orwell perpetually sneering at "They"—a Marxist-Shavian concept which included Masters, Old Collegers, the Church and Senior
reactionaries. This did not prevent him knocking Highworth down
once when he found him tormenting me. One day at the end of
my sixth term I found myself "staying out" in the sick-room with
Roger Mynors. Day by long day we made friends, discovering in
each other the inevitable passion for the Isle of Purbeck, for chalk
streams and geography and for the first time I underwent the
civilising influence of my senior election. They were a most remarkable set of boys, and included a batch of five scholar athletes,
animated, unlike the rulers of college, by post-war opinions. They
hated bullying, beating, fagging, the election system, militarism,
and all infringements of liberty and they believed in the ultimate
victory of human reason. They were polite to each other and formed
an oasis of enlightenment, with one set of baby reactionaries underneath them and another, more dangerous, in the year above.

Mynors did not drop me when we came out of the sick-room
and an epidemic of mumps thinned out my own election, enabling
Charles Milligan, Jackie O'Dwyer and myself to push forward
together. Jacky was clever, lazy, good at games and attractive. He
represented a type which is found in every school, the affable
genial kind of boy whose life is a succession of enthusiasms; for
dab cricket, for learning all the peers by sight, the variations of
the house colours, the results of the Harrow matches or the batting
averages of the eleven. He was sunny and tolerant, suspected of
"not going hard" in the more painful sports and like myself,
greedy. We ate quantities of bananas and cream and all day played
a game called "passage fives" under a white fused light in the

echoing mump-stricken corridor. Roger Mynors walked about with me and called me the "little ray of sunshine". The affectionate and civilised head boy of St. Wulfric's tentatively reappeared and that Easter, after my fourth term, I wrote O'Dwyer a letter. The dark ages were over.

CHAPTER XXI

RENAISSANCE

≫≪

IT WAS NOW THE SUMMER OF NINETEEN-TWENTY. I WAS NO longer a fag and had a room of my own. Neither ruler nor serf, I now formed part of the central bourgeoisie of College. I first saw Nigel by the letter slab and from that moment I was as much changed as Godfrey by pneumonia. The "pair system" reappeared in my life, the faun, the dream brother. That afternoon we played in a knock-up cricket match and each made twenty-five. Nigel had all the familiar features, dark hair, green eyes, yellow skin and a classic head with the wistfulness of a minor angel in a Botticelli, but, being a colleger, he was not stupid like Wilfrid or Tony; in spite of the year and a half between our ages, companionship was possible.

To say I was in love again will vex the reader beyond endurance, but he must remember that being in love had a peculiar meaning for me. I had never even been kissed and love was an ideal based on the exhibitionism of the only-child. It meant a desire to lay my personality at someone's feet as a puppy deposits a slobbery ball; it meant a non-stop daydream, a planning of surprises, an exchange of confidences, a giving of presents, an agony of expectation, a delirium of impatience, ending with the premonition of boredom more drastic than the loneliness which it set out to cure. I was now entering adolescence and for long was to suffer from that disfiguring ailment. My sense of values was to be affected, my emotions falsified, my mind put out of focus, my idea

190

of reality imposed on reality and where they did not tally, reality would be cut to fit.

Nigel was in my sub-junior election. This meant that although I could be seen about with my junior election, I could not be seen alone with him. One way I could talk to him was by availing myself of co-ordinated visits to the shooting gallery, glimpses on the way to meals, leaving chapel, at absence or other ceremonies of the community. The other was to frequent my junior election and make use of the etiquette by which they were allowed to go about with him. This meant altering my ideas about the election system, in fact, ceasing to be a reactionary. The change in emotional life led, as is often the case, to a new political alignment.

I first made friends with the two civilised members of my junior election, Peter Loxley and Walter Le Strange and through them was able to see something of Nigel and his red-haired friend Freddie Langham. At the same time, growing more liberal, I became more acceptable to the election above. Denis Dannreuther and Robert Longden took me up and afterwards King-Farlow and George Wansbrough. At the end of the term I sat next Nigel at a house-match. (I could not give a picture of Eton if I did not emphasise how much time was devoted to planning meetings with people of another year or in another house; the intrigues were worthy of Versailles or Yildiz.) At the house-match I asked Nigel who he liked best in the school. Langham? "Second best," Loxley? "Fourth best," and so on. He also asked me. We realised that we had both omitted "first best" and that the only people we had not mentioned had been each other. I experienced the thrill not untinged with apprehension by which the romantic recognises reciprocated love.

Then came Camp, where my parents who lived near, gave dinner-parties for Godfrey and my new friends, Mynors, Runciman, Wansbrough, Longden, and Dadie Rylands. Our house was a refuge from Camp and, making up my little dinner parties, I tasted the joys of being a political hostess and laid my plans for the future.

The Christmas term of 1920 I was launched. Looking back at my schooldays I am conscious of a rhythm about them, every year culminated in the summer term; it was the term when things happened, the climax of emotions, successes, and failures. I never felt well in the summer term. The Thames Valley climate was lowering, I was enervated by the profusion of elms and buttercups and sheep-turds, the heat and the leisure. The summers at Eton were too pagan, one collapsed half-way through. Those hot afternoons punctuated by the "toc toc" of bat hitting ball when I sat with a book in the shade of Poets' walk, a green tunnel that has etiolated so many generations of poets, or wandered through the deserted college buildings, where the chalky sunbeam lay aslant the desk, were deleterious. Christmas terms meant consolidation and new beginnings; Easter was a season of promise; the games that I was good at were fives and squash; I liked the Easter terms best. Christmas was a primitive, Easter the quattrocento, and summer the decadence.

To this day I can tell whether a person is school-minded: whether they are cowardly, gregarious, sensitive to pupil-teacher relationships, warm, competitive and adolescent—or whether they are schoolproof. The art of getting on at school depends on a mixture of enthusiasm with moral cowardice and social sense. The enthusiasm is for personalities and gossip about them, for a schoolboy is a novelist too busy to write. Orwell, for example, with his "non serviam", or Steven Runciman who divided the world into two groups, the stupid and the sillies, lack the ape-like virtues without which no one can enjoy a public school. I possessed them, and from now on was happy and successful. I joined the College Literary Society for which we wrote poems, and criticism.

Two of my new friends in super-senior election belonged, Dadie Rylands and Terence Beddard, whom I called, as one was so much more censorious than the other, the Old and the New Testament. Dadie was a charming, feline boy; he lent me modern poetry to read in the Chap Books which were then coming out. He liked Rupert Brooke and introduced me to the Georgians. My possession of these Chap Books awoke in Highworth envy tinged with incomprehension. "My God, Cyril—if I'd known you were going to turn into a bloody æsthete and go bumsucking after people like Rylands! There's Godfrey turned pi as hell and all the rest of our election without any guts—and now you start letting your hair grow long and reading those bloody chapbooks. Rupert Brooke! Ow boo-hoo boo-hoo, stands the church clock at ten to bloody three and is there honey still for bloody tea!" After this I lost my temper and for the next year never spoke to him. Handsome and neat as ever, with several cricket colours and many Oppidan friends, he had hopes of getting into Pop, and yet was bewildered, isolated from the rest of us by his lack of adolescence.

One day I wrote a pines-and-heather poem myself for the Literary Society which was favourably criticised. The last couplet was:

> And, winging down the evening sky,
> The herons come to the heronry.

Dadie said that by accident I had written a couplet as good as anything in Rupert Brooke. Godfrey took me aside and said that he wished he could have written the poem, that it expressed everything he felt and that he did not know anyone else could feel. Even Terence Beddard, a dandy with a romantic side and a gift for satire, was impressed—but Highworth never saw it.

Terence and I did classics up to Mr. Headlam in the same division, we satirised Georgian poetry and the literary society in our spare time and invented a Georgian poet called Percy Beauregard Biles. Terence was a Byronic character, the first one I had met; he was a Mercutio, a foppish, melancholy and ironical dandy. I used to go along to talk in his room and we discovered a common interest in Nigel. By then I liked Freddie Langham almost as much; he was more engaging, intelligent, and whole-hearted than Nigel who could embarrass me by displaying a sentimentality which I shared. He was also inclined to grow weepy, and religious. We sometimes walked across School Yard at night and lay on our backs looking up at the buttresses of the chapel for it was a discovery of

mine that the height of the Gothic could be appreciated in that
way.

"I suppose we are the only people in College," said Nigel, "who
ever look at the stars. The others are all fools. We are the only
two who are humble."

By the next term Terence had left. He had had great influence
on me, bringing out a side—Don Juan with a touch of Wilde—
whose development made my life more interesting but also more
theatrical and egocentric. For years afterwards I wrote to him,
about "Le Rouge et Le Noir" as I called Freddie and Nigel. Nigel
sulked that term and grew more religious than ever. My friends
were Denis Dannreuther (the head of my senior election), Charles
Milligan and Freddie Langham; the Dark Friend, the Extreme
Blond and the Redhead were rallying.

Denis was an exquisite classical scholar, one of those rare people
who combine a brilliant and logical mind with genuine moral feeling and who become more than a careerist. We talked ethics and
College politics, for the political situation was fascinating. There
was party government in the struggle between pre-war and post-
war—between right and left. The armistice and the end of the war
had released a wave of scepticism and revolutionary feeling over
Eton where a book like *Eminent Victorians* made a particular sensation. The Left Wing or Liberals, as we called ourselves, in opposition to the Reactionaries, had a clear view of the situation.

(1) The war and the corresponding increase of militarism had
affected the freedom of Eton boys. Emergency measures had been
enforced and not repealed, lights went out earlier, discipline was
stricter and privileges had been given up in the crisis which had
never been restored. The tightening up of discipline involved a
cynical view of boy nature, which, especially in College, was to be
deplored. Those responsible were the ushers, among whom were
certain Vile Old Men who wished to wrest from the boys all liberty and independence and who were aided by our vacillating
Master, a sex-obsessed prude who extorted information about boys'
morals from hysterical confirmation candidates and practised other

jesuitical abuses. Behind him was that fine casuist the Headmaster
and of course the Old Tugs—old collegers who belonged to the
stoic pre-war generations, the pillars of the *ancien régime*.

(2) The corner-stone of this régime was the election system
which did not exist in the houses, was of quite recent origin, and
harmful in that it created a false authority, separating people who
ought to be mixing with each other, preventing a "bad" election
being improved by a "good" one and creating a sense of guilt in
those who had innocent relationships outside. The theory that the
election system prevented bullying was untrue, since bullying, like
immorality, was commonest among boys of the same age. The
election system therefore must be abolished from the top, and boys
be allowed to talk to whom they liked. In this daylight the danger
of immorality would be less than in the present atmosphere of
privilege and intrigue.

(3) Corporal punishment was a relic of barbarism. It was as
bad for those who administered as for those who received it. That
torture also must be abolished from the top while mass floggings
and generality beatings of the kind we had been subjected to were
inexcusable.

(4) The fagging system must be modified. The summoning of
boys from Chamber to distant parts of College, the last one to
arrive being sent off to Windsor for a walnut cake, made too great
inroads on their time and the knight-and-squire relationship between fagmaster and fag was sentimental.

(5) The privileges of College Pop or Debating Society were
invidious. There was too much canvassing and blackballing, the
elections made too many people unhappy.

(6) Games and colours were over important. Their influence
was exaggerated and must be fought. They should not be competitive or compulsory.

(7) The Corps was a joke; it had no business to be compulsory
and any tendency to increase militarism among a war-weary generation must be exposed and ridiculed.

(8) Boys must be appealed to through reason. They must be

given the benefit of the doubt; their fundamental goodness and good sense must be believed in, however contrary to appearances.

To this the reactionaries replied as they always have; that human nature could not be changed, give people an inch and they would take an ell, that "one must draw the line somewhere", that if games and discipline were relaxed orgies would break out, that corporal punishment was the only check on self-satisfaction and answered a bully in his own coin, that boys were conservative and hated giving up any of their hard-won privileges, that life was a Vale of Tears in which liberalism did not work.

At that time College Pop, unlike School Pop, still had debates and some of my senior election had been elected members of it. There had been two classic debates, on the "election system" and on corporal punishment that had almost ended in blows. The liberals at the bottom, Denis, King-Farlow, Roger Mynors, Bobbie Longden and Gibson had been supported by Miles Clausen and Christopher Hollis, the liberals at the top. The election in between that would shortly be coming into power was reactionary, except for Rylands and for one or two others who were non-political.

As the last liberals left the top of the school and my reactionary super-senior election came into office, the position of the liberals in senior election, and the few others, like myself, Charles Milligan, Le Strange, and Loxley grew unpleasant. Reprisals were due and our few protectors were leaving. Without Beddard and Rylands I had no friends among those coming into power and at the advanced age of seventeen I received a beating for "uppishness". Here are two letters of the time.

Easter, 1921.

MY DEAR TERENCE,

Home and Morbid. Since I wrote I have become clean gone on Nigel again. It's really too awful. I told you his attitude this half has been sulky with flashes of niceness—well, Monday I lectured him about it, and got out from him—A, the fact that he despised me. B, that his ideal was to be completely indifferent—this he kept up continually till on Thursday afternoon I got him alone in Lower Tea Room and discovered that "he was aiming at obtaining spiritual perfection, and that he regarded me as a distraction to be avoided, that I brought along other distractions (Loxley and Le Strange) and tried to talk about nothing with him and Langham."

All of which is true. I spent the last three days trying not to show him (Freddie) that I liked N. more (which I did since last Monday). N. told me that he thought it impossible to like everyone and that he wanted to cut down his acquaintances to a small but select circle and he did not want me to be one but he was afraid my personality was too strong. Well, I then had him on toast. I said that he must have a pretty rotten sort of perfection if it had to be guarded from plausible antichrists like me (that is his unexpressed idea of me), that he treated me like a muck-heap in the corner of his room which he shunned instead of trying to clear up—that he was running away from temptation instead of fighting it, that he was completely selfish, and instead of trying to make others better was only trying to safeguard himself—as for his beastly set, he, I suppose, believed in the parable of the good Shepherd? Yes he did—Well, which did the shepherd admire most, the 99 good sheep or the wandering one? He had to admit he would admire the 99 more. But which did he like most and take most steps over? Moreover who did he suppose liked the shepherd best, the 99 good sheep or the wandering one?

He had to give in and admit he was quite wrong and unchristian . . . I showed him that, temporarily at any rate, I preferred him to Langham. This morning I found him in Lower Tea Room and said goodbye, he asked me to write to him and seemed to have forgiven me. Now I can think of no-one else. Do you know the Greek epigram "delicate are the fosterlings of Tyre but Myiscus outshines them as the sun the stars"; it seems to me that suits him, there is a husky look about him which the name Myiscus brings out and his good looks are typical sun products, not rosy or effeminate. Langham is now very nice and attractive but relegated to second place, and now I am not glad at getting home but sorry at not seeing N. I am altogether rather fed with last half—I talked exclusively to a set consisting of Dannreuther, Minns, Milligan, Eastwood, Langham and N., with no one else have I talked anything but trivialities. I got on badly with N. and quarrelled with Highworth. However I got my first "stinker" [Distinction in Trials] the story of which I must tell you when I have more time.

I never dreamt I could go clean gone on the *same* person. Wish me luck in my new venture. I hope I can get him gone on me again but I dread lest I should then cool myself. N. despises you I think even more than me. χαῖρε.

Tuesday.

MY DEAR TERRY,

I wrote you two letters lately. Re N. I think it was being treated the right way set me gone on him again. What I like is a winning fight—well at first I got that, then nothing to fight for, then a losing one. Now I am straight again. It is not true to say the unattainable is the spice of life, it is attaining the unattainable. I never enjoy doing a thing until I have made sufficient difficulties—given that I am colossally conceited, I only realised it lately. Tuppa (Headlam) and Crace both saying I was v. able bucked me up enormously. I used to think I could never do more than obtain a superficial knowledge of a few things. Now I think there is *nothing* I cannot do, though very few things worth taking the trouble to (don't end sentences with prepositions).

You ask how life is? Chaos. I am in the state of mind of not being able to get at anything, the only thing that is true is that (*a*) *everything is true* (*b*) everything is false.

Tuppa's formula of Some People . . . Others . . . seems to be the only generality worthy of acceptance. I am house-hunting for a way of life, it is fun in a way but the agents do not know what I want and the houses that sound most attractive are hideous to look at close, others are beyond my income.

I wrote to N. and sent him my photo, with a lot of explanation of my present state, which seems to worry him. I said I thought I lived for the best form of happiness: learning to appreciate the first rate and know the sham, learning to look for beauty in everything, sampling every outlook and every interest (bar stinks and maths), trying to stop people being lukewarm and liking the second rate, trying to make other people happy, but not doing so at the cost of my own happiness, or concealing it when I am being generous. Publishing all the good I do. I suppose I am too cautious to risk investing in treasure in heaven. Roughly these are my ideals. I said how much more I liked him than I used to, and that he must treat me as a nice dog, not worship or despise, but sympathise. I said I really had no aim in life (by the way I am trying to analyse after doing anything my motives for doing it and so deduce what my outlook is—unwilling to accept my own introspective failure). I think the fact that one does things and cannot analyse motives or reconcile them to averred principles goes a long way to proving fatalism. I love extremes, either I would be a Catholic fatalist, or an atheist. (I did not say that to N. at the time.) I began "Dear Nigel" and signed my photo "Cyril". I got:

Dear Conolly, I feel very honoured that you (then in pencil) *consider me worthy of ink. You see that I don't think you are. I did not ask for the picture, but as you have sent it there remains no other course for me than to say "Thank you"* (you notice the improvement in style on the last letter!). *By the way I wish you would leave paragraphs in your so-called letters.*

I want you to understand that I consider your spiritual welfare a thing that it is my duty to improve. I will allow that I have felt a certain amount of pitying affection for you. I saw last half that you were a waste paper basket for wrong ideas and that something ought to be done for you. I should have tried to do this had I had a chance of seeing you alone and discussing. But you, quite blindly and utterly incapable of putting yourself in my position, always brought company with you and went into Langham's room, where your frivolity, barely keeping within the bounds of decency, was to me so utterly despicable and repulsive to my principles, that I was bound to adopt the attitude which you called a pose. If it hadn't been for Langham I might have quarrelled with you quite nastily—but of course you are not appreciating anything I say. Think of all the millions of times last half you came into MY stall ALONE.

If you come next half alone I shall not generally consider you a distraction, but you must be quite prepared to be sent away, and I want you to understand you are not going to come before either my work or my religion and I want you to realise that anything in the nature of company or popularity is quite repugnant to me. Langham is quite nice and sociable, but as yet I do not know much about him and am beginning to wonder if there is much beneath the surface. Be it far from me to worship you! You state that you have no aim in life as yet and are trying to find one, well why not take the plain one with

which you have been fed from your youth up. (A. Because it is plain.
B. Because I have been fed with it from my youth up.) *I.E. The
Christian One. You can form a pretty average good ideal from this I
should have thought. Of course you must know all about it and you
can do this by systematic bible reading. Form your principles on what
you read, and do everything on principle. Imagine your ideal, which
after all is set down in the N.T. You need not call it God, if you dislike
the word, but think of it and act on it always. If you like, take it as a
matter of interest. Think how frightfully dull your present aimless
life is* (is house-hunting dull?) *compared with what it might be. If
you have an aim in everything you do you will find you have an
extraordinary pleasure at every success achieved, renewed confidence,
and firmer principles. For instance I can assure you I gain real genuine
pleasure in turning you out of my stall when I want to talk to you,
but have some work to do. In your condition you are perfectly lonely
and whenever you are in trouble you have nothing to fall back on, no
one to help you, and you act on inspiration. When I am in trouble I
always know what to do through my principles. I consult with God
and so am acting definitely, and not in an aimless helpless way.*

*Try this, will you? Call it imagination at first if you like, but if you
are sincere you will soon be convinced that it is more than that.*

*You must see for yourself how thoroughly unsatisfactory your present
state is.*

Now I am sure you will laugh at me for all this.

N.

A wonderful letter for a boy of fifteen and I think he means it. I
wonder why he is so deliberately rude and impersonal. I don't think
his ideal is so very good, he says God is his principle while the
Christian idea of God is Love. His is more Petrine than Joannine Christianity. I think unless I can make him take an interest in poetry, painting, etc. he will become an awful Puritan. If he cares only about religion he will become narrow-minded too. I know he does despise all
popularity, but then he is good-looking enough to be able to. The
only respectable Christianity is Broad Church or R.C., and here we
have a modern P. father in embryo. Moreover he talks as if he will
drop Freddy as soon as he is sure there is nothing in him, though
Langham likes him best in the election. I want to make Langham

interesting and wrote to him telling him to go to the National Gallery before he answered. He has not answered but I think he is too young to enjoy writing letters.

I am becoming quite a Socrates in the lower half of college. I do want people to like talking religion and morals, to read good books, like poetry and pictures, and think for themselves. N. merely retires further into his shell as when he wouldn't answer my questionnaire for my religion chart. You see I think my ideals are superior to his. Of course they are founded on the assumption that there is no conscious immortality, that happiness is the mean between good and evil (in their usual sense) that the greatest happiness is to be found in novelty. I think self-sacrifice is the greatest happiness when you are at an age to appreciate it, at present it must be ostentatious and announced to everyone. I think in Art it is at first necessary to accept the decisions of others. I have to go before a picture and say "that is a great picture, I must learn to like it", till, aided by my own good taste, I do like it. I think my ideals have deteriorated. I used to think Perfection the aim of life, now I think it is Perfection in Happiness. Adversity is like a purge, it is good for you at the time and you are the more able to enjoy life when you have done with it, and it gives me a chance to demonstrate my atheism. I think I must try and be a stoic in adversity, and Epicurean in prosperity. Baudelaire says somewhere:

> From the crude ore of each minute
> Draw the pure gold that is in it.

Gangue is the word for "ore".

I would love to have tea with you at Rumpelmayer's when you come back on the 24th when I go to stay with Loxley in town. I am so hard up for a sufficiently debauched confidant that you must excuse these long rambling epistles. Biles has written a bawdy ballad in exile. It begins—

> O to be back at school again
> To gossip and laugh and swear—

I must go to bed now. A Riverderci.
PS.

> Is it so small a thing to have enjoyed the sun
> To have lived light in the spring

To have loved, to have thought, to have done,
To have advanced true friends, and beat down baffling foes?
That we must feign a bliss
Of doubtful future date
And in pursuit of this
Lose all our present state
And relegate to worlds yet distant our repose?

The summer of 1921 my life was once again changed by Nigel. At first we got on well. We agreed that I should introduce him to art while he would convert me to religion. But the relations between adolescents are variable, and Nigel, who had perhaps over-reached himself with religion, cared that summer only for cricket, and despised all who were not cricketers. One day we quarrelled. I said our friendship must be All or Nothing; he said, "Very well, I choose nothing", and I left his room. After a day I tried to make it up. "Nothing" was not having the effect I hoped for. Nigel was brutal and called me a dirty scug (boy without a colour). I left him in a hysterical mood and went and broke a chair in Upper Tea Room. Then I rushed to Freddie and Denis for sympathy. I was fond of Nigel and fond of myself, and he had injured both these idols.

The rest of the half I kept on making overtures to him which he rudely ignored. Sometimes I was rude too and used to seek him out in order to cut him. He would make loud personal remarks and kick Walter Le Strange if he was walking with me for he had now got a cricket colour and made Oppidan friends. The effect of this quarrel on me was threefold. I was unhappy and for the first time in my life rebuffed; the guardian angel who looked after my relationships had forsaken me. My one ambition was to get over my feeling for Nigel and avenge myself by making him regret having quarrelled with me. I wanted to become the most useful and desirable person in his world, indispensable to his vulgar ambitions which I would help him to gratify as contemptuously as Lord Steyne assisted Becky Sharp to a new necklace. In my day-dreams I acquired all the colours under the sun. I put him up for Pop.

The three results were that I became more social, that I worked harder, that I grew sceptical and pessimistic about the world. I was determined that Nigel must see me only with people he would himself like to know. I hugged closer to Denis and to King-Farlow, who was my fellow history specialist. He was robust, tough, cynical, good at games, energetic, and vulgar. We were both absorbed in Renaissance history and translated everything we learnt into our own lives; after reading Machiavelli I practised Machiavellianism, drawing up analyses of whom I should sit next, whom make friends with; of how to separate So-and-so, how to win over somebody else. Every man had a price. It was necessary to discover his ruling passion and play on it. The test of action was whether it led to one's own advantage, i.e. was justified by political necessity. One must learn to keep "one's thoughts secret in an open face".

Thus all college must be cultivated for I could never tell who might prove an asset in the humiliation of Nigel—that humiliation which was to consist in giving him the things he valued and which I despised and in being the only person who could give them him. He now went around with my enemy Highworth. They talked invariably of cricket and cast black looks in my direction so I made friends with Highworth again. Machiavelli would have approved. Highworth, outwardly successful, was still bewildered, and oppressed, I discovered, by the thought of the Vale or official leaving poem he would be expected to write at the end of the term and to which his attitude to poetry could scarcely contribute. I offered to compose it for him. I tried to make Nigel jealous by cultivating Freddie Langham whom I liked more and more; I could not make friends with cricketers as College did not possess any but I made up to our rowing men, two of whom were in the Eight. Farlow also had some rowing and football colours, and I felt less of a scug as I swaggered with him past Nigel's room.

It was the fashion to have photographs of our friends signed

and installed on the mantelpiece. I had sent Nigel mine. He refused to give me his. I took one and he said that I had stolen it.
I collected photos after that like an old hostess collecting celebri-
ties. I cultivated anyone who was a rarity or who had not been
taken, persuading them to get done for me and rushing off with
the new scalp. Machiavelli functioned. I found I could charm
people merely by asking them questions, and seeming interested
in them, and at the end of the term I was elected to College Pop.

The election had been stormy and it was through my friendship
with the rowing men that I got in for had I been put up by any
of the liberals I would certainly have been blackballed. The
political situation was now acute. Super-senior election were in
power and beatings were frequent. To our indignation they beat
Orwell for being late for prayers then another member of senior
election whom they considered uppish finally and on the most
flimsy pretexts, Whittome and myself. Orwell and Whittome were
boys of eighteen; they were just outside Sixth Form, and were
beaten by boys of the same age in their own senior election, as
if they were fags.

The feeling ran so high against the Captain of the School, the
odious Cliffe, and the six other reactionaries in his election that they
were cut to a man. Denis's speeches at college Pop debates were
reinforced by the contempt of Mynors, the intransigence of Farlow,
the indignation of Cazalet and Gibson. At the end of the term it
was customary to pass votes of thanks on those who were leaving
from College Pop, on the President Treasurer and Secretary, the
Keepers of College Wall and Field. For the first time in history
these votes of thanks were blackballed. The genial ceremony collapsed; Cliffe the Captain of the School, Lea the Cadet officer of
the Corps, Babington-Smith and the boys who beat Farlow and
Orwell and Whittome on trumped-up charges for political reasons
faced the unprecedented verdict. Name after name was read out,
the vote of thanks proposed and seconded, the ballet box passed,
the blackballs counted, and the transaction noted down in the
annals. At Farlow's "leaving tea" a day or two afterwards a lam-

poem of mine which drew attention to the idiosyncrasies of the seven blackballed reactionaries was sung with rapture. The Master in College protested against the breach of tradition, the Old Tugs got to hear of it, the Vile Old Men took it up, and there were whispers about Bolshevism which almost reached the newspapers. Meanwhile I had succumbed to the disease of scepticism. My health was excellent but I could not get rid of ideas of mortality, futility, and death. What was the use of existence? Why did one do anything? All was vanity. Stupidity governed the world and human life was a blot on creation. I searched the classics for confirmation of my scepticism and found an overwhelming support. Job and Ecclesiastes and the author of the Wisdom of Solomon agreed with me; the Greek lyric poets and philosophers proclaimed it, Horace confirmed them as did Voltaire and Gibbon and Villon and Verlaine. I wrote a paper on Pessimism for the Essay Society. Only two kinds of thought existed, a pessimism which anticipated better things (Christianity) and my own—which did not. But if one believed this then one should kill oneself, which, of course, I was not prepared to do. Why not? Because of the consolations of friendship and learning, because suicide played into the hands of the Jealous God. One lived on to spite him.

For years I throve on this black doctrine for although it originated with me owing to a rebuff from Nigel and a Thames Valley summer more virulent than usual, it happened that I had caught the fashionable malady of the period. Futility was the rage. With Farlow I concocted a play which was to expose history. We had been set a "work of the imagination" to show to housemaster and history tutor, and we collaborated on a revue about the Renaissance, interspersed with songs and satirical sketches which showed knowledge and reading, vast cynicism and an unsuspected talent for horseplay. The Popes, the Emperors, the Medici, the Doges, the Kings of France and England, the Constable of Bourbon, Calvin, Luther, Zwingli and Savonarola, the King of Spain, the Borgias, Leonardo and Michelangelo were treated to the same knock-about. It was the first creation of my new-born scepticism and the most important. Nobody liked it but ourselves, least of all our tutors, who refused to sign it, Mr. Gow making only the ambiguous comment "perveni ad umbilicum" and I had instead to write a little purple essay "On a Crucifixion attributed to Antonello da Messina". But in the Specialists examination called the "Grand July" I did well and came out eleventh in the whole school. My gloom was not proof against this although my philosophy withstood it. What did it matter, eleventh or eleven hundredth? Was death deferred a day? Would anyone care in a hundred years? *Cui bono?* "Can I forget Myiscus, who is in all beautiful things?"

> Now years three and "halves" ten
> Have hastened by and flown
> And soon there will be other men
> But I shall be forgotten then
> My very name unknown.
> And no more careless evening hours
> Of slippered armchair ease
> No glimpse of tea things in the towers,
> No cans, no steam, no shouts from showers,
> No shorts, nor mudded knees.

as I made Highworth protest, echoing Mimnermus, in his commissioned Vale. At Camp that year my depression was entire, Nigel was not there nor Freddie nor Denis; I was glad to be able to get away on a motor-bicycle and drink a glass of port with one of my rowing friends at Ludgershall. I could only bear to talk to Jackie O'Dwyer; like some mad monarch with his favorite; even Farlow, in whose tent I was, lost patience with me, for like many Etonians, although cynical, he detested inefficiency. Nothing was worth doing but it was not worth doing badly. We argued till he used to yell, "Here, Private Connolly, you who appreciate the beauty of our English hedgerows, you who claim that pleasure and pain are the same thing, go and empty this bucket." I kept a volume of Gibbon in my uniform and read it when I could. My other bible was La Rochefoucauld whom I remember reading when the victorious Eight came back drunk from Henley. I found his opinions most reasonable for I was one to whom the existence of good seemed already more mysterious than the problem of evil. In an old French exercise book of mine during this summer Walter Le Strange, my Anglo-Irish æsthetic friend in Junior Election was keeping a diary, a valuable contemporary document.

June 9th. *In the afternoon repaired with Satyr and Apollo to the Stoa.*[1] *Pride was leading forth his chorus of Athleticism's devotees. "Ora pro nobis," he cried. "No anglo-catholicism" thought Man. Satyr fed him on strawberries while he read* Wuthering Heights, *and, that finished,* The Newcomes. *Discussions on Socialism and Tyrannus followed. Yesterday Man and Calm and Conservation and Calculus discussed Slavery and Fagging. Both are utterly foul. Everybody here seems to think*

(a) *White men are better than others.*

(b) *England is everything.*

(c) *a "gentleman" is the thing. Also all or mostly all worship Athleticism.*

Cynicus and Man listened to a revue—"The Renaissance"—by Apollo and Cato, Apollo good, especially the lyrics, Cato inclined to drag but his horseplay satire superb. The conversation in Hall turned on the peerage. How ignorant they all are, even Pride.

June 11th.

> *Barnaby bright*
> *Barnaby bright*
> *The longest day*
> *And the shortest night.*

A bright day indeed. The trees along the field and by Jordan looked splendid from the Stoa where I lay throughout the afternoon, near the Ball Alleys. Apollo was on my right. He too knows my loved acacia and has apostrophised it, he says, in verse. I am glad I did not try Shaw before. I am just in the state to understand him. Two years ago the

---

[1] The Stoa was the group of lookers-on at College cricket. They read and talked under the elms, which constituted "taking exercise." Pride is a boy called John Carter who leads his side out to field. I am Apollo, Man is the author, Tyrannus the Master in College, Satyr Clutton-Brock, Cato Farlow, Rome Gibson, and Cynicus Orwell.

preface to Androcles would have shocked me and upset me. A year ago I should have fallen too easy a prey to it. To-day I rejoice. Shaw wants just what I want. An equalising philosophy of life—politically and intellectually, morally, and socially a panacea, in fact an elixir. Stevenson's Velasquez is very interesting. I looked at the Prado reproductions with Apollo again to-day. How ravissant is Mercury and Argus. An English hamlet may be pretty, the country here—take Chamber Field overstrewn with buttercups and clover, or Fellows Eyot with its poplars—is beautiful. But O, for the Wicklow hills. I never realised till now the true glory of the sugar loaf—of Gilt Spear's top, or of the heights between Glencullen and the Scalp.

Evening full of the linnet's wings.

Sunday. *Tea with the Alabasters. Then talk turned on the* Beggar's Opera, *which I have not seen. Apollo—with whom I walked in the evening—talked of introspection and confidences. Is introspection a good thing? I think it is. Why, I wonder, does one always feel a superiority to others? Not always, but frequently at least. Apollo, I fear, does it too much. Yet I like him.*

June 13th. *Apollo, Beatrice d'Este, Rome* [1] *and I argued most of the afternoon about religion. Very interesting. The result: "Man must worship something by an inborn instinct." Surely he can drive this instinct out of him. Later on Satyr, Beatrice d'Este, Scaife and I gossiped with Rome. The conversation turning on Pride, Scaife gave demonstrations of his foul ways and words, whereupon Tyrannus entered and in his hypocritical friendly way adjured Rome to cease. Rome with much coldness, though quite politely, dismissed him, and we continued our conversation. This evening, however, Greedy-for-Power* (Lea) *"wanted" Rome and Scaife, accused the one of filthy talk and the other of encouraging it. Rome told the story of how it happened. He was dismissed. But—and I burn to think of it—Scaife was whipt— whipt like a mere slave—that is, an oppressed fag, or lower boy, by that unutterable brute, Greedy-for-Power, for a sin of which Rome had proved him guiltless. O may all tyranny perish. May everyone be free! Let not the wretched new boy be oppressed and mishandled just for*

[1] Beatrice d'Este = Raymond Coghlan.
Rome = Gibson, who was a Catholic.
Scaife = "Cully" Cox.

the convenience of the idle Capitalists, that is to say, the self-made priests of Athleticism, of the Public School Spirit of Imperialism.

June 27th. *Peter (Loxley) came back to-night. Full of racing and tennis. I wish sometimes I could interest myself in such things. Of course not worship them. I have been reading the Loom of Youth. It is all so true in its way. Everything seems melancholy. Is life worth living? Where can one get help? One cannot paint for ever, it only makes you into that æsthete, loose tie, velvet coat sort of thing. Poetry makes you excited, or else sadder. O to do something! But how can a Nobody do anything worth while? Help is from within. Perhaps if one saw everybody as good. It is so hard—but it is beautiful. Therefore it is meet and right to do. "Les sanglots longs"—but they do it always. "I will arise and go now, and go to Innisfree . . ." O if only I could quit this place, with its society, its "gentlemen", its absurd church. Where is a true religion? O for peace. Even this journal is hypocritical.*

July 2nd. *There is only one God here. Athleticism and his law is "Believe—or Be Cast out." Even now I hear the shouts and cheers, as of barbarism. Baths are banged. Boys shout. Such a display of rowdyism I have seldom heard. The Mob! The Howling of an Angry Mob. Awful. But a joyful mob is worse. The Eight have won the Ladies' Plate at Henley. Three of them are in College—"jolly boating weather —we'll cheer for the best of schools". It seems sad to think that a great crowd of boys—of cultured boys—should pour out their spirits thus. O Athleticism! Athleticism! The din is now outside my door. Horror! Horror! Baths are banged and banged—cheers—cheers. So help me!*

The noise has been quelled. It is sad that N. (Nigel) should have been so completely corrupted by athleticism. We were quite friendly once. But now he is so devilish superior. And rude, too. What have I done? I despise Athleticism—but not Athletics, yet I have never said he should not worship it just because I am interested in the things that really matter. Need he be so really uncivil?

July 3rd. *A boiling Sunday. The heat was most oppressive. I talked chiefly to Cyril, Peter and Farlow. These questions of fagging and of College Politics are very interesting. So is reading the Greek gospel. Belief seems to be based on such slender grounds. It is extraordinary how unchristian are the lives of all those boys who "profess and call themselves Christians" Carter, Maud, N. But there is an awful danger for us too. One is so inclined to become a Pharisee—an utter prig. The milder forms of this athleticism are not harmful for the young. They do no lasting good. But they tend to present happiness. But everyone seems to imagine that athletics mean success. Get a cricket colour and you are made for life. Half a dozen people come up to you. "I say, isn't it good for College having two Sixpennies." What could be more ridiculous? No one seems to take any interest in the fact that a Colleger has bought a Dürer, or that the Hervey English Verse Prize was won by a Colleger in C.*

Carter's ignorance showed itself again yesterday. "Why Lord John Russell and not Lord Russell?" he asked. But I mustn't be a snob. The Hermit (Martineau)—it appears from a conversation of this evening—is an ultra-reactionary. He disapproves of boys in B playing ping-pong in Sixth Form Passage.

Last Sunday Farlow gave a tea-party in Lower Tea Room, after which the party sang songs, including a topical one by Cyril. All very pleasant, but Carter made himself somewhat objectionable to his host. On the Friday evening there had been the usual College Pop election. Cyril got in. Peter was put up three times and blackballed, I ditto twice, Carter was put up and got seven (five excludes). All this gave us much subject for conceited conversation. Peter seemed rather sad not to have got in. I was also sorry for myself. Our conceit grew vehemently. On Monday, to the general consternation of many, Carter was awarded his College Cricket. This means he will be second keeper next summer, and so in a position to make even more of himself than at present.

.   .   .   .

That summer I went abroad for the first time. My father took me to Paris and the Belgian coast. We stayed off the Rue de Rivoli and ate in restaurants with purple menus, screened from the pavement by tubs of sooty privet. I did not care for Paris, I was frightened there, it was too hot and I thought people's feet smelt, I liked only the Louvre where I felt at home, Notre Dame and Versailles which, as I wrote at the time, "suited my mood". "French revues are funnier than English," I wrote to O'Dwyer, "but after eight o'clock this town is as full of whores as camp was of wasps"—then I reverted to the interminable College politics. Carter, Nigel's great friend, in my junior election disliked me and my two cronies there, Loxley and Le Strange. There was a chance of him getting into College Pop. It was against my principles to blackball anyone yet somehow five people had to be found who would; Cazalet and Farlow, alas, had left—"You have to remember, my boy," I enjoined O'Dwyer, "that nowadays you are Cazalet, and I am Farlow."

One event in Paris upset me. On a sultry evening as I was walking back to my hotel after dinner, I was accosted outside the Café de la Paix by a pimp with a straw hat and an umbrella. He offered to take me to a music-hall. I was too nervous to refuse and he then informed me it would be "rather a rough kind of place, you understand". I was now too frightened and excited to turn back and he took me to a brothel in the Rue Colbert. I was overcome with guilt and apprehension as I sat with the pimp in the little gilded *salon* while he spoke to the Madame. The mechanical piano played, at last the girls filed in and I was asked to choose two of them. Voiceless I pointed with a trembling finger. They stayed behind and a bottle of champagne appeared. We all had a glass and then another bottle. Drink made no impression, I was paralysed with fear, partly of being hit on the head and waking up in Buenos Aires, partly of saying the wrong thing. Then it was suggested that I should go upstairs with the two ladies. It was then a new panic arose. How much was all this? In a shrunken voice I asked for the bill. *"Quoi. Déjà?" "Oui, oui, oui. Toute suite."* I explained to Madame that I did not know if I would have enough money to pay. She was astounded. "But I thought Monsieur was a gentleman!" When the bill arrived it was for almost ten pounds, mostly for champagne and with a bonus of course for the pimp. I explained that I could not pay at once, that the ladies must leave immediately, that I would give her all the money I had (about four pounds), and find the rest within the week. I gave her my card, on which I had written the address of my hotel. My father was waiting up for me and I told him I had lost my way.

The rest of my time in Paris was spent in anguish. At any moment I expected to see Madame and the pimp arrive to ask for me. Meals in the hotel were a torture which I could not bear for I would be sure to see the pimp with his umbrella or Madame with my visiting card directed to our table by the concierge. No time of day was safe. I wrote to my grandmother who, I knew, was giving me five pounds for my birthday and asked her to send it to Paris in advance as the shops were better there than they would be in Belgium and I wanted to buy some presents for my friends. It seemed as if her letter would never arrive; my worst moment was in the Musée de Cluny, beside the iron crown of Receswinth. I went out and sat in a cold sweat on a bench in the garden.

Next day the money arrived and I rushed round to the brothel. It was eleven o'clock in the morning; no one remembered me, another Madame was on duty and listened in bewilderment while I explained, stuffing money into her hand, and wondering if it would seem impertinent to ask for my card back. At last I was safe. I bought Charles Milligan, Denis, and Freddie a few cheap presents and shortly afterwards attained my eighteenth birthday, still without having kissed anyone. The Belgian coast was a relief after this nightmare, and Bruges, with its brackish canals and Flemish primitives, like Versailles, "suited my mood", for I would try no more conclusions with the Present.

Boys do not grow up gradually. They move forward in spurts like the hands of clocks in railway stations. Most of those in College advanced in this wise though in many the sap of youth ran down after their efforts. In my own case the autumn of 1921 and spring of 1922 were a high renaissance. They were not the happiest days of my life but I was as happy then as I was able to be.

I started the new term as "a bit of a chap". I was in a "mess", that is to say I took tea in Charles Milligan's room with him and Minns and a fag to look after us, instead of having it in Tea-room. This was an advance in civilisation as one had privacy and could have masters to tea and get on better terms with them. I was also in College Pop and got my "shorts" for football, whereupon Nigel spoke to me again. We were delighted to be friends, my scepticism was now permanent but I had accepted the vanity of life and the worthlessness of human nature so fundamentally that I no longer felt bitter or with a grievance against society. "Our mess has china tea—down by the streamside" I used to sing, and we gave exclusive tea-parties. Denis was in Sixth Form. All the election above him had now left except the youngest member, who was Captain of the School, a clerical reactionary held in check by Denis, Mynors, Gibson and Longden.

CHAPTER XXII

THE BACKGROUND OF THE LILIES

SO FAR IT WOULD APPEAR THAT WORK PLAYED A SMALL PART IN
our lives; this was not so, however for the first two years most boys
did not enjoy their work and found it a tedious drudgery. It was not
smart at Eton to work; to be a "sap" was a disgrace and to compete
for prizes eccentric. Everybody used cribs though the punishments
for being caught were severe. For boys at Eton wanted one thing,
popularity and the flaw in the Eton education was that work was unpopular. Indeed for twenty years I was never to grasp that the love
and friendship which I sought were in this world the rewards not of
seeking them but of hard work and success.

It is hard to see how such conditions arise. They are prevalent
in most schools although boys are more bored and more unhappy
than ever when they do not work. Even in College, among the seventy
scholars, "sapping" was discredited and we were infected by the
fashion from without, behind which lay the English distrust of the
intellect and prejudice in favour of the amateur. A child in Ireland,
a boy at St. Wulfric's, a scholar at Eton, I had learnt the same lesson.
To be "highbrow" was to be different, to be set apart and so excluded from the ruling class of which one was either a potential
enemy or a potential servant. Intelligence was a deformity which
must be concealed; a public school taught one to conceal it as a
good tailor hides a paunch or a hump. As opposed to ability, it was
a handicap in life.

At Eton this was emphasised by the stigma attaching to Collegers which although an economic prejudice found expression as an anti-intellectual one and of which a ridiculous aspect was the contempt in which boys held masters, a relic of the eighteenth century when boys brought their own tutors to Eton and treated them, as the term "usher" still indicated, little better than their servants. In this direction the feeling was strong; masters who were old Etonians, who were rich like John Christie or well-born like Georgie Lyttelton escaped but in general the boys assumed that most of the staff had never held a gun or worn a tailcoat, that they were racked by snobbery, by the desire to be asked to stay with important parents or to be condescended to by popular boys. An Eton division consisted of thirty boys, five of whom wished to learn something, ten of whom wished to do what everybody else wanted and fifteen of whom spent their time searching for the usher's weak points and then exploiting them with the patience of prisoners of war tunnelling out of a camp. What Proust called the *"lâcheté des gens du monde"* was never so apparent as at Eton, where the life of a teacher like Aldous Huxley was made intolerable because of his defective sight.

The teachers in the middle parts of the school devoted themselves to cramming and keeping order; inspired teaching, owing to the intransigence of the boys, could appear only at the top, where there were five real teachers: the Headmaster, Mr. C. M. Wells, Mr. G. W. Headlam, Mr. G. H. K. Marten, and Mr. Hugh Macnaghten. They are worth considering.

At Eton, as at other schools, there existed the ordinary education for the average boy but there grew up as well an inner culture, the eleusinian mysteries of learning, to which favoured boys were admitted and which was maintained by teachers such as these and by a few important outside figures, the Provost, Mr. Luxmoore, Mr. Broadbent; the pure eighteenth-century Etonian tradition of classical humanism, which could be learnt nowhere else. Most of the boys went through the school without knowing of its existence, without having heard of esoteric figures like William Johnson Cory or Mrs. Warre-Cornish, Howard Sturgis or Austen Leigh, but by 1921 (the year for me when "modern history" begins), I was being initiated; I would dine with the Provost and the Headmaster, or Mr. Headlam and Mr. Marten would come to tea.

The first of the big five a Colleger came up to, when about sixteen, was Hugh Macnaghten. Although a fine teacher, his learning possessed the faults or rather the literary vices of his time. He was an ogre for the purple patch, the jewel five words long, the allusion, the quotation, the moment of ecstasy. In fact he was embedded in the Milton-Keats-Tennysonian culture, that profuse and blooming romanticism of the "bowery loneliness",

> The brooks of Eden mazily murmuring
> And gloom profuse and cedar arches

which had dominated English literature until the death of Flecker and Rupert Brooke.

The Eton variety was diluted with Pre-Raphaelitism. Watts' "Sir Galahad" hung in College Chapel, Burne-Jones and William Morris had been Eton figures, and Mr. Luxmoore painted fastidious water colours of his riverside garden in which the fair Rosamund would not have disdained to take her medicine. He was a disciple of Ruskin, the forgotten man of the nineteenth century.

Another field for the Pre-Raphaelite influence was in translating. Homer and Virgil were the pillars of an Eton education; it would be hard to derive more pleasure then or now than we obtain from reading them. But we read them with the help of two officials cribs, Butcher and Lang for Homer, Mackail for Virgil. Lang believed that Homer must be translated into the nearest English equivalent which was an Anglo-Saxon prose reminiscent of the Sagas. He tried to manage on a Bronze-Age vocabulary, and the Mediterranean clarity of the *Odyssey* was blurred by a Wardour Street Nordic fog. Homer, in short, was slightly Wagnerised. Mackail, who had married Burne-Jones' daughter, gave to his Virgil an eightyish air, the *lacrimæ rerum* spilled over and his Christian attitude to paganism, that it was consciously pathetic and incomplete, like an animal that wishes it could talk, infected everything which he translated with a morbid distress. Dido became a bull-throated *Mater Dolorosa* by Rossetti. His translations from the *Greek Anthology*, one of the sacred books of the inner culture, the very soil of the Eton lilies, were even more deleterious. They exhaled pessimism and despair, an overripe perfection in which it was always the late afternoon or the last stormy sunset of the ancient world, in which the authentic gloom of Palladas was outdone by that attributed to Simonides, Callimachus or Plato. Meleager was the typical Pre-Raphaelite lover.

To put it in another way, a sensitive Etonian with a knowledge of Homer and Virgil through these translations and a good ear, would be unable to detect in poems like *Tithonus, Ulysses* or the *Lotus Eaters* any note foreign to the work of Homer and Virgil. If he had been told that "a spirit haunts the year's last hours" was a word for word translation of Virgil, he would have accepted the fact. The two classics had been "romanticised" for him, impregnated with the cult of strangeness, of the particular rather than the general and of the conception of beauty characteristic of the Æsthetic Movement as something akin to disease and evil.

Macnaghten accentuated this. He told us that the most beautiful word in the English language was "little", he liquidated his "r's" in reciting and intoned poetry in a special way . . .

> and hear the bweeze
> Sobbing in ver little twees.

Jolly good! He would exclaim, and to hear him chant "Ah, poor Faun—ah, poor Faun" was a study in pity which made his severe and even harsh discipline appear the more surprising.

The other object of this inner cult was Plato. His humour and sophistry were the delight of those who expounded them to the bewilderment of those who listened. His theory of ideas and essences, his conception of body and spirit, the romantic dualism on which he insisted formed the ruling philosophy. Platonism was everywhere, popping up in sermons and Sunday questions, in allusions to Neoplatonism, in essays by Dean Inge, at the head-master's dinner-parties or in my tutor's pupil-room. Socrates roamed through the classes like a Government inspector and even Virgil and Tennyson withdrew before him. But it will be re-membered that Plato himself, in the Republic, turned against the poets and advocated censorship and discipline. This contradiction extended through our school-life and emerged in its attitude to sex.

For there was no doubt that homosexuality formed an ingredient in this ancient wisdom. It was the forbidden tree round which our little Eden dizzily revolved. In a teaching conscious and somewhat decadently conscious of visual beauty, its presence in the classics was taken for granted; it was implicit in Plato's humour and æsthetic. Yet Eton, like all public schools, had no solution for sex. If boys had such intercourse between the ages of fourteen and eighteen, no matter with whom or with what, they had better go. The School could do nothing for them. "Created sick, commanded to be sound", the majority floundered through on surreptitious ex-periments and dirty jokes but there were always a number who, going further, were found out and expelled.

The extent to which sex-life is necessary and should be per-mitted to growing boys remains uncertain. The Eton attitude was in line with that of other authorities and with the wishes of most parents, for the dilemma is inherent in all education, lurking in the playing-fields and vinegar-scented cloisters of our seats of learn-ing as, in the preaching of the careful Pater, beckon the practices of Wilde.

The result was that boys learnt to walk a tightrope; the senti-mental friendship was permitted in some houses and forbidden in others, allowed to some boys and denied to their fellows or per-mitted and then suppressed according to the changing views and vigilance of the housemaster. No one could be sure on what ground they trod. There was Macnaghten who, spartan in body as he was soft in mind, would give an annual and long-anticipated lecture attacking those friendships at a point in Plato's *Euthyphro;* at the same time we were made to put into Latin verses a sentimental poem addressed by Dolben to the then Captain of the Eleven. One thing was certain; the potentially homosexual boy was the one who benefited, whose love of beauty was stimulated, whose appreciation was widened and whose critical powers were developed; the normal boy, free from adolescent fevers, missed both the perils and the prizes; he was apt to find himself left out.

There is much celibacy in public schools and, where many housemasters are not married, it is possible to say that their teaching will encourage continence officially and homosexuality by implication, sending up to the universities, from whence they will immediately rebound as masters, that repressed and familiar type, the English male virgin.

Another effect of Macnaghten's teaching was to associate English literature with Latin verses. We came to think of poetry in terms of tags and useful epithets, and to consider the best poetry as being in the form of the sonnet or sixteen-line lyric. Macnaghten would not treat Latin verses as a cross-word puzzle; he insisted that we put feeling into them, that we exercised our dreams of literary composition through the medium of another language. In his taste he was a true escapist; everything he admired reeked of the death-wish, port after stormy seas, holy quiet and romantic fatigue. No one who did his verses well could write poetry afterwards. There would be one slim Eton-blue volume with a few translations a *Vale,* and a couple of epigrams, then silence. For the culture of the lilies, rooted in the past, divorced from reality and dependent on a dead foreign tongue, was by nature sterile.

It may be wondered why I call Macnaghten a good teacher. The reason is that although he concentrated on moments of beauty, he did not neglect the encircling drudgery, and because, although his taste was uncertain, he would permit no blasphemy. To laugh at anything he thought good meant punishment. He chastened the hooligans (even Highworth could but mumble) and he insisted on the modesty, the abnegation without which great art cannot be appreciated. "Up" to him boys for the first time had the experience of literature and every now and then, in the dusty classroom, grew aware of the presence of a god.

Wells taught the classical specialists; he was a fine cricketer and a judge of claret, a man of taste with a humour of understatement in the Cambridge style. The Headmaster was theatrical, he liked knotty points and great issues, puns and dramatic gestures. He was a worldly teacher, a Ciceronian, an All Souls Fellow and we felt we were learning Divinity from a Prince of the Church. He was fond of paradoxes and we learnt to turn out a bright essay on such a subject as "Nothing succeeds like failure" or "Nothing fails like success". The exaggeration of his teaching was repugnant to the classical specialists and such was the moral weight of William Egerton, Denis, or Roger Mynors, that he became a naughty boy "showing off" in their presence although his entry into any other class-room would petrify us with fear.

His was the cult of that light verse which had always been the official poetry for despite Gray, Shelley, Swinburne and Bridges, the kind of poetry which Eton took to its heart was either the sentimental lyric, the translation (of which Cory's *Heraclitus* is the example) or the facetious. Praed, Clough, Calverley, W. S. Gilbert and the sacred J. K. Stephen were the official bards and if the Headmaster had had to include a living writer he would have added Father Ronald Knox.

Thus, although the *Eton College Chronicle* made an appeal to premature essayists and the fourth leader of *The Times* was within the grasp of its editors, critical or creative writing there was none. Humorous "Ephemerals" had a sale but in spite of tradition, and the encouragement given to them, the Arts at Eton were under a blight. Figures of the post-war world such as Aldous Huxley, and Maynard Keynes had been in College, but.we would never have known it. They were not recognised, they did not wear like Maurice Baring, Arthur Benson, Percy Lubbock or J. K. Stephen, a halo in the pale-blue canon.

Into this world the history teachers introduced a note of realism. Marten was a model of clarity and enthusiasm; he was the sanest of schoolmasters but for that reason had less influence on us than a teacher like Headlam who did not aspire to be impartial.

If the Headmaster epitomised All Souls, Headlam was typical of Balliol but it was not Balliol that made him impressive, so much as the fact that in his class-room there was at last evidence of a Pre-Ruskinian culture, of the eighteenth century. His favourite writer was Horace, the book he gave to us on leaving was *Boswell's Life of Johnson*. To us he was an enigmatic figure, he seemed to go some of the way towards futility and yet while our conclusions from the axiom All is Vanity were "nothing is worth while, except art", "except friendship", "except pleasure", or "except wisdom", his seemed to be "except success—except doing a job efficiently". He appeared cynical but that may have been only because he was un-Tennysonian. Although irritable in the early morning he was more tolerant than other masters; his tolerance at times seemed apathy, a product of disillusion, yet he hated idleness, dishonesty and that frivolous complacency to which growing boys are addicted. He brought common sense and reasonable worldly values into his relations with boys with the result that his house was the best at Eton and, as he surveyed the row of Pops in it with affected vagueness, he must have enjoyed the bewilderment of other housemasters.

All the history specialists imitated him, his affectations of saying "Erse" instead of "Yes" and "Toosda" for Tuesday, his apparent lack of interest in games and exercise (although he was a good fives player and his house held the football cup), his attitude of *nil admirari*. He was a Tory in politics, where again he seemed to stand for tolerance, efficiency and a hatred of fuss. "You must learn that there is no justice in this world," he was fond of saying, perhaps setting the wrong boy a punishment to illustrate it and "You must always remember that nobody is indispensable," was another of his maxims.

Was he a Balliol careerist, with the affectation of laziness and indifference that was considered the Balliol manner and by which we were taken in or a split-man in whom an efficient and ambitious self was being watched by a cynical spectator? Or was he an evocation of the eighteenth-century Tory or of ancient Rome? In appearance he was dark, handsome and rather fat, not unlike the Roman poet whom he interpreted; his expression was blasé and judicial, his voice and smile were charming, his eyes, sombre in repose, when angry, kindled into fire.

All masters lost their tempers; there were some whose rages were comic spectacles, others who became maniacs, fascinating to watch but dangerous if one got in the way; with the Headmaster or Macnaghten there was a sensation of panic owing to the severity of the penalties which they could enforce, but with Marten and Headlam alone did one get a feeling of shame; they were teachers whose rebukes of one boy enlisted against him the sympathy of the class, and "To do poorly" up to Headlam, or be "tiresome" with Marten, was distressing for at last we were attaining a level where it was not impermissible to work.

In the æstheticism which was gathering round me, part backwash of the nineties, part consequence of my Celtic romanticism being worked upon by the Pre-Raphaelite background of the Eton lilies, Headlam's sober intellectual energy, his Roman values, offered a gleam of mental health. But, to an æsthete, what appealed in Headlam was his irony, his way of making a reference to authority sound ridiculous (due, one suspected, to an antipathy to the Headmaster which was pronounced among the senior old Etonian housemasters) and to his fondness for what he called gestures—"That would be a good gesture—the Massacre of St. Bartholomew was a bad gesture." The good gesture, the noisy piece of self-sacrifice, was one of the few lines of conduct sanctioned by my futilitarianism. It must be like Sidney Carton's, magnanimous, public, and useless.

By the time I had left Eton I knew by heart something of the literature of five civilisations. It was a lopsided knowledge since we were not taught literature and since the only literature which appealed to me was pessimistic but it is worth analysing, since, although many of the books had been read for hundreds of years and others seemed my own discoveries, taken together, they give a picture of fashionable reading-matter just after the last war.

I was fond of the Old Testament, disliked the New. My favourite books were Ecclesiastes and the Wisdom of Solomon in which I recognised the melancholy and tired distinction of an old race, the mysterious Ezekiel and that earthy mystic, the first Isaiah. Job was too much thrust upon me and the Lamentations of Jeremiah I found in faulty taste. All these I read with more pleasure in the sonorous Latin of the Vulgate. They were among the books I lived in through the winter evenings.

In Greek literature I had read the *Odyssey* with passion, but not the *Iliad*, I admired Æschylus, particularly the *Agamemnon*, and Sophocles, particularly *Œdipus Rex*; Euripides and Aristophanes I disliked, and Plato, except his epigrams and the *Symposium*. I enjoyed the lyric poets, Sappho and Archilochus, and adored the Mackail selection of the *Greek Anthology*, Theognis, Plato, Callimachus, Palladas, and Meleager; I knew all the sceptical epigrams by heart and most of those about love and death and "the fate of youth and beauty". In all my books I had written after my name "τίς τίνι ταῦτα λέγεις" (Who are you that say this, and to whom?) Mackail's *Anthology* (in the one-volume edition with the long preface), might have been described as the Sceptic's Bible. I was also fond of the bloomy Theocritus and the *Lament for Bion*.

In Latin Literature I read Horace and Virgil but did not enjoy them till later for Horace, except by Headlam, was not inspiringly taught and Virgil associated with too many punishments and in his moments of beauty with Macnaghten's vatic trances. Although I had learnt Latin all my life I still could not appreciate it without a crib and it was the arrival at the end of my time of the Loeb translations, sanctioned by the authorities, that put its deeper enjoyment within my grasp. Virgil and Horace, without them, had been too difficult, too tearstained. Horace besides was more connected with character than with prettiness. We were slow to appreciate him as a verbal artist

Fortes creantur fortibus et bonis
Est in juvencis, est in equis patrum
Virtus

"Brave men are bred from the good and brave, there is in cattle, there is in horses," Headlam would rasp, "the virtue of their sires," and the history specialists, conscious that though not poets, they were the stuff about which poetry was written, seemed to preen themselves for a moment in the afternoon drowse.

My favourite was Catullus, whose poetry "suited my mood," and therefore the mood of the age. It was cynical, romantic, passionate and bawdy and I could substitute my own name for his. *"Otium, Cyrille, tibi molestum est"*, *"Sed tu, Cyrille, destinatus obdura"*. I liked the world of Suetonius and Tacitus but the Latin prose-writer for me was Petronius Arbiter. I had four editions of the *Satyricon*. The best I had bound in black crushed levant and kept on my pew in chapel where it looked like some solemn book of devotion and was never disturbed. To sit reading it during the sermon, looking reverently towards the headmaster scintillating from the pulpit and then returning to the racy Latin, "the smoke and wealth and noise of Rome" was "rather a gesture".

I also liked Martial, crisp and Iberian but resented the sancti-monious Juvenal, I was excited by the *Pervigilium,* I struggled through the convolutions of Apuleius and admired the pagan chapters of the *Confessions* of Saint Augustine.

In French I cultivated the Troubadours but was disappointed, as I was by those four old bores, Montaigne, Rabelais, Boccaccio and Burton. The deceptively simple verses of Villon I loved, with the Poussin landscapes of Chénier and the garden sadness of Ronsard and Du Bellay. Then came a few lines of Racine, all Candide and Manon Lescaut and an unrepresentative selection of Flaubert, Gautier, Hugo and Baudelaire, no Rimbaud but a close study of Verlaine, Hérédia, and Mallarmé.

I was fortunate to read French with Mr. de Satgé, he loved beauty and while working with him, I apprehended that remoteness of great poetry from life which is inherent in the exaction of the form and creates literature, "la treille où le pampre à la rose s'allie."

In English I began with Spenser sleeping in his coils, I knew little Shakespeare but I worshipped Hamlet, who seemed the Prince of Scepticism and Gestures ("How now, a rat in the arras!"), and of course Marlowe. Shakespeare's sonnets I absorbed. They formed, with Omar Khayyám and the *Shropshire Lad,* limited editions called "the Medici Books", which, unhealthy though they were in bulk, one could yet obtain as prizes. Webster was my favourite Elizabethan, then came Donne and after him Marvell, Herrick and Sir Thomas Browne. Milton was the poet in whom my appreciation culminated. Then a gap until Blake, the *Marriage of Heaven and Hell,* and, still later, Tennyson and Matthew Arnold. I knew nothing of Pope, Dryden and Crabbe, and I had a prejudice against the romantics; Keats turned my stomach, Shelley was ethereal, Byron vulgar and Wordsworth prosy. What I required from an author was the authentic romantic thrill and the prestige of obscurity. After Tennyson was Housman, who came down to lecture to us on Erasmus Darwin and then Bridges, Yeats, Brooke, de la Mare, Flecker, Masefield, *The Spirit of Man* and a repository of Georgian cliché called *Poems of To-Day.*

In prose, after Sir Thomas Browne, came Boswell, Gibbon and Sterne, then Pater (so clear in his thought, so evasive in his conclusions), in whose Sebastian van Storck, with his refusal "to be or do any limited thing," we recognised a fellow sufferer—lastly the usual modern mixture—Samuel Butler, Shaw, Compton Mackenzie, James Stephens, Belloc, Buchan, Conrad, Lytton Strachey and Aldous Huxley. Orwell lent me *The Picture of Dorian Gray.* But I could not swallow it. It was not necessary.

I was as fond of painting as of poetry and haunted the National Gallery. My taste was conservative. I knew of no French painter except Corot and it was typical of the civilisation of the lilies, the limitations of good taste, that I had such knowledge of the masterpieces of the past yet remained timidly at sea among the creations of the present.

CHAPTER XXIII

GLITTERING PRIZES

❦

THE RESULT OF SCEPTICISM, OF ESCAPING FROM THE WORLD VIA
the pursuit of knowledge, was that I unexpectedly won the Rosebery History Prize. The gain was about twenty pounds' worth of
books, but those available, with their horrible bindings, so shocked
me that I obtained special permission to get Medici prints. The
Man with the Glove, Beatrice D'Este and The Duke of Cleves now
looked down on my bureau. After an intrigue with Denis I was
given my "liberties", the privileges of not wearing a hat, of
fagging boys, of having supper by themselves, accorded to the next
six in college, after Sixth Form. When a boy not in Division One
(Sixth Form and Liberty) won the Newcastle, a classical prize, he
was co-opted into it; in getting the same reward for the Rosebery
I had advanced the prestige of the History Specialists, a prestige
which was rising at the expense of classics, languages and science.
History was easier and more interesting, it was the fashion. Most
of the important boys were history specialists, and Mr. Headlam's
division had ended by becoming a field of the cloth of gold for
the feudal chieftains. Of the eleven hundred boys about twenty-
five were in Pop and eight of these were "up" to him. After I got
the Rosebery they began to notice me.

In every division there is room for one boy to reconcile popularity with hard work. He is the brilliant idler, a by-product of
dandyism. "Petronius deserves a word in retrospect. He was a man
who passed his days in sleep, his nights in the ordinary duties and

226

recreations of life: others had achieved greatness by the sweat of their brows—Petronius idled into fame." This archetype of scepticism came to my aid; by imitating his example and doing my work illicitly at night by candle my days were left free for social intercourse. I had an excellent memory, I could learn by heart easily, gut a book in an hour and a half of arguments, allusions and quotations, like a Danube fisherman removing caviare from the smoking sturgeon and remember them for just long enough to get down in an examination paper. I was the perfect examinee. The Oppidans began to take me up. I answered difficult questions and discovered smutty passages for them and if I was caught reading a book in class, it would be something as spectacular as the *Epistolæ Obscurorum Virorum*. Once a week we had to recite a few lines of poetry that we learnt by heart; most boys depended on poems they had learnt before.

> Thereisswee musichere thasofterfalls
> Thanpetalsof blowroseson the grass . . .
> On the grass. . . .

At the end I would stroll up with modest confusion and recite a long Greek chorus chosen for its pessimism, for not to be born was best of all.

My strong point was still being funny. I was working hard enough to be permitted some licence, and I could make jokes about our subject—for the history we studied was the history of personalities—in which even Oppidans could join. I was at my best when being taken up, grateful but not servile, sunny but not familiar and with the schoolboy's knack of living in the moment. I had the advantage of beginning at the top, the only Oppidans I knew were already in Pop, I had no inferiors with whom I had been associated, no ladders to kick down. Antony Knebworth was the first to make friends with me. He had won the other Rosebery prize and was a Byronic figure of overpowering vitality who with his crony, Nico Davies, seemed to make more noise than a whole division. He and Nico were the most successful types of normal schoolboy; they were in all the elevens, ran their houses, were able and rather lazy at their work, conventional, intolerant and senti-mental; they were easily moved to laughter, rage or tears, strict enforcers of privilege and always appealed to by the headmaster when there was a question of Pop "using its influence".

A less schoolminded couple were Teddy Jessel and Edward Woodall; they were dandies in the pure sense, with a sober worldly gravity. Jessel had a touch of the "Arbiter" himself, he was criti-cal of errors of taste, especially on the part of masters whom he treated, with two exceptions, as a set of lower-middle-class lunatics. He disliked Collegers, finding them dowdy and "pi" and he was fond of remarking how swiftly their cleverness evaporated. "A brilliant scholar, won the Newcastle three times running", he would exclaim, imitating a master's complacent tones, "and now he has passed second into the Office of Works." With me, however, he was more tolerant, Horace Walpole to Gray, Townley to Ponti-fex. The other important Pop was Alec Dunglass, who was Presi-dent and also Keeper of the Field and Captain of the Eleven. He was a votary of the esoteric Eton religion, the kind of graceful, tolerant, sleepy boy who is showered with favours and crowned with all the laurels, who is liked by the masters and admired by the boys without any apparent exertion on his part, without ex-periencing the ill-effects of success himself or arousing the pangs of envy in others. In the eighteenth century he would have become Prime Minister before he was thirty; as it was he appeared hon-ourably ineligible for the struggle of life.

Relations with Oppidans were more superficial than with Col-legers. They were easy-going extroverts lacking in super-ego who regarded friendship as a question of equality and shared interests; only Collegers treated it as a philosophy, an end in itself. Meeting Oppidans was like going to smart luncheons where people seem more intimate than they are; returning to College was going on from lunch to spend all the afternoon with a bourgeois intellectual friend of long standing. Friendship, among Oppidans, was a lux-ury—a touch of failure, inequality, absence and it perished. In

College it was a necessity of our strange monastic society, a religion invented by sensitive boys under hard conditions and which existed to combat them.

The term which was my happiest now drew to an end. College politics were absorbing and occupied our anxious elders outside to the extent that we christened these busybodies "The College Investigation Society" and wrote bawdy songs about them. Le Strange summed up the feeling of the minority:

Nov. 20th. There are two great troubles: political and religious. What is one to believe? The religious services here are just awful. Singing absurd meaningless hymns among ugly windows and pictures, with hopeless tunes, and then the intoned droned prayers—all meaningless.

If there is a God he can't be like the Yahweh of the Old Testament. Yet was Christ God? I think not. If there is no God—only a fiction of man's brain, what are we to do with life? Is there another life? Will it be a punishment or reward for this life? No! Then must we be good? Why not rest—peace is what I need. To get away from all the noise and squalor of the world out on to the hills—if there is any god it is Pan— but we cannot worship him except by letting ourselves be absorbed. He is deaf to prayers. He goes on his way regardless. There cannot be a benevolent God. It is impossible in all this squalor. Should one try to improve the squalor? Dorian Gray is an extremely interesting book but of course Lord Henry Wotton must be wrong. I have also just read Potterism. It is dreadful the morbid state into which people get whatever they do. Either they become jingoists like Kipling or else they think of a vanished golden age—like those patriot poets in Ireland.

All the questions of freedom—ethnologically, and of Disarmament are so interesting, but the world is so parochial that one can never think of them.

All my time is taken up with talking of: Athleticism, College Pop, and Fagging. They all run into one another.

Peter and I were both elected to Coll. Pop at the beginning of this half, after being blackballed last summer. So was R. Cyril got in last half. We all arranged to keep Carter out. He was so awful, sarcastic, reactionary, etc. After all, he had his College Cricket, that was sufficient. Now he has got his Wall too. Poor R. has been turned out of that, he

is a barbarian and to be foiled of his barbar triumphs must be hard.
Everything here is done on an athletic standard. I am still in Lower
College with those small boys, good enough in themselves—But O!
the ignominy of it. Thank God Peter is also in L.C. O Peter is
splendid! unselfish, generous. It must be wretched for him too. But
I can't make myself think of that.

I want to reform College when my time comes—to make the fagging
better if I can't abolish it, and corporal punishment too. Why should
this heaven be made a hell just for the sake of old traditions and to
make the British public school type? Ought I to keep Carter out? He
has been good to me—but his influence is bad in College. He stands
for Athleticism and Good Form and all the rubbish joined with that.
And still at the back of all these questions of reform and improve-
ment and an intellectual rather than an athletic standard and so on, is
the moral question.

Is anything worth while?

Should one live for the greatest happiness of the greatest number,
avoiding all classes and creeds—or live so as to get the greatest peace
for oneself. The second is so easy, and yet conscience goes against it.
What is conscience? Is it only some hereditary tradition to be spurned
with patriotism, etc.? The English Gentleman. What an opprobrium
that is. O pray, if you have a God, for peace of mind. If we live for
others we spoil ourselves. If we live for ourselves we harm others.
The only course is to give oneself up to art or literature or such. But
then that doesn't pay, and I suppose—Il faut vivre.

We shared Walter's contempt for the politics of the outside
world; politicians were monsters of inefficiency and self-interest,
we underwent the general post-war disillusion and would have
been surprised and humiliated to be told that through the medium
of college politics we had ourselves become politically-minded. I
was fond of quoting Halifax: "The Government of the world is
a very great thing, but it is a very coarse thing compared with the
fineness of speculative knowledge."

My mother took me to Switzerland for the Christmas holidays
of 1921. We spent them at Mürren. I was mad about ski-ing, the
hotel was full of pretty girls. I skied, made friends and fell in love

but still managed to work for some part of the day. I had often met girls in the holidays but when I was back at Eton they had failed to retain a hold on my imagination; if I had asked them to come down to see me I would then find excuses to put them off. Their reign would come later. Staying in the same hotel however was Antony Knebworth and we saw something of each other. For the first time I was aware of that layer of blubber which encases an English peer, the sediment of permanent adulation. Antony was high-spirited and even when he rearranged all the shoes outside the hotel's two hundred bedrooms he could do no wrong. The meeting had consequences for me. The alpine heights, unfriendly, like too healthy climates, to all forms of art, were also unpropitious to philosophic doubt. My scepticism retreated; the shutter between myself and the rest of the world was raised and under Antony's protection, I enjoyed a social success.

It was now decided I must try for a history scholarship; at first Cambridge was indicated. Most Collegers went on to Kings, where there were safe scholarships for them and a reprieve for several more years from expulsion from the womb; Farlow was there and Rylands, Walter Le Strange was going on and eventually Nigel and Freddie. Some of us had been to Cambridge the term before to see the production of the *Oresteia,* and we had found it exhilarating and cosy, for, subject to a little permutation, the sentimental friendships from College continued unabated with undergraduates from other schools forming an audience, who, at a pinch, could contribute new blood to the cast.

On the other hand, Headlam advised Oxford of which we had caught a glimpse marching down the High on a wintry field-day, while the old Etonians waved to us from their college porches. Denis and Roger Mynors and Bobbie Longden were all going up for scholarships there and besides Oxford was "better for history". In the end out of admiration for Headlam I chose to try for Balliol and as a gesture because it was the more difficult. For the same reason I concentrated on mediæval history; we were taught European history from the Renaissance and "mediæval" history

meant teaching myself, another "gesture", which also provided the
escape that I wanted my work to be. In history I was on the side of
the underdog; I liked the past, the personal element, the Ages of
Faith, the policies with no future. Most stimulating were the Dark
Ages, there was "no damned merit" about them, they were obscure, their futility a standing criticism of humanity. I admired the
Childerics and Chilperics of the Merovingian dynasty, the chronicles of Liutprand, the crimes of Brunnhild and Fredegonde.

Each night, by my outlawed candle, I read all Gibbon, all Mil-
man's *History of Latin Christianity*. I specialised in the heresies of
anarchists and Albigensians but I was interested in them all, in the
Manichæans, in the heresies of Abelard, of my hero Frederic Stu-
pormundi, the Flagellants and in my favorite Neminians who
believed in a religion of "No Man" because "No Man living hath
seen God", and "To No Man is it given to escape Death".

Reading late by candle was bad for the nerves for it had to be
hidden in one's bed or a chink of light might be seen under the
door and, like many lazy people, once I started working I could not
stop; perhaps that is why we avoid it.

The result of cramming was that a noise of any kind sent me
into a temper and that ordinary schoolboy chatter drove me mad.
I could speak only to Denis, Charles Milligan and Jackie O'Dwyer;
in other company I would glower and pull out a book. With the
Oppidans however my ill humour vanished, I became engaging
and witty.

I now admitted to myself my ambition to get into Pop and
planned my campaign. My handicap was that I had no athletic
distinctions, nor was I in Sixth Form from which a certain number
of Pops invariably had to be chosen. My only hope was to be
elected as a wit. Although it was but a small section of Pop who
thought me funny, they were influential. My tactics were to seem
as important as I could in College, so that my Oppidan friends
would not feel that I was too powerless in my own fief to deserve
recognition abroad. There were two Pops already in College, the
lion-hearted Gibson, a fellow history specialist and Robert Longden,

one of those angel-faced Athenians whom the school delighted to honour. I was very fond of both of them and had known them for a long time. I would walk away with Gibson, arm-in-arm, from divisions and seeing me with the only two "possible" people in College, the Oppidans felt they were safe in going about with me by themselves. I mention this technique in case others who wish to be elected to things may find it helpful. It was not very difficult for if the Oppidans observed me with the right Collegers, the latter also saw me with the right Oppidans and both felt pleased with their discrimination.

Deeper than this lay my friendship with Teddy Jessel which arose out of a certain boredom he felt at Eton through not being adolescent. I amused him because he stimulated me.

If I should get into Pop I told my conscience, my morbid spiritual director, I would make amends, for I should be free to talk to whom I liked, and then no one could stop me. There could be no further social ambition. Meanwhile I watched my step.

The scholarship examinations drew near. With Denis, Robert Longden and Roger Mynors I stayed in Balliol and did two papers a day, of which the most important was the English Essay. The subject was *Compromise* which was a favourite of mine for I had already written one essay on it and had quotations ready by which I could prove that compromises were failures and that, even if they were successes, it was one's duty to remain uncompromising. The ages of Faith came to life under my pen. But as Denis and I walked about the Quad or lunched with the Balliol contingent of Old Collegers, as we inspected the dingy rooms with no pictures and few books whose furniture was a dark green tablecloth burnt by cigarette ends, a blokey armchair and a small cold bedroom looking out on a Neo-Gothic quad, a doubt assailed us. Here we were, urbanely pouring out the content of our well-stocked minds for six hours every day. *And for what?*

The sheets had not been aired in my bedroom. I got rheumatism in my shoulder and could hardly hold a pen during the later papers. The dons impressed me but the undergraduates I encountered made me long to return to my suspended boyhood, to Charles and Jackie and Nigel and Freddie, my books and Medici prints, the view from my window of wine-dark brick and the chestnut tree in Weston's Yard.

College spirit [I noted down] is antagonistic to Balliol spirit in its suppression of the political, lack of emphasis on conversation, hatred of "giants at play" and in its attention to reading and the reading of dead rather than living authors. It appears more akin to Cambridge, but with less emphasis on the bawdy Elizabethans.

We were all four school-sick (Oxford reminded me of Wellington) and radiant when the train brought us back down the Thames valley. The term ended in athletics. I went in for school fives with Longden and then the scholarship results came out. Denis and Roger had got classical scholarships at Balliol, Robert at Trinity and I had won the Brackenbury History Scholarship. There was excitement, the history specialists cheered, and a whole holiday was given. Then came the last Sunday of term and the morning of the Pop election. I sat in my room with Charles. We had planned to go abroad together for Easter, our parents had given permission and in a few days we would realise our dream of a visit to Provence. I longed to see Avignon, the scandalous history of whose popes was as clear to me as the lines on my hand, for although I had now been abroad twice, to Paris and to Switzerland, I had never travelled alone before.

We knew that Gibson and Longden planned to put me up for Pop. The suspense grew heavy, our voices languished. Pop elections took hours, for the same boy would be put up and blackballed seven or eight times, a caucus of voters keeping out everybody till their favourite got in. Only the necessity of lunch ended these ordeals. Suddenly there was a noise of footsteps thudding up the wooden staircase of the tower. The door burst open and about twenty Pops, many of whom had never spoken to me before, with bright coloured waistcoats, rolled umbrellas, buttonholes, braid, and "spongebag" trousers, came reeling in, like the college of car-

dinals arriving to congratulate some pious old freak whom fate
had elevated to the throne of St. Peter. They made a great noise,
shouting and slapping me on the back in the elation of their gesture and Charles drifted away. I had got in on the first round,
being put up by Knebworth, but after they had left only the faint
smell of Balkan Sobranie and Honey and Flowers mixture remained to prove it was not a dream.

At that time Pop were the rulers of Eton, fawned on by masters
and the helpless Sixth Form. Such was their prestige that some
boys who failed to get in never recovered; one was rumoured to
have procured his sister for the influential members. Besides privilege—for they could beat anyone, fag any lower boy, walk arm-
in-arm, wear pretty clothes, sit in their own club and get away with
minor breaches of discipline, they also possessed executive power
which their members tasted, often for the only time in their lives.
To elect a boy without a colour, a Colleger too, was a departure
for them; it made them feel that they appreciated intellectual worth
and could not be accused of athleticism; they felt like the Viceroy
after entertaining Gandhi. The rest of the school could not understand that a boy could be elected because he was amusing; if I got
in without a colour it must be because I was a "bitch"; yet by Eton
standards I was too unattractive to be a "bitch"—unless my very
ugliness provided, for the jaded appetites of the Eton Society, the
final attraction!

When I went to chapel I was conscious of eyes being upon me;
some were masters, cold and censorious, they believed the worst;
others were friendly and admiring. Those of the older boys were
incredulous but the younger ones stared hardest for they could be
beaten for not knowing all the Pops by sight and mine was a mug
they must learn by heart. Everybody congratulated me. The only
person not to was Denis. He himself had been co-opted in as
future Captain of the School and he could not believe that my
election to such an anti-intellectual and reactionary body could give
me pleasure. I thought that it was because he was envious, since

he had been elected *ex officio.* My intravenous injection of success
had begun to take.

Before we went abroad I visited St. Wulfric's. I was now Old
Wulfrician No. 1 whose triumphs were chronicled in the school
magazine but although Flip and Sambo were charming, I was uneasy as I surveyed the eighty little boys in their green jerseys and
corduroy knickers. I taught the Sixth Form, I wandered round
classrooms and playing fields, the drill ground, the gooseberry
bushes, the chapel. It seemed inconceivable that I could have felt
so deeply, that I could have been a boy there myself, that Tony
Watson had existed or the Manx Shearwater. Flip was confidential; I saw her angry with one or two boys, then when they had
gone, she would laugh about them and say what a lot of nonsense
one had to tell them at that age, how difficult it was to keep them
in order. Had I dreamt then about my favour-charts? Had I imagined it all, like a savage who believes that a tree or an old bone
is ill-disposed to him? I could not be sure for it was clear that these
monsters whom I had feared when I was ten had become delightful and reasonable people now I was eighteen—or would my "favour" change and Flip be revealed again as Avenging Juno? I
was bewildered.

All the boys seemed happy; there were several peers and a
Siamese prince; once more the School had won the shooting trophy
and the Harrow History Prize. It was a mystery. I felt like the
English lady at the Paris exhibition whose mother was taken ill
in her hotel and who came back with a doctor to find her name
absent from the register, the rooms re-let, re-papered, refurnished
and the hotel staff adamant that mother and daughter had never
been seen. I wired to Charles to fetch me a day early and we
crossed to Dieppe. Sambo's farewell was vivid. "Don't forget, Tim.
A Balliol scholar has the ball at his feet." Already I felt embarrassed to know what to do with it.

We stayed our first night near the Gare St. Lazare and visited
the Folies Bergères. In the interval we roamed about the Prome-

noir and sat down at a table with two thin dark prostitutes. It was
a great moment and seemed to wipe out my humiliation of the
year before. We gave them drinks and were extremely polite, in
the *Sinister Street* manner, for who knew, they might have as many
different editions of Petronius as I? We wore blue suits, camel's
hair waistcoats and dark blue overcoats with a waist at the back;
we smoked cigars and drawled a little, for I was now in Pop, and
Charles, in Sixth Form, was blonder and neater and vaguer than
ever. He might have entertained prostitutes at the Folies Bergères
all his life.

Suddenly Egerton and Rylands came up. We were uneasy and
left our guests, for "Pussy" Egerton, now a scholar of Trinity, had
been the Captain of the School and in the Eleven; he was "the hell
of a chap" and the Colleger who had best fitted into the background of the lilies, correcting the headmaster, sleeping through
difficult construes, to wake up and suggest an emendation with that
bloom of laziness which was a trait in the "To him that hath shall
be given" Eton type. Rylands, his great friend, was more exaggerated, more literary. He was going to be the Duchess in the *Duchess
of Malfi* next year, he told us, and he talked of "Lytton" and
"A.C.B."

Afterwards we went back to the hotel and lay awake in the
dark. My face itched, and I could feel lumps under my fingers. I
scratched, and heard a noise in the silence. Charles was scratching
too.

"Charles."
"Yes."
"Are you awake?"
"Yes."
"So am I."
"Charles."
"Yes."
"Do you know how one catches it?"
"Yes. I think so. From shaking hands—or touching them or
drinking out of the same glass."

"My God—it's come out on my face already."

"And mine."

"I shook hands with mine."

"Mine wore gloves—I felt fairly safe."

"But don't you think she wore them because she *had it there?*"

"Christ! How awful—and my face itches too."

"Have you got anything we can put on?"

"Only some Icilma."

"It's better than nothing—in the morning we can go to a doctor."

"Or should we go now?"

We put on the light and looked at each other. Charles sat up in his white Egyptian cotton pyjamas. They were mosquito bites. We joked about them with nervous vigour, and caught the morning train to Avignon.

There is the first time we go abroad and there is the first time we set eyes on Provence. For me they almost coincided and it would be hard to express what I felt that evening, in the garden above the Papal Palace. The frogs croaked, the silver Rhone flowed underneath, the Mediterranean spring was advancing. I have been back so many times, as a spring ritual, to that palace, to Hiely's restaurant with its plate-glass windows, to the Greek Theatre at Arles, the hills of Les Baux, the ruins of St. Remy, to the Rhone with its eddies and islands and the cypress hedges where the cicadas charge the batteries of summer that I can no longer remember what they looked like for the first time. I know only that they are sacred places, that the country between the Mont Ventoux and the Canigou, from Avignon and Vaucluse to Figueras and Puigcerdá, is the expression of the complete south, the cradle of my civilisation.

We hired bicycles at Villeneuve-les-Avignon and visited Nîmes and Tarascon and Beaucaire. Then we had to make a decision. Should we go on to the Riviera or down the east coast of France towards Spain? Charles inclined to casinos but we chose Spain because it was cheaper and spent the next night at Narbonne. The town was gloomy, the mistral blew, Charles broke the chandelier in our room and tried to hide the pieces. At the last moment they were found and a large item added to the bill. The mistral made travelling impossible. We sat in the train going past platforms where the acacias and cypresses were plastered back by the wind and where even the names of the stations seemed fretted by the mistral; Agde, Leucate, Fitou, Palau del Vidre. The lagoons fascinated us, for it was the country of *Mariana in the South*. The strip of sand, the reeds, the sea lavender, the wind and sun brought back South Africa; there was the Mediterranean, a dark streak beyond the lagoons like the edge of a pineta and close at hand the stakes in the water, the white beds of flaking salt, the barren rocks of the Corbières. We reached the red soil of Roussillon, the fortress of Salses, the cathedral of Elne where a Byzantine empress lay buried, Collioure with its phallic church tower, dingy Port Vendres, Banyuls and after many tunnels the frontier at Cerbère. We could go no farther without a visa.

Next morning we scrambled up to the top of the hill from the beach, blown flat against the ground by the mistral but able to feel we had looked into Spain. Below us was an identical stony hillside dotted with asphodel, Port Bou with its cove, Cullera and Llansa, the mountain peninsula that runs out to Cadaqués and the plain of the Ampurdán. For one moment we surveyed it, then we were blown off our feet. Unable to stay on in Cerbère, we retreated, still battered by the mistral, from the station with its queues of Catalans, in berets and rope-soled shoes, their rugs slung over their shoulders, to the palms and cafés of Perpignan. I was getting school-sick for Eton.

> *Où sont les gracieux galants*
> Whom I saw last a month ago?
> And here at Perpignan I want
> To see them all again, although
> 'Twas not with such an easy flow
> Of mutual intercourse enjoyed. . . .
> In fact I often was, I know,
> By ἔρις not ἐρῶς destroyed.

And how does my dear Denis fare
Called "proud" by Dadie, whom we met
The prey of the Folies Bergères
And wooed by many an Amoret
Who said *"Dormirez-vous,* you pet"
But Egerton, with visage *noir*
Repulsed the sirenaic set
Who circle in the Promenoir.

Our journeys back were unpleasant. We both ran out of money and because of our tickets had to return by different ways. I travelled by Toulouse, carried my suitcase across Paris, got to London in the evening and rather than confess that I was penniless, spent my last five shillings on dining alone in Soho and then retired for the night to St. Martin's-in-the-Fields. It was cold and uncomfortable, the people coughing all round me and wrapping themselves up in newspapers, kept me awake. The next morning I met Charles at Victoria. He was coming back by Avignon but had overslept and gone on to Marseilles where they had tried to make him pay the difference. He had only a bag of dates on which he had been living and we took them to the Park and finished them before going round to his home in Upper Brook Street.

CHAPTER XXIV

VALE

❧❦

WHEN WE WENT BACK TO ETON THE NEWS OF OUR TRAVELS
had preceded us. We were sent for by the Headmaster and rebuked
for having visited the Folies Bergères which was not the sort of
place where Etonians go. Charles's visit in his sleep to Marseilles
was misconstrued by his tutor who asked him if he was aware that
it was a centre of the white slave trade? I had been staying on my
way back with my aunt and her butler had packed the magazines
which were by my bed, including a copy of *La Vie Parisienne*. My
tutor was horrified, it was bad enough to glance at such drawings
he explained, what made it worse was that they were so "diaboli-
cally clever". He also took away *Tristram Shandy* and an uncut
Rabelais.

Denis, Robert Longden and Roger Mynors now formed the
principal mess. Charles and I now messed alone; Denis was Captain of the School but for the first month of my last term I lived
among Oppidans. "Since God has given us the Popacy let us enjoy
it," was my motto after Leo the Tenth's. I was ashamed to hire
classical records now from the music shop and on summer mornings I would go down there with Edward Woodall, Robin Gurdon
and Teddy Jessel to play "Say it with Music" while the fox-trot
floated away on the sunlight and we commented on the looks of
the passers by.

It was a custom to walk up to a hotel in Windsor and sit in
the garden, drinking and smoking. These were serious offences

but the Pops took them for granted and never went about without
a full cigarette case. At lunch they sat beside their housemasters,
breathing port and tobacco over them and making patronising conversation. I soon discovered that my notion of being careful whom
I went about with till I was in Pop and then making friends with
whom I liked was quite impracticable. The Pops like all tyrants
clung together as afraid of what the school thought of them as
the rest were of the Pops; those who had nothing in common and
disliked each other hurried when they met to link arms against
an invisible danger.

Thus only boys in Pop were allowed to walk arm-in-arm. When
I was not in Pop but was walking with Teddy Jessel or Robert
Longden I would await the gesture, the arm first raised and then
shot forward to bring the sleeve and cuff down within grip of the
fingers and then the whole arm inserted, like a bishop laying on
hands, with a sacred stealing motion through my own. It was a
solemn moment when this public favour was conferred but when
I was in Pop and enjoyed the same privilege I found that my arm
seemed unwilling to experiment, and felt at ease only when another braided Pop sleeve reposed in mine.

Soon everybody in College began to seem insipid and dowdy
for I saw them through Oppidan eyes and only the fastidious
Charles and the genial Jackie were proof against that insolent
fashionable stare. "How petty everything is," wrote Walter Le
Strange. "Even people one would never suspect of it seem afraid
of Cyril, speaking of him only in hushed whispers."

Some of the Pops had been worried about my not having a
colour and the Captain of the Boats was persuaded to give me a
rowing one; like any oligarchy the Eton Society went in terror of
letting itself down. For a month I was a model member of that
corrupt and glittering eighteenth-century clique and I forgot for
the first time in my life that I was a "highbrow", and that highbrows are cut off from the world.

During this month I managed to emancipate myself from the
Irish bogey through the Anglo-Irish boys at school who were

cousins of mine and whom I met at my aunt's. Being in Pop was a distinction even the Anglo-Irish had to recognise and one day I realised that I was the most important boy there, that they wanted to know me not I them, that I need not rack my brains to think of something to say about horses, it was for them to try to talk about the all-Colleger performance of *She Stoops to Conquer* in which I was playing an exhibitionist role.[1] A voice told me that Clontarf, rebuilt with livid stained glass in the Isle of Wight Gothic of the sixties round an old ivied tower, was an ugly and unimportant house in a Dublin suburb, that History, after taking one look at the Vernons, had moved across the Channel and that whoever might now receive her favours, it would not be the lately landed Anglo-Irish Gentry.

Alas, in my excursion into the ruling class I had reckoned without an old enemy—the Thames Valley summer. Buttercups, lilac, elms and steamy evenings had returned and were preparing their annual coup. They used a roundabout method.

It was the privilege of College Pop not to have to stamp their own letters. One member offered to "keep the stamps" and to him a fag would bring the letters from the letter-box, stamp them there and enter the amounts due in a book. When stamps ran out, the stamp-keeper would go round and ask people for what they owed him. At that time I kept the stamps for College Pop but I spurned the dunning of people for money and announced that I would pay for the stamps myself. One or two conscientious boys gave something, the rest accepted this typical "gesture" as a mixture of idealism, laziness and the desire to show off. "Qui veut faire l'ange fait la bête!" I soon ran out of stamps and having some letters brought to me to post, I remembered that any placed in the

---

[1] *Mrs. Hardcastle.* The signatures on my programme at this extreme moment of dandyism are revealing. Dunglass, Knebworth, Teddy Jessel, Robin Gurdon, Maurice Bridgman, Edward Woodall, Greville Worthington, Guy Wainwright—all history specialist members of Pop, Brian Howard (æsthete), Bernard Brassey (toast of the day) and three fags, Alsop, Coleridge and Ford to represent College with Nigel and his friend O'Connor. Five of these and three members of the cast would meet violent deaths before they were forty. *Quel époque!*

letter-box in the rooms of the Eton Society were franked in the same way. I sent the fag down with them. That afternoon, when the letters were collected, somebody in Pop chanced to go through them, and noticed that several were to the parents of Collegers. The old hostility broke out. "Why the hell should those bloody bastards in College post their letters here—why should we stamp letters addressed to all the bloody villas in Tooting, etc., etc." The Pops assumed that they had been posted by Denis, whom they disliked, to oblige his friends and made remarks about him. I heard of the proceedings but at some time in the St. Wulfric's or Dark Ages period my nerve had gone. I felt the old panic about "owning up", "going straight", "generality", and "being wanted" —I could not explain, only wait for it to blow over. Eventually— by elimination—they discovered who it was. Nico Davies and Knebworth rebuked me in a friendly way. I tried to apologise but was seized with a hopeless feeling of guilt. How could I explain? I had betrayed Pop; I had let down the friends who had made the experiment of electing me.

From that moment my vitality failed as I had seen it fail in others, I felt uneasy whenever I was with Pops, and could no longer face the rakes in the Hotel Garden. I made the mistake, common in youth, of not understanding that people who like one for oneself, will overlook occasional lapses. I felt that the Members of the Eton Society liked me only in so far as I conformed while someone more mature would have known that the affair was trivial and that they liked me because they knew I could never conform. Driven underground for a year by success, my persecution mania had found an outlet.

In College my self-confidence still held out but even as I had fallen victim to scepticism a summer before, so now I succumbed to æstheticism. It was in the air; the season, the lime-flowered summer evenings undermined me and I fell. I wore, instead of a blazer, with my grey flannel trousers, a black dinner-jacket and a panama hat. The fashion was not followed. I read *Marius the Epicurean* and *A Rebours* which sent me on to silver Latin and *"faisandé"* prose. I studied the philosophy of Aristippus of Cyrene and smouldered with the "hard gem-like flame". I believed in living for "golden moments", in "anything for a sensation" and read Baudelaire, Verlaine, Hérédia, Moréas, and Mallarmé at French Extra Studies with de Satgé, from whom I borrowed *Limbo* and *Crome Yellow* which I got into trouble for reading.

I went to the rose-show at Windsor and had an intense experience looking at the whitest of white roses; after that I always had some Frau Karl Druschki's in my room. Rancid with boredom, I burnt melancholy texts round the wall with a poker. "Let us crown ourselves with roses before they be withered" (*Coronemus nos rosis antequam marcescant*) from the *Wisdom of Solomon*, "*Finis venit, venit finis, evigilavit adversum te et ecce venit*" from Ezekiel, and from Mallarmé "*La chair est triste, hélas, et j'ai lu tous les livres*".

I now admired the twelve Cæsars with their enigmatic deathbed sayings charged with power and satiety and the last king of France— "mettons-nous à la fenêtre et ennuyons nous," exclaimed Louis XIII, "Nous ne sommes pas heureux à notre âge" added Louis XIV. Lous XV left no wisdom, but I learnt that on receiving the news of each defeat in the Seven Years War "Il ouvre ses grands yeux tristes, et tout est dit."

A favourite and succulent character was Audubon, in Lowes Dickinson's *Modern Symposium*.

"And just there is the final demonstration of the malignity of the scheme of things. Time itself works against us. The moments that are evil it eternalises; the moments that might be good it hurries to annihilation. All that is most precious is most precarious. Vainly do we cry to the moment, "Verweile doch, du bist so schön!" Only the heavy hours are heavy-footed. The winged Psyche, even at the moment of birth, is sick with the pangs of dissolution."

Walter Le Strange corroborated.

June 25th. *Seven months since I have seen you, sweet book! Cyril has had you—thank God they were no profane hands that touched you, or unholy eyes that read my heart. When I last confided to you I had sunk to depths of æsthetic affectation deeper than I realised at the time. Now I am (I flatter myself) more level-headed. Cyril has once more consented to know me, after some months of estrangement. His conversation is as butter and honey after bread and dripping. Unfortunately, instead of what was, for me at least, friendship, there is now worship. For then we were outwardly (I flatter myself again) equal, now I am (to the world, not mentally, I hope) unchanged, while he has Success. Niké disdains me. I let Cyril influence me more than I mean to. I know all influence (especially an enervating one like his) is bad. But Cyril is so pleasant I cannot resist him even if I wished to try. (O Hypocrite that I am, this is written for his eyes.)*

July 12th. *Life should be lived, wildly and feverishly within, outwardly with absolute calm and composure. Nor ought one's true opinions to be given to anyone. Everything should bow to expediency and efficiency. How weak I am! In the evening I make huge resolves, in the morning I remember them and disregard them.*

July 15th. *Since last I wrote the whole world seems to have been spread before me. I have seen incense burnt on the altar of Dionysus and heard the Antigone acted in the original tongue of Sophocles. I have dined with the Headmaster and talked of Italian Art. Cyril has shown me the most beautiful flowers in the world. I have knelt on the floor looking at a mediæval map beside a Prince Palatine. I have had my 18th birthday. I have four ambitions of which only the third is likely to come true.*

(1) *To get a scholarship at Kings in December.*

(2) *To get my College Wall.*

(3) *To see Florence and Venice.*

(4) *To be in Pop next summer half.*

To myself I appear a Messiah.

To my friends an ineffectual angel with a touch of the idiot.

To my enemies a negligible knave.

Coronemus nos rosis antequam marcescant. *But I only do it because it is the thing to do.*

Vain attempts to attract Maud.

The Beggar's Opera *and* Dear Brutus *both tend to show "the utter futility of doing anything under any circumstances."*

Le Strange at least kept his diary but all my own attempts to write were doomed to failure. I didn't see how one could well write in English, and my Greek and Latin were still not good enough. I took to writing jingles in which a Greek verse was brought in to rhyme with the English; it was not till a year or two later that I was able to discard English and express myself in Greek epigrams for to compose in a dead language was the creative activity toward which my education was inexorably tending. Meanwhile there was French.

Roses blanches
Qui se penchent
En songes
Elles m'ont chanté
Des enchantés
Mensonges.

Que la vie est brêve
Rêve d'un rêve, etc. etc.

This was the summer's only inspiration.

Meanwhile a strange pink album had appeared called the *Eton Candle*. It contained poems and some precious stories, contributions from Max Beerbohm and those suspect old Etonians, Aldous Huxley, Osbert and Sacheverell Sitwell. One day Teddy Jessel introduced me to the editor, a boy in his house with a distinguished impertinent face, a sensual mouth and dark eyes with long lashes. He wrote to ask me to tea. I accepted, on Pop writing paper, and went round one summer afternoon to find *foie gras* sandwiches, strawberries and cream and my postcard of acceptance prominently displayed on the mantelpiece. Seeing it up there for the world to know that Brian Howard had had a Pop to tea with him, I was miserable. I felt that once again I had let the Eton Society down. It was natural for Teddy Jessel to know Brian who was in the same house. The question was, *Who else did?* I swallowed down my tea like a lady who is offered a swig by a madman in a railway tunnel and bolted.

Afterwards when I saw Brian alone I would talk to him; when I was with other Pops I avoided him, as in the Dark Ages Wilfrid had avoided me. I need not have worried for he soon became the most fashionable boy in the school but, as it was, though I grew to know him better, his politeness overwhelmed me. He belonged to a set of boys who were literary and artistic but too lazy to gargle quotations and become inoculated with the virus of good taste latent in Eton teaching and too disorderly and bad at games to be overburdened with responsibility and who in fact gained most from Eton because of the little they gave. There was Harold Acton, a prince of courtesy, his brother William, Robert Byron who was aggressive, and played jokes on the Corps, the two Messels; Antony Powell, the author of *Afternoon Men* and Henry Green who has since described them in his novel, *Blindness*. They were the most vigorous group at Eton for they lived within their strength, yet my moral cowardice and academic outlook debarred me from making friends with them.

College politics were now less exciting, for we were not in opposition but in office. Denis was Captain of the School; beatings stopped, fagging was light, the election system languished. College Pop had now extended the privilege of using its library to the Upper Half of College, and so to belong no longer brought that increase of privacy which, at Eton, formed the substance of promotion. Being in Liberty and in Pop but not in Sixth Form, I was in an irresponsible position, a school but not a house prefect. I looked on myself as a kind of Charles James Fox or Wilkes, a Whig to the left of the Whig position although I was more of an anarchist than a Liberal for I disbelieved in power and authority and thought them evil and believed that the natural goodness of human reason must triumph without them.

The deadly sin, since I was in Pop, was "Worldliness" and I preached against it whenever I could. As with many anarchists, there was some vanity in my make-up. I did not want to co-operate or be co-operated with and began to take umbrage with Denis, Roger, Robert Longden, the Periclean Caucus who governed College.

Thus after the reform of College Pop into a debating society, I resigned as a protest against compulsory debates although the motion, "that death was preferable to life", was one very dear to me. A blasé *grand seigneur* I called everybody in College by their Christian name and at Liberty Supper I would hold "wantings" which were parodies of the dread affairs of my youth and on occasion a mock beating in which the victims kept their gowns on, and the canes, carefully notched beforehand, broke in half at the first stroke. It was a silly way to behave as rumours spread which made more difficult the genuine reforms of the Caucus. Anybody could play about with discipline in that way since however much one might rag "wantings" and fagging, there was no question of boys not turning up for the wanting or not running to be fagged.

I made friends with many of the fags; in my jaundiced state I enjoyed their simplicity and vitality, besides, I wanted them to be happier than I had been myself. I was sometimes suspected of other motives by my ambivalent housemaster which made me scornful and defiant. He had complained once of my "infernal pride" and I at last lived up to it. I hated history by now; it stank of success, and I buried myself in the classics. I was bored and unhappy but there was no equal in whom I could confide. I was afraid Denis would fail to understand, the virtuous Caucus might lecture me, my housemaster was antipathetic, Headlam could have helped me but I was too frightened of him. He had pointed out to me the seats which the Sitwells had occupied in his class-room but on the other hand he had condemned as morbid "Ere blowsy tediousness of summer days", the last line of a sonnet I wrote.

Urquhart came down from Balliol and had tea with me; he seemed with his easy-going good-mannered confidence and aroma of the days of Greville and Palmerston to promise release into an adult world of intellectual excitement and sensible activity—but after he had gone the white roses, the green bananas, the clove carnation soap and the dismal mottoes resumed their power, and I even engaged a fag to sing Gregorian chants outside my room, like Saul with David.

I was eighteen and a half, I had never had sexual intercourse,
I had never masturbated. "Lilies that fester smell far worse than
weeds," perhaps even St. Wulfric's, even the Eton authorities had
not required a chastity so strict.

The end of term arrived. There was still Camp, which was one
long operatic farewell for me but parting was imminent. I had a
spectacular leaving tea, to which my friends were invited in platonic couples and where I played the *Après Midi d'un Faune* on
my gramophone.

Cyril's leaving tea. A beautiful evening, tea and fair faces and good
music [wrote Le Strange]. Then Liberty Supper, the last alas! How
banal Liberty suppers will seem next half—*Cyril est épatant, mais
comme toujours à la grande manière.* N. got his 22 to-day. He has
gone completely off, as has Maud who used to be so very nice.

There was the last chapel where for the last time I refused to
bow my head in the creed and read Petronius through the leaving
hymn, walking afterwards under the limes with Teddy Jessel. The
cant of leaving infuriated him, the sentimental farewells, the warnings against the prostitutes of Jermyn Street and the hypocritical
anxiety of the stupider Pops worrying about their successors. The
gruelling election had lasted all that morning, with partisans of
one boy putting in two or three blackballs each against nominees
of others until one understood why the College of Cardinals, on
such occasions, was locked in and given no food. My principles
still kept me from blackballing anyone but I enjoyed the excitement. Charles my old friend and mess-mate was elected, and the
second time round I put up Nigel to realise my insolent day-dream
of the year before.

In spite of the reconciliation our friendship was in abeyance, it
would seem that in the quarrel I had expended all the emotion I
was capable of feeling. I remembered how at one time noticing the
shape of his ear in chapel had moved me and now he was only a
bouncing fellow who had just missed the Eleven. He was not
elected till a year later but his gratitude put me to shame.

In *College Annals* Denis wrote the account of his stewardship.

The past year has been conspicuous more for an alteration in the general tone of College than for any remarkable achievements. It has always been the hope of my own Election to destroy the inter-election enmity, as it existed a few years ago, to abolish the scandals of College Pop, to reduce the number of beatings to a minimum, and generally to substitute a more harmonious system of government for the old methods of repressions and spite.

The actual changes that have occurred may be summed up thus:— When I was a fag it was considered a poor night for the "senior" if no one was beaten, and "wantings" occurred every night, whereas this last half it does not happen to have been necessary to use corporal punishment at all, scarcely a dozen to twenty "wantings" the whole half. As regards College Pop, instead of being a miniature Eton society with exclusive right to Reading Room, it has been reformed with the intention of making it a debating society proper, and I have hopes that the new rules will not allow it again to degenerate into a selfish body of College "chaps", like School Pop. . . . It is early yet to judge of the success of these experiments, and the universal prediction of the "old men" may be verified, but I can at least honestly record that College has been in every way happier this year than at any time in the last six years.

The verdict of subsequent Captains of the School on our short-lived and unpopular experiment in happiness can be found in Mr. Eric Parker's *College at Eton* (Macmillan, 1933). *College Annals* also included a short autobiography of every colleger, usually a list of his athletic distinctions, but, under our decadent administration, more general in tone. Thus Farlow added his slogan *"cui bono"* to his list of triumphs, Charles included his gesture in resigning from the Corps and Le Strange ended up "other minor scholastic achievements there were too, which it would be tedious to enumerate." I added a list of favourite authors, favourite flower, rose (white) and my new motto, "I hate everything public" (σιχαίνω πάντα τὰ δημόσια), concluding: "A sentimental cynic, superstitious atheist and Brackenbury scholar of Balliol College Oxford."

Although I affected not to care I dreaded leaving; one part of me was bored and looked forward to moving on, the other clung to the past. Once more I had built up a private civilisation of reason and love at a temperature warmer than the world outside; once again it had to be shattered. "We whose generations are ordained in this setting part of time are providentially taken off from such imaginations"—but I could not repress a dread of the future, of the uglification of life, of Oxford bedrooms and dour undergraduates. Eton is one of the few schools where the standard of comfort is almost in advance of the universities and unlike most boys, Denis and Robert and I were not looking forward to more liberty than we enjoyed already, to more interesting friendships, or to a room of our own for the first time. Also we were attached to the past and used to a world of boys, boys with a certain grace who like the portraits in the Provost's Lodge wore their eighteenth-century clothes with elegance. The world of matey young men with their pipes and grey bags, the blokeries to which we had been allotted, filled us with despair; we mourned with apprehension, "Not the dead but the ἥβας ἄνθος απολλύμενον—the flower of youth perishing."

I was now entering the third hot room of English education; from St. Wulfric's I had got a scholarship to Eton, from Eton to Balliol and from thence there would, I supposed, be other scholarships awaiting me; I could not imagine a moment when I should not be receiving marks for something, when "poor" or "very fair" or "Beta plus" was not being scrawled across my conduct-sheet by the Great Examiner. And yet already I was a defeatist, I remembered Teddy Jessel saying to me by the fives courts, in my hour of triumph: "Well, you've got a Balliol scholarship and you've got into Pop—you know I shouldn't be at all surprised if you never did anything else the rest of your life. After all, what happens to old tugs? If they're clever they become dons or civil servants, if not they come back here as ushers; when they're about forty they go to bed with someone, if it's a boy they get sacked, if it's a woman they marry them. The pi ones go into the church and may become bishops. There goes Connolly, K.S., a brilliant fellow, an alpha mind, he got the Rosebery and the Brackenbury, and all the other berries, and passed top into the Office of Rears!"

There was much truth in this, in fact were I to deduce any system from my feelings on leaving Eton, it might be called *The Theory of Permanent Adolescence*. It is the theory that the experiences undergone by boys at the great public schools, their glories and disappointments, are so intense as to dominate their lives and to arrest their development. From these it results that the greater part of the ruling class remains adolescent, school-minded, self-conscious, cowardly, sentimental and in the last analysis homosexual. Early laurels weigh like lead and of many of the boys whom I knew at Eton, I can say that their lives are over. Those who knew them then knew them at their best and fullest; now, in their early thirties, they are haunted ruins. When we meet we look at each other, there is a pause of recognition, which gives way to a moment of guilt and fear. "I won't tell on you", our eyes say, "if you won't tell on me"—and when we do speak, it is to discover peculiar evidence of this obsession. For a nightmare I have often had has been that of finding myeslf back; I am still a boy at Eton, still in Pop, still in my old room in Sixth Form Passage but nobody remembers me, nobody tells me where to go. I am worse than a newboy, I am a new oldboy. I go into Hall and search for a place to eat, I wander in schoolrooms trying to find a class where I am expected. When I first used to have this dream I had only just left Eton, I knew most of the boys and the masters and the nightmare then took the form of everyone, after my place had been filled, my gap closed over, having to pretend they were glad I had come back. As time went on nobody remembered me and the dream ended with my ignominious ejection. I have found other old Etonians who have had the same experience; some dream they are back in their old rooms while their wives and children hang about outside to disgrace them.

Once again romanticism with its deathwish is to blame for it lays an emphasis on childhood, on a fall from grace which is not compensated for by any doctrine of future redemption; we enter the world, trailing clouds of glory, childhood and boyhood follow and we are damned. Certainly growing up seems a hurdle which most of us are unable to take and the lot of the artist is unpleasant in England because he is one of the few who, bending but not breaking, is able to throw off these early experiences for maturity is the quality that the English dislike most and the fault of artists is that, like certain foreigners, they are mature.[1] For my own part I was long dominated by impressions of school. The plopping of gas mantles in the class-rooms, the refrain of psalm tunes, the smell of plaster on the stairs, the walk through the fields to the bathing places or to chapel across the cobbles of School Yard, evoked a vanished Eden of grace and security; the intimate noises of College, the striking of the clock at night from Agar's plough, the showers running after games of football, the housemaster's squeak, the rattle of tea-things, the poking of fires as I sat talking with Denis or Charles or Freddie on some evening when everybody else was away at a lecture, were recollected with anguish and College, after I left, seemed to me like one of those humming fortified paradises in an Italian primitive outside which the angry Master in College stood with his flaming sword.

> Procul abest Fridericus, Fridericus capite rubro
> Procul abest Nigel, qui solebat mecum ire
> Procul absunt pueri qui clamant in cubiculis eorum
> Qui sedent super focos pulchri sine arte
> Pulchri sunt sed nesciunt, nec decoris eorum habent scientiam—
> O Roma, urbs beata, lumen ultra mare.

Since I was unable to write in any living language when I left Eton I was already on the way to becoming a critic. My ambition was to be a poet but I could not succeed when poetry was immersed in the Georgian or Neo-Tennysonian tradition. I could but have imitated Housman, Flecker, Brooke, de la Mare or Ralph Hodgson. By the time Eliot and Valéry came to save my generation from

---

[1] Even the Jews in England are boyish, like Disraeli, and not the creators of adult philosophies like Marx or Freud.

the romantic dragon it had already devoured me. I was however well grounded enough to become a critic and drifted into it through unemployability.

In other respects I had been more deeply scarred. The true religion I had learnt at Eton and St. Wulfric's had not been Christianity nor even Imperialism but the primitive gospel of the Jealous God, of το φθονερόν—a gospel which emerged as much from the old Testament as from Greek tragedy and was confirmed by experience. Human beings, it taught, are perpetually getting above themselves and presuming to rise superior to the limitations of their nature; when they reach this state of insolence or ὕβρις, they are visited with some catastrophe, the destruction of Sodom or the Sicilian expedition, the fate of Œdipus or Agamemnon, the Fall of Troy or the Tower of Babel. The happiness, to which we aspire, is not well thought of and is visited with retribution; though some accounts are allowed to run on longer than others, everything in life has to be paid for.

Even when we say "I am happy" we mean "I was" for the moment is past, besides, when we are enjoying ourselves most, when we feel secure of our strength and beloved by our friends, we are intolerable and our punishment—a beating for generality, a yellow ticket, a blackball or a summons from the Headmaster, is in preparation. All we can do is to walk delicately, to live modestly and obscurely like the Greek chorus and to pay a careful attention to omens—counting our paces, observing all conventions, taking quotations at random from Homer or the Bible, and acting on them while doing our best to "keep in favour"—for misfortunes never come alone.

Consider Jacky; playing fives with me one afternoon he said "Damn and blast" when he missed a ball. The Headmaster, who was passing, heard him and told Sixth Form. That night he was beaten. In the excitement of the game he had forgotten to prepare his construe. Others had prepared theirs but after the silence before boys are put on to construe, when all diversions have been tried in vain, it was he who was called upon. He was ploughed and given

a "ticket" "Failed in Construe" to get signed by his tutor. He had
not the courage to show it him, forged his tutor's initials on the
bottom and handed it back. By chance the two masters met, the
ticket was mentioned and the fraud discovered. Within three days
of the game of fives the Praepostor came with the terrible summons.
"Is O'Dwyer K.S. in this division? He is to go to the Headmaster
at a quarter to twelve." The wide doors are open which means
a birching will take place. The block is put out. Two boys in Sixth
Form are there to see the Headmaster does not raise his arm above
the shoulder, and an old College servant to lower his trousers and
hold him down. "Call no man happy till he's dead. Next time it
may be me."

Morally I was not in advance of this abject religion; I rejected
Christian ethics yet was not enough of a stoic to adopt pagan standards in their place. I was a *vierge folle* full of neurotic pride and
this gave to my thinking a morbid tinge.

Politically I was a liberal individualist with a passion for freedom and justice and a hatred of power and authority but I disliked politics and wished for nothing better than to talk to my
friends, travel abroad, look at Old Masters and romanesque cathe-
drals, read old books and devote myself to lost causes and controversies of the Past.

The cause of the unhappiness I had come across I put down as
Competition. It was Competition that turned friends into enemies,
that exhausted the scholars in heart-breaking sprints and rendered
the athletes disappointed and bitter. "Never compete" was my new
commandment, never again to go in for things, to be put up and
blackballed, to score off anyone; only in that way could the sin of
Worldliness be combated, the Splendid Failure be prepared which
was the ultimate "gesture". Otherwise when free from guilt and
fear I was gay, with evening high spirits hardly distinguishable
from intoxication and which rose and rose until the shutter fell,
a glass which cut me off from loving friends and imagined enemies
and behind which I prepared for that interview with the moment,

that sacred breathless confrontation from which so little always results, and so much is vainly expected. I was also an affected lover of sensations which I often faked, a satirist in self-defence, a sceptical believer in the Heraclitan flux, an introspective romantic-sensitive, conceited, affectionate, gregarious and, at the time of leaving Eton, the outstanding moral coward of my generation.

Sometimes I imagine Eton replying to these criticisms, the voice of "Henry's holy shade" answering me with the serenity of a dowager.

"Yes. Very interesting. It was one of my masters, I think, who said, 'Connolly has a vulgar streak'—but we won't discuss that. As I understand, you blame us because our teaching encouraged aestheticism and the vices that are found with it and then punished them when they occurred. Has it ever occurred to you to blame yourself? You say winning a scholarship and getting into Pop turned your head, and set you back ten years. Well, I'm sorry for you. Other boys achieved this and more and were not harmed by it. Look at Robert Longden. The same age as you are and Headmaster of Wellington and Lord Dufferin, almost in the Cabinet. You complain that my teaching is cynical and concentrates on success. Don't forget what Jowett said. 'There are few ways in which a young man can be more harmlessly employed than in making money.' Not that I altogether approve of Pop myself, but since your time its morals have improved and its powers been restricted. The state of College has improved too, that Bolshy epoch, when some of the post-war unrest reached our little backwater, is a thing of the past.

"I think if you had been less vain, less full of the wrong sort of pride and with a little more stuffing, you would not have been attracted to the 'primrose path'. You would not have let a little success get the better of you. Don't forget we put you in a strong position. The great world is not unlike the Eton Society. Their values are the same. You could have made lasting friendships with people who will govern the country—not flashy people but those from whose lodges, in a Scotch deer-forest, great decisions are taken. You Bolshies keep on thinking the things we stand for—cricket, shooting, Ascot, Lords, the Guards, the House of Commons and the Empire are dead. But you all want to put your sons down for Eton. It's twenty years now since you came here. Even then people talked about this world being dead but what is more alive to-day? your Bolshevism or the English governing class, the Tory Party?

"But let's leave Pop, let's suppose it is no good in after life to a boy—excuse me—with your income. There was always a Balliol scholarship. Why didn't you follow that up? I see you show a tendency to sneer at the government offices and the diplomatic service. And yet they rule the country more than ever. If "Pop" leads to the Cabinet, "College" leads to the Permanent Under Secretaryships, the plums of the administration. It was the old Colleger type, prelate, judge or civil servant who turned out the late king (not an old Etonian) with such absence of friction. They decide who's to be given a visa or permitted to land; they open the mail and tap the telephones. I shouldn't sneer at them. You imply our education is of no use to you in after life. But no education is. We are not an employment agency; all we can do is to give you a grounding in the art of mixing with your fellow men, to tell you what to expect from life and give you an outward manner and inward poise, an old prescription from the eighteenth century which we call a classical education, an education which confers the infrequent virtues of good sense and good taste and the benefit of dual nationality, English and Mediterranean and which, taking into account the difficulties of modern life, we find the philosophy best able to overcome them.

"You complain that Ruskin's cult of beauty and Tennyson's imagery of water and summer still predominate; but we can't help our buildings being beautiful or our elms stately. If you think boys are happier for a retarded development in unfriendly surroundings, you should have gone to Wellington. You say we are sterile and encourage composition only in dead languages. Shelley and Swinburne and Dr. Bridges wouldn't agree with you. And what matter, if the spirit is alive. Take this:

Quam breve tempus abit quod amando degitur! Instar [1]
Momenti fugiens somnia vix superat.

Exquisite! It is by Mr. Broadbent. Something you were too bathed in your masochist Celtic twilight to appreciate. You were never a very good classical scholar. Too lazy. You would not grasp that, as one of my masters writes, 'No education is worth having that does not teach the lesson of concentration on a task, however un-attractive. These lessons, if not learnt early, will be learnt, if at all, with pain and grief in later life.' Now I expect you have found that out, as you will one day find out about character, too.

"About the civilisation of the lilies, Percy Lubbock and Santayana say very different things from you. However, we bear no ill-will. We shall be here when you have gone. Come down and see us some time. I admit we have been disappointed in you. We hoped that you would conquer your faults but we can't all be Pitt or J. K. Stephen and, in spite of what you say, we have since turned out a writer who has been able to reconcile being a 'live wire', with loyalty to the school tradition, even on the Amazon."

I have concluded at this point, for it marks the end of my un-conscious absorption of ideas, besides there was now nothing new which could happen to me. Although to the world I appeared a young man going up to Oxford "with the ball at his feet", I was, in fact, as promising as the Emperor Tiberius retiring to Capri. I knew all about power and popularity, success and failure, beauty and time, I was familiar with the sadness of the lover and the bleak ultimatums of the beloved. I had formed my ideas and made my

[1] Que l'heure est donc brève
Qu'on passe en aimant
C'est moins qu'un moment
Un peu plus qu'un rêve
Le temps nous enlève
Notre enchantement.   Anon.

friends and it was to be years before I could change them. I lived entirely in the past, exhausted by the emotions of adolescence, of understanding, loving and learning. Denis' fearless intellectual justice, Robert's seventeenth-century face, mysterious in its conventionality, the scorn of Nigel, the gaiety of Freddie, the languor of Charles, were permanent symbols which would confront me fortunately for many years afterwards, unlike the old red-brick box and elmy landscape which contained them. I was to continue on my useless assignment, falling in love, going to Spain and being promising indefinitely.

Somewhere in the facts I have recorded lurk the causes of that sloth by which I have been disabled, somewhere lies the sin whose guilt is at my door, increasing by compound interest faster than promise (for promise is guilt—promise is the capacity for letting people down); and through them run those romantic ideas and fallacies, those errors of judgment against which the validity of my criticism must be measured.

For the critic's role was implicit in this Georgian boyhood.

> Beneath the hot incurious sun
> Past stronger beats and fairer,
> He picks his way, a living gun
> With gun and lens and bible
> A militant enquirer;
> The friend, the rash, the enemy,
> The essayist, the able,
> Able at times to cry.

It is too early to tell if he has been misled by the instinct for survival. It may be that, having laid the ghost of his past, he will be able to declare himself and come out in the open—or it may be that, having discarded the alibi of promise, it will only be to end up in the trenches or the concentration camp.

> Determined on time's honest shield
> The lamb must face the Tigress,

and the Tigress may win for in spite of the slow conversion of progressive ideas into the fact of history, the Dark Ages have a way of coming back. Civilisation—the world of affection and reason and freedom and justice—is a luxury which must be fought for, as dangerous to possess as an oil-field or an unlucky diamond.

Or so now I think; whom ill-famed Coventry bore, a mother of bicycles, whom England enlightened and Ireland deluded, round-faced, irritable, sun-loving, a man as old as his Redeemer, meditating at this time of year when wars break out, when Europe trembles and dictators thunder, inglorious under the plane.

July 1937—Aug. 1938
"Post fanum putre Vacunae."

INDEX

Addison, 11-12, 119 n.
Advertising, 21-22, 88
Aristippus, 38, 245
Arnold, 21 n., 45, 94, 108, 201-202
Auden, W. H., 40-41, 72, 78-79, 99, 131, 132, quoted 171, 260
Axel's Castle, 56-57

Balliol, 221-222, 233-234, 249, 251, 252, 258
Baring, Maurice, 63, 120, 220
Baudelaire, 30, 112, quoted 122, 201, 224, 245
Beach, Sylvia, 58-59
Beaton, Cecil, 164-165
Beddard (Terry), 192, 193 *et seq.*
Bennett, Arnold, 4, 49, 58, 119
Blake, title page part II, 68, 101, 104, 118, 127, 225
Boru, Brian, 154, 156
Bowen, E., 27, 129
Broadbent, 215, 259
Brooke, Rupert, 15, 23, 192-193, 216, 217
Brooks, Van Wyck, 123-124
Browne, Sir T., 46, 225, quoted 252, title page, part I
Butler, S., 21, 25, 86, 87, 125
Byron, Lord, 97, 127, 225

Cambridge, 73, 231
Campbell, Roy, 60
Campbell, Tom, 120
Catullus, 97, 224
Celtic Twilight, 3, 180, 187, 259
Character, 160, 167, 174-175, 259
Civil Service, 88, 258
Clever Young Men, 43

College Pop, 204, 243-244, 248-249, 251
Competition, 256
Congreve, 34, 35, 39, 94, 129-131
Conrad, 19, 23, 225
Conversation, 106-107
Cowley, Malcolm, 133
Crabbe, 85-86, 127, quoted 147

Dannreuther ("Denis"), 194, 233, 240, 241, 244, 248, 251, 252, 254, 260
Dolben, 219
Douglas, Norman, 23, 25-26
Dryden, 11, 30, 41-42, 97
Dunglass, Lord, 228

Ecclesiastes, 205, 223
Egerton, 220, 237
Eliot, 40-41, 79, 131, 254
Eminent Victorians, 46-48, 194
Escapism, 105
Expatriation, 105 n.
Ezekiel, 223, 245

Farlow, 188, 203, 204, 205, 206, 209, 210, 251
Fifteen, 187
Firbank, 33-38, 41
Flaubert, 29, 42, 224
Forster, 6, 26-27, 49, 81, 92, 119
Futility, 41-42, 205-207, 222

Garnett, David, 27, 60
Gibbon, 46, 206, 232
Gide, 71, 114, 138
Graves, R., 60

263